THE THING ABOUT SECOND CHANCES IS...

OTHER BOOKS BY POLYPHONY PRESS:

The Thing About Love Is…

WORDS FROM

THE THING ABOUT SECOND CHANCES IS...

*The wildbearded man
on the corner waves his sign:
Buy your property now
the glaciers are coming!
He's taking the short view:
things matter.*

—"Glaciers"

I had fallen asleep when the cat escaped. I still don't know how it pushed its frenzied head under the flap and through the yards and yards of masking tape. But the dozing passengers were awakened to a howling, spastic feline gymnastic show in the main aisle. As Claire would later remind me, yelling "Rabies!" at that point was premature....

—"Providence"

My mother is tearing our house down with her bare hands. And she's doing a pretty good job of it, too, for someone who has never lifted a hammer before. Last week she hacked all the furniture in half, and yesterday she dismantled the front door.

—"Sawdust and Camellias"

The history of art is, as I said, chiefly commercial. And political. The spoils of war have always included art. The British Museum has the Parthenon tablets; the Louvre has the Mona Lisa; even the Metropolitan has its share of back-door pieces. I'm not an opportunist... but I do understand that the world we live in is messy. We can either retreat from its dilemmas, or do our best.

—"On a Certain Morning"

Kenneth Collins is doing what Kenneth Collins always does when Kenneth Collins is anxious: repeating a silent prayer, the "Hail Mary," again and again until the boredom of repetition subdues his nerves. Of course, boredom is not the point of the prayer, but boredom is what Kenneth Collins desires. Dull, plain, safe, boredom.

—"The Jonquils"

She was the stepdaughter who sat in the cinders and watched the ogre terrorize the mother. She was the stepdaughter who spun straw into gold to supplement the money the ogre threw at the mother. She was the stepdaughter who now watched his body degenerate into her freedom.

—"Song of the Jeweled Bird"

"Armed robbery, Boss Man," said the assistant warden.
"That's what I said," said Gabriel.
"You didn't say 'Boss Man.'"
"Is it necessary I do?"
"If you want to get along with me, it is."

—"Gabriel and the Boss Man"

For 150 years, the Sorrentino family has marched together in the procession of Sant'Agnello. You cannot leave. Sunday, we must march in the Sant'Agnello procession, all of us together. Then I will be happy to die.

—"My Father's Shoes"

He was surrounded by too many women, my mother thinks. The aunts. His mother. Even herself. They made him crazy, she thinks. Or he just wasn't strong enough to come out of it.

—"Another Son"

The smoke from the woman's cigarette, combined with the thick, musty air of the club, caught in Jo's lungs. Then she felt it move down and spread out into her body—just as Damien had told her happened to him in India. She understood what he'd meant now. Only it wasn't love that was filling up her insides; it was this woman's deep, unapologetic laugh.

—"Fun House"

Poets are liars
Ordinary guys
With extraordinary
Sensibilities talking
To other ordinary guys in
Ordinary language.

—"Poets"

THE THING ABOUT SECOND CHANCES IS...

AN ANTHOLOGY OF FICTION, POETRY AND DRAMA

——— ◆ ———

ROBERT N. GEORGALAS, EDITOR

JO-ANN LEDGER, ASSOCIATE EDITOR

POLYPHONY PRESS™

THE THING ABOUT SECOND CHANCES IS...

Copyright © 2000 Polyphony Press

All rights reserved. No portion of this book may be reproduced or transmitted in any form or by any means, electronic or mechanical, including photocopying, recording or by any information-retrieval system without written permission of Polyphony Press.

For information, contact:

Polyphony Press
PMB 317
207 E. Ohio St.
Chicago, IL 60611

Publisher's Note

The works that follow are fiction. Names, characters, places and incidents are either the product of the author's imagination or are used fictitiously. Any resemblance to actual persons, living or dead, events or locales is entirely coincidental.

ISBN 0-9673109-1-1
Library of Congress Card Number 00-109052

First Edition

Printed in Chicago by Fisheye Graphics.
The text was set in 11-point Adobe Garamond.

Cover design: Lee Nagan
Cover photo: *The Window of Time* © Robert N. Georgalas, 2000.

ACKNOWLEDGMENTS

This anthology is the child of many parents. In addition to the authors represented, the 300-plus pages that follow owe much to people absent from the table of contents. Among those who donated technical assistance, proofreading skills, marketing advice, legal counsel, advertising space, objective ears and generous doses of enthusiasm are: Joanne Pepe, Lee Nagan, Ed Underhill, Robert Creason, Chris Carlsen, Ben Aylesworth, Linda Wilkins, Susan Strong-Dowd, Katy Schwartz, William Meiners, Freyda Libman, Theresa and Charles Pepe, Marianne McGrath, Marco Benassi, and Tuckie Pillar.

I'd also like to acknowledge Barnes & Noble, Hudson Street Papers, Roosevelt University Bookstore, Amazon.com and the College of DuPage Bookstore for showcasing both *The Thing About Love Is...* and *The Thing About Second Chances Is....* Finally, I'd be remiss not to express my gratitude to everyone on the advisory board. Your unflinching contribution of time and wisdom deserves nothing less than a standing ovation. In specific, I'd like to thank Brooke Bergan for her impeccable sense of the poetic; Michael Burke for the clarity of vision he helps Polyphony to retain; David McGrath for his stimulating insights and perceptive critiques; Mark Wukas for his encyclopedic understanding of all things literary; and last (but far from least), a special bow to Jo-Ann Ledger whose diligence, goodwill and can-do attitude never flagged. Without each of you, this anthology would not have been possible.

Robert N. Georgalas
November 2000

CONTENTS

PREFACE	xv
THE TOURIST — Nicolette Roberts	1
THE DOGS OF POMPEII — Robert N. Georgalas	2
PIG ROAST — Dorothy Terry	18
SONG OF THE JEWELED BIRD — Cris Burks	20
THE NOO NOO — Mary Ruth Clarke	30
LULLABY FOR TWO — George Einar Nelson	33
CLOSE HARMONY — Glenna Holloway	42
LA LOCA — Deborah Adelman	44
WRITER'S WORKSHOP — Glenna Holloway	61
PROVIDENCE — Tom Montgomery-Fate	63
MILES FROM HOME — Ellen Zalewski	77
GABRIEL AND THE BOSS MAN — E. Donald Two-Rivers	78
THE PILOT STUDY — Deborah E. Ryel	85
THE JONQUILS — Michael Burke	88
HAIKU — Connie Scanlon	99
ON A CERTAIN MORNING — Edward Underhill	100
FELIX CULPA — Scott Grunow	214

THE FIRST SUPPER — Scott Mintzer	215
AN EARLY WORK — M. J. Rychlewski	236
FUN HOUSE — Sari Wilson	239
GLACIERS — Peter Meinke	255
THE WAY IT REALLY WENT — Patricia Ann McNair	256
SMOOTH SAILING — Jo-Ann Ledger	268
I DIDN'T — Mary Ruth Clarke	269
BROKEN WING — David McGrath	273
BREAK — Tom Montgomery-Fate	290
SAWDUST AND CAMELLIAS — Daisy Lin Shapiro	292
THE GIFT — Peter Meinke	301
ANOTHER SON — Michele Weber Hurwitz	302
MUSE — Brooke Bergan	307
MY FATHER'S SHOES — Marco Benassi	308
POETS — Brooke Bergan	337
CONTRIBUTORS' NOTES	341

PREFACE

"You go back Jack do it again"
Steely Dan

Though diverse in style, form and content, the works that follow seem linked by a mutual belief. Each of us, they suggest, is an agent of history, someone whose choices affect the destinies of others, as well as of ourselves. For many, the responsibilities inherent in that idea trigger sleepless nights and angst-drenched days. Slices of time in which choice, chance or misfortune prod us to revisit the crash sites that punctuate our past. Once there, we're assailed by a brushfire of "what ifs," and begin to wonder what we'd do if given the occasion to redraft a segment of our lives.

Well, suppose such an opportunity presented itself. Would we recognize it for what it was? Or have the courage to take it? And if so, what would we do to assure the happiness, redemption, forgiveness or love that we sought? Listen more closely? Banish denial? Opt for speech over silence? Choose our hearts over our heads? Run?

It is questions such as those which the writers in this book address. And their answers lead them to locales rife with either plenitude or paucity, clarity or blindness, joy or anguish.

Whether painting visions of victory, stalemate or defeat, the poets, short story writers and dramatists we've gathered remind us how deep the oceans of desire run. Indeed, when we leave this anthology's pages, we exit both elated and fearful. Awed on the one hand by the resiliency of human nature, and humbled on the other by its capacity to create tidal waves of physical and emotional ruin.

Robert N. Georgalas
November 2000

THE TOURIST

—Nicolette Roberts

In Paris,

>huddled in a doorway,
>angry at the rain.

>Time taunts. Three days
>to absorb the city's heart.

Step out.

>Retreat.

>>My reflection dumb in the glass.

>>Behind the window, olive oil in
>>slender bottles: sunshine pressed
>>into amber, its silky blood bright
>>against the walnut shelves.

>>On the floor, an orange cat curled
>>warm in a mouse rich dream.

THE DOGS OF POMPEII

──Robert N. Georgalas

Adam has just paid their entrance fee, 16,000 *lire*, and is stuffing the change into the lower pocket of his cargo shorts when he glimpses them at the base of the ramp that winds toward the city.

"That's strange," he says. "I'd swear they weren't here last time."

He is referring to a cohort of dogs, some of whom sprawl like commas among the toasted weeds, while others sniff busily at the ash grey plaza that bakes in the Italian sun. Black, brown, spotted or white, each is a mangy cur, its fur matted and dull, its eyes a blend of hunger and distrust. Jennifer assesses them quickly. She is bothered less by the saliva-slick tongues that overlap their maws than by his use of the phrase "last time." Once a day, sometimes more, he reminds her that the ports of call on their ship's itinerary are not new to him. And though she admires him for having seen parts of the world she knows only from textbooks, she realizes that "last time" is simply a code.

Adam unfurls a yellow and green map. His eyes skate across its glossy surface, searching for the pictograph that approximates their location.

"Was Deanna afraid of dogs?" she asks.

"What?" His finger zigs across the paper as the group with which they came trundles *en masse* toward the city gate.

"Perhaps we'd better stick with the others," Jennifer says.

Adam shakes his head, unwilling to give up on the map.

"C'mon," Jennifer says. She wraps her hand around his forearm. "Let's not lag behind."

Reluctantly, Adam folds the map and wedges it into the waistband of his shorts. One of the dogs trails them as they climb the incline that leads toward the ramparts. Its untrimmed claws click on the cobblestones. Jennifer glances at it over her shoulder. The dog raises its snout, its nostrils twitching. "Just ignore it," Adam says. After a few paces, the beast loses interest and halts to snap at a fly.

"I was once bitten by a dog," Jennifer says. Adam registers interest. "It was my seventh birthday," Jennifer continues, "and my parents had arranged a party for me in the park across from our house. At one point, my friends and I were playing atop a small hill. Part of our game was to see how fast each of us could roll to the bottom. As I hit the ground a German shepherd squeezed through a row of bushes. I ignored it and began to tumble down the hill. The dog raced alongside me as I rolled. Its breath was hot on my face and the jangle of its neck tags mixed with my laughter. The faster I spun, the closer it came. Then it started to paw at me and bark. The next thing I knew my leg was in its mouth."

"What happened?" Adam asks.

Jennifer feels her calves tighten as the incline steepens. "My father was cooking burgers on a portable grill. When he heard me scream, he dashed toward us, shouting at the dog and waving his spatula. If I had to guess, I'd say the shepherd was distracted more by the smell of flaming beef than my father's threats. Either way, he released me."

"Were you badly hurt?"

"There were teeth marks on my ankle," Jennifer says, "but the skin wasn't broken."

Adam nods to the pack in the *piazza*. "Are you worried about these mutts?"

"No," she says. "Just thinking about my father."

Ahead, Rafaela, their tour guide, marches the bulk of their group through the Porta Marina, a wide barrel vault that tunnels through the city's outer wall. Extended high above her head is the red umbrella she carries as a beacon for stragglers.

"I think I'll tell her we're going off alone," Adam says when they exit the cool of the vault. "I mean, if it's just two hours, I'd rather spend them on something I haven't seen before."

He opens his camera bag and loops the strap of his Canon EOS under the collar of his light blue shirt. Years ago, when he had first visited here with Deanna, he owned a pocket-sized Olympus, and though it was adequate, he was certain that the pictures he had taken then would be nothing like those he could take now.

Jennifer stops and leans against a shadowed wall. It is only after he has removed the lens cap and set the command dial to full auto that he senses she is no longer beside him.

"Jenn?" He glances over his shoulder. "Are you all right?"

Jennifer removes her sunglasses and rubs a wrist across her forehead. Despite the long-billed cap that shades her features, her complexion has blanched. She bends forward, her buttocks pressed to the wall.

"Jenn?"

Beads of sweat erupt along her upper lip. "All of a sudden," she says, "I don't…" She draws a breath and circles her stomach with the flat of her hand. Adam snaps shut the camera bag and steps toward her. "I was a bit seasick last night," Jennifer says. "Perhaps…"

The arid air stabs at her nostrils. She slumps to a squat, then sits on the ground, her back propped against stones from the Temple of Venus.

Adam hovers above her. "Why didn't you say something?"

"You were playing blackjack," she whispers. "I didn't want to distract you."

"Hell." He presses his palm against the temple's outer wall. "I was losing. It would have been better if you had."

A squirt of bile sears her throat. Jennifer removes her cap, unleashing a river of raven hair. "Adam?" She squeezes her eyes shut. "I want to go back to the ship."

Adam stares up the street. The last of their group has entered the ruins of the Basilica, and he has yet to inform Rafaela that they plan to explore on their own.

"Jenn," he coaxes, "this place is all you've talked about since Istanbul. Maybe if you take some water." He unhooks the canteen of *acqua minerale* tied to his belt. "Here."

Jennifer pushes the offering aside. "If I drink, I'll vomit."

Adam kneels in front of her. Her face is sallow, her sleeveless arms stretched limp on her tan thighs. He turns the palms of her hands upward, pushing them together, curling her fingers to form a cup. A shiver spiders through Jennifer's limbs. He waits for it to pass, then pours from the canteen and urges her to splash the liquid onto her face.

"Better?" he asks.

Tendrils of water snake past her chin. "I don't know."

"Look," he says. "It's all right. We can wait here awhile, then go on."

"The ship?" Jennifer asks.

He dabs her forehead with his handkerchief. "There's no getting back there before the bus returns."

"A train," she says. "There must be a train to Naples."

He rubs the dampened handkerchief along her neck. "Perhaps, but by the time we find it and then make it back to the docks…"

Jennifer sits in silence, waiting for the wave of nausea to pass. When it does, she opens her eyes again.

"Better?" he smiles.

She shakes her head. "I think we should just wait here."

Adam rises and looks toward the forum. Given the hour, the streets are devoid of oohing and aahing visitors. He rakes a hand through his hair, calculating the ground they could cover while the others dally in the public baths or troop through the House of the Vettii.

Jennifer knuckles her watery eyes. "Adam?"

"Listen," he says. "How about we stroll down the Via del'Abbondanza? Just a street or two. You might feel better if you walk."

Jennifer fans herself with her cap. "You go," she says. "It's okay. I'll stay here."

He wrestles the urge to stomp his heel on the road. "Don't be stupid," he says. "I'm not going to leave you."

"But you want to go. I understand."

"Yes, I want to go, but you should go too."

Jennifer rests the hat on her lap. "I can't."

Adam lifts a stone and flings it into the distance. It careens off the iron gate that fronts a weed-choked house. "Come on, Jenn. Try. One block. Then if you still feel ill…"

"I can't."

Adam slaps the wall of the temple. "How stupid," he chides himself. "The thermal pack in my camera bag. Maybe if you held it to the base of your neck."

He ferrets past lenses and rolls of unexposed film. Jennifer extends her hand. Adam reads the directions on the pack, then snaps it in the appropriate place. Jennifer shudders as the cold penetrates her skin.

"Good?" he asks.

She nods, then circles the pack across her face before settling it on her stomach.

Adam crouches beside her and gently kneads her shoulders. "A minute or so, you'll be fine," he says.

Jennifer fans herself again with her cap. The motion of his fingers is pleasurable against her muscles, the kiss he plants on her cheek as electric as the brush of a dragonfly's wings. While his hands meander down her spine, she conjures images of their lovemaking: his tongue rapid and eager as she straddles his face, his penis thick in her mouth. That they should have gotten this far amazes her. Not because romances between younger women and older men were unique. It was more that the gap between them seemed vast, he inhabiting one world, she another.

Three years ago, she had returned to college and enrolled in two of his classes. Short Fiction in the fall, The Novel in the spring. Each began the same. For the first few sessions, he shielded himself behind the podium, his hands clutching tight to its sides as he spoke of Flaubert's struggle for *le mot juste* or Hemingway's quest for the one true sentence. Then, about two weeks in, when it was evident that the students seated before him were more intrigued than bored, he ventured among them, fingers and shirt powdered with chalk, pacing the aisles, dramatizing paragraphs from the text, stopping to address them individually, encouraging those who hazarded responses to his questions, prodding the introverts who cloaked themselves in silence.

Later, in the waning days of a grim and snow-dense winter, after he and she had begun to address each other by their first names, she joked about those initial lectures, her knuckles white as she imitated his grip on the podium. At ease in the warmth of a local Starbucks, she said: "It's as if you thought yourself an impostor about to be exposed." He swirled the espresso in his cup and laughed at how near her observation had come to finding the mark. "I'm always like that at the start of a new semester," he explained. "It's the burden of knowing that what I say can alter your perception of certain authors for life." Had the response come from anyone else, it would have struck her as snide or self-serving. The words of someone who overestimated his importance in the hierarchy of another's life. But her experience with him over the last six months had validated its sincerity. Unlike others in whose classes she had sat, he was not enamored with the sound of his own voice. Nor was he amused by his own cleverness. Instead, he truly seemed to honor those of whom he spoke and his passion for their artistic achievements was infectious.

Sometime in May, they edged across the boundary that separated student and teacher. Not that they hadn't spoken of personal things before. A comment she had once made about the photo of him and his wife that sat beneath his desk lamp prompted him to reveal the widening fissure in their relationship. "To paraphrase Arthur Miller," he said, "a marriage ends when its basic illusions are exhausted."

Perhaps wishing him to know that she too had been violated by grief, she told him of that Tuesday in early September. Four years ago. The sun dipping into a blue-pink twilight. She returning home from her first day as a clerk in the local Borders, anxious to tell her mother about the boy she'd met, the tall, sandy haired one with the sonorous voice and the neon smile.

Forgetful that her mother had left that afternoon to attend a convention of direct marketers in New Orleans. Turning into the drive, she tapped the remote on her dash. The garage door rose with a metallic rattle, the thinning light of evening stooping beneath it to replace the darkness inside. At first, she thought her eyes were playing tricks. But once the door passed the midpoint there was no mistaking what she saw: her father strung from a cross beam, his head crooked at an awkward angle, the tip of his bloated tongue overlapping his bottom lip, the slim grey rope embedded in his neck, his shoes pointed toward the ground like a dancer's.

"My father," she said, "the guy with all the answers, the man who went to his job every day and smiled at the neighbors and held me to his shoulder each time some boy broke my heart. For weeks, I refused to believe the police. I mean, I was sure it had been murder. It wasn't, of course. So I turned on my mother. 'Was it you?' I said. 'Did you push him too hard?' She slapped me for that. And she was right to. Truth was, she was as clueless as I. A few months later, I tried a priest. Then a shrink. The first was full of clichés. You know, the mystery of God's plan and such. The other did what he could for a hundred an hour. Neither dulled the pain, but somehow they convinced me to move on. So I did what my father had always wanted, I returned to college. And lo and behold, I ended up in your class."

There was nothing between them that year. Nor the next when his marriage splintered like crystal dropped from a precipitous height. It was only when Jennifer's mother remarried midway through her daughter's junior year that fate shifted. Unable to coexist with her stepfather, Jennifer opted to change schools, resettling in a small liberal arts college in Colorado. Yet the splendor of the Rockies failed to counter the loneliness she felt and after a semester, she returned. Not to her mother's house, but to a studio apartment in the city.

By then, he had finished the novel he had been working on, a story about a boxer who possessed the will, but not the talent, to succeed. Though surprised by her reappearance on campus, he was pleased when she consented to read his book. "The honor's mine," she said.

They met every Thursday to discuss individual chapters. During their third session, the air-conditioning in his small, monk-like office failed and he suggested continuing over lunch in a nearby restaurant. There, in the dim lighted comfort of a red leather booth, the conversation shifted from academic to social and by meal's end, she had agreed to accompany him that Saturday to a performance of Euripides' *Electra*.

Over the weeks that followed, their meetings lengthened, she espying the man who lay beneath the professor's mask and he becoming enamored of her vivacity, a quality of which he said age and circumstance had conspired to rob him. When he finally invited her to his apartment, she hesitated, fearful that the remnants of his wife's aura would be too much for her to handle. A forgotten sweater hung in the recesses of a coat closet. An unfinished tube of lipstick wedged between the peroxide and the shampoo in the medicine chest. "No worries," he told her. "Deanna took everything that was hers. Besides, I've moved since then."

On their sixth date, a Tori Amos concert he'd selected in what she was certain was deference to her age, Jennifer initiated the transition from languorous kisses to sweat-soaked intercourse. Restrained at first, he offered the defense that his wife had been the only woman with whom he had made love in the last dozen years.

"Wait," she said. "This isn't about some college by-law, is it?"

"No, but…"

"Adam, you're not my teacher anymore," she reminded. "Nor am I one to kiss and tell."

From then on, infatuation swept them forward. And as fall hardened into winter and winter melted into spring, she began to believe that she could love him. Not that he was perfect. Indeed, as her awe for him softened into mundane familiarity, his vulnerabilities crystallized. There were the fits of melancholy when his novel was rejected and the intermittent outbursts of jealousy whenever he found her lazing on the quad, or studying in the library with one of her male peers. "Look, if you want to break this off.…" Then, too, there were the cigars he puffed as he wrote, hand-rolled robustos whose smoky tang caused her head to throb and whose tar and nicotine content led her to fret for his health. "Must you always?" she would say. To which he would reply, "Jenn, there is no such thing as a safe life."

As irksome as these and other of his habits were, their negativity was offset by the leeway he gave her to make her own mistakes. Something her mother had never done. Either for her or her father. Having accepted her as a woman and not a child, Adam spoke to her as an equal, trusting her judgments and listening intently as she spoke. More than that, she helped him to reawaken his senses, he following her lead in the bedroom and relinquishing himself to her sexual experiments.

That June they spoke about living together. "It's not something you just do," he said.

"Does that mean you're bored with me?" She had asked him this more than once, afraid that his twenty-year advantage in knowledge and experience would eventually reveal her as trite and repetitive.

"Of course not. It's just different than a night here or there. It takes work. And if it ends, it may be harder for me to recover than you."

"How can you say that?" she challenged. "You think I don't feel as deeply as you?"

"Not at all. It's just that your heart's younger and more resilient than mine."

"Don't kid yourself, Adam. I need you as much as you need me."

And so, on the heels of such an interlude, he proposed that they take a vacation, a two-week cruise of the Mediterranean. Istanbul, the Greek Islands, Sicily, Naples, Rome.

"Think of it as both an adventure and a trial. Two weeks together from dawn till nightfall. If we can stand each other by the finish, then maybe we should give it a go."

For the first few days, shipboard life was carefree and relaxed, the two of them touring the sites of ancient civilizations (Ephesus, Delos, Akrotiri) in the morning, then basking under the midday sun as the ship journeyed to its next port of call. Half a world from home, they discovered their final inhibitions about one another eroding as naturally as soil in a heavy rain. And Jennifer began to notice that he was less and less bothered by the stares of those who were wont to peg them as father and daughter.

Still, the bliss she felt with him as they wandered through once great cities was undercut by his intermittent references to his ex-wife. And one night, during an idle stroll on a deck canopied by a million stars, she anticipating the sex that would follow, he let slip that years ago he and Deanna had done this same cruise for their honeymoon.

She pried his arm from her shoulder, her anger fueled by the thought that he'd taken her abroad so that he could match her against his first wife. "I am not Deanna," she said.

He drew her to him and kissed the hollow of her neck. "I'm glad you're not her."

"Then why did you tell me that?"

He continued to nibble at her perfumed flesh. "I don't know. I thought the happiness I felt then could be added to what I feel now. And if that happened, maybe this time it would last."

Until that night he had spoken of his divorce only in fits and starts, a detail here, an unfinished sentence there. But in the hour that followed, as the ship's propellers churned the ebony sea a phosphorescent white, he gave the story shape.

"Deanna wasn't one to abide the death of a dream," he said. "Once she was convinced that my novels would never sell, the sands began to shift. I understood that. You have money all your life, you tend to think the planets waltz to your violin. But when I refused to join her father's real estate firm, her response was incendiary. At faculty socials, she would bait my colleagues, or mock the dean for his ill-fitting suits, then pinch my ear and abandon me to a round of red-faced apologies as she wiggled her ass toward the wine bar. When it became clear that I wouldn't leave academia for sales, she'd visit me unannounced between classes, shut the door to my office, and fuck me on the desk. After which, she'd proclaim to anyone within earshot that I'd failed to bring her to orgasm."

"So that was it? The money?"

"Partly," Adam said.

"And the rest?"

A white-jacketed waiter returned with the *grappas* Adam had ordered.

"Children should not be born into those circumstances," he said. He downed his drink in a single swallow, the *grappa* singeing his throat.

"I don't want to see the remains of the dead," Jennifer says. She's leaning against his chest now, his arms anchoring the cold pack to her middle, his legs stretched alongside hers.

"What?"

"I mean, if we walk on."

Adam brightens. "They're not really the dead. Just plaster casts of…"

"Still." Jennifer frees herself from his grasp and rises slowly to her feet.

"Where to?" she asks.

Adam brushes dust from the seat of his shorts. "Well, I thought we'd skip some of the tourist magnets and stroll toward the amphitheater."

"But I was interested in the villas, Adam. The House of the Gilded Cupids. The House of the Silver Wedding."

Adam checks his watch. "I don't know, Jenn. If we do those, we may not…"

Jennifer dons her cap and begins to walk. "Look, I know you've seen them before, but this is my first time. Besides, you promised me on the ship."

"Yes," he says, "but I didn't anticipate the delay. I had my heart set on covering some new ground. I mean, you'd like to see the Gladiator School and the Large Theater, wouldn't you?"

Jennifer presses the cold pack to her cheek. "Perhaps if I'm still okay after the villas."

They enter the forum. Despite the luminance of the day, Vesuvius is veiled in a smoky haze to the north. Adam opens his guidebook as Jennifer's eyes sweep the time-bleached bricks and columns that frame the rectangular expanse. "Here," Adam says. He directs her attention to a page of color photographs. "If we go my way, there'll be things for us both. Houses, shops, mosaics, frescos."

"Wait," Jennifer counters. "Wasn't it you who once said that someone should know the major works before turning to the minor?"

"Jenn, everything here is major."

She switches the cold pack to her other cheek. "Look, I'm a bit too unsteady for this. Just point me in the right direction. Maybe I can catch up with the group."

"But I wanted you to be with me."

"Adam," she says, "there's no need to argue. Each of us can have what we want."

"Good. Then you'll come with me."

The sun has climbed another rung in the azure sky and Jennifer's cold pack has gone soggy. "Fuck it," she says. "Let's just move before I get heat stroke."

Stung, Adam agrees to a compromise. They'll visit the House of the Vettii then proceed south to the newer excavations.

They walk along the thick grey cobblestones, he indicating the ruts and grooves carved by the heavy wheels of carts and chariots, she dazzled by the mosaic floors of the wine bars and the brilliance of the paint that remains on many of the buildings' walls.

"'Our sympathy is cold to the relation of distant misery,'" Adam says.

"What?"

"Gibbon," he answers.

Jennifer holds him in the corner of her eye. It's something he's begun to do a lot as of late, quote from books or authors he knows she has not read, closing his comments with advice that she investigate them.

Once inside the Vettii's villa, Adam attempts to rush her visit, but the friezes in the various chambers exert too strong a hold.

"Odd," Jennifer says as they leave the women's quarters. "Somehow this feels so illicit."

"What? The pornography on the walls?"

"No. Wandering in and out of someone else's rooms. It's like rummaging in your mother's drawers and finding a dildo beneath the sweatsocks."

Adam smiles and guides her to an exit. "Reminds you how carefully we need to draw the line between our public and our private selves."

Outside, Jennifer readjusts her sunglasses, following a step or two behind him as his finger traces the route on his laminated map. A ways on, her stomach begins to twitch again. "Adam." Adam turns and snaps a picture of her seated atop the retaining well of what was once a public fountain.

"Waste of film," she says. "The way I feel, I must look like shit."

Adam uncaps his canteen. She takes it from him and drinks, but the tepid water does little to still the nausea. Trying to ignore it, she focuses on the impressive length of the sun dried street, the weathered taverns and temples and bakeries along its sides too numerous to count. "Imagine," she says. "One day you're the most prized resort in Italy. Then…"

Adam kneels to compose a long shot of the dissipated glory. "Chaos will have its way," he says.

Jennifer belches, the knot inside her tightening. Adam lets the Canon fall against his chest then points to a distant doorway. "What if you stepped through there and it was 79 A.D.?" he asks. "Even if you could speak the language, what would you tell them? That Vesuvius would erupt? That they should abandon what they have and run?"

"I don't know, Adam." She doubles forward. "But this is as far as I can go."

"We're just at the corner." He extends his arm. "There's a whole city down there."

"Go," she says. "Just leave me the canteen."

"But there's no shade," he protests. "Maybe if we go on a bit, you can find an alcove or something."

A chill slithers through her arms. "Adam, if you want to go, go. Otherwise, take me back."

"All right," he says. "I won't be long. Twenty minutes. Half hour. Promise."

Jennifer watches him trot down the street, his head flitting from this side to that. Then the bile returns and she closes her eyes. For a moment, she wonders what he would have done had she been Deanna. Would they have ventured this far or would her money have stopped them at the Venus temple?

Jennifer's thoughts are shriven by a scream. She opens her eyes and turns to the sound. Behind and to her left, a man and a woman race toward her, their faces mottled with sweat and fright. Jennifer angles herself on the fountain and looks beyond them. Coming fast on their heels are the dogs. Some barking, others snapping wildly at the roasted air. The woman screams something. The man glances over his shoulder at the galloping pack. Their coats are gluey with pebbles and dust, their beards thick with drool. Seeing no escape, the man orders her to stop. "Stand still," he says. "Don't show them you're afraid." Despite the panic varnished on her face, the woman heeds him, trembling in the man's arms as the dogs circle them. "Easy," the man says. "Easy."

Unsure of what to do, Jennifer eyes the ground for a rock or a stick. No sooner does she spy one than she senses the dog. Its lips are drawn back over its fangs and a string of spittle drips from its lower jaw. Jennifer meets the animal's gaze. A guttural growl rumbles in its throat. Suddenly, the dog is joined by others who abandon the man and the woman. Jennifer places her feet under her so that she can stand on the fountain's rectangular rim. As she rises, the dogs move closer, their noses inches below the soles of her feet. "Scat," Jennifer shouts. "Go away." The dogs refuse to obey. Intent on retaining her balance, Jennifer hesitates to turn toward the man and the woman. "Are you free?" she calls. "Can you get help?" There is no answer.

An engine of brown fur and yellow teeth leaps for her. She hurls the cold pack at its head, knocking him to the ground. The other dogs surround the missile and tear at it. Then one scratches at another and his victim pivots to engage. Within moments, the fight claims the interest of the pack. Jennifer twists her torso to address the man and the woman. To her surprise, the two have vanished.

When Adam returns, she is yards from where he left her. "I see you found some shade," he says, pointing to the overhang of grass and weeds that darkens the corner of the house in which she stands.

Jennifer informs him that her nausea has subsided, but says nothing about the dogs.

"*Nihil dorare potest tempore perpetuo,*" he says.

"What?"

"Nothing lasts forever. It's a line of poetry that was painted on one of the houses."

"Prophetic," Jennifer says.

They continue toward the gate that will lead them to the buses. Excited, Adam tells her what he's seen: the political graffiti on the house of Paquius Proculus; the marble polychrome tiles that top the counter of a wine bar; the large theater, built to fit a curve in the sloping ground; the arcaded court where the gladiators lived; the names of prostitutes written on a tavern wall. "And the amphitheater, Jenn. You walk in there it's as if you can hear the crowd, half shouting for blood, the other for mercy."

Jennifer is in the bathroom of their cabin, drying her hair. A long afternoon nap alone in the cool of her bed has made the world clear again.

Adam knots his tie in the dresser mirror. "Was it what you expected?" he asks.

She unplugs the blow dryer and steps to the doorway. "Sorry."

Adam ingests her nakedness. The firmness of her body stiffens his cock.

"Pompeii," he says.

Jennifer dons her robe. "Not really," she replies.

Adam tosses her the panties that lay on her bed. "That's too bad," he says. "I was certain you could learn something from that city."

Jennifer sits in an armchair, her fingers splitting the plastic that encases a pair of pantyhose. On the dresser across from her stands a photo of them taken by the ship's photographer when they boarded in Istanbul. In it, she and Adam are positioned behind a life preserver emblazoned with the ship's name. Adam's arm is draped about her shoulders and the two of them are laughing. After first seeing it, she had decided to frame it and hang it in their bedroom. Now, as they cut through the evening waters bound for Rome, the image seems to pale and the space on Adam's wall seems better left blank.

PIG ROAST

──Dorothy Terry

I

Saturday pig roast, in a noisy churchyard.
Rain anoints our humid green tent—
wine becomes beer and friends bless the old days
as the relentless thrum of gypsy anthems
crucifies us with too much bass.

I have my cards read
by an acolyte of the Tarot,
seated on a rickety card table throne,
a lucky crystal dropping from her neck—
seer with the large, moist eyes,
of a consumptive Madonna.

Tattered wings of curled black hair
hover over the cards
as she turns them over, one by one,
on the sticky oilcloth
to disclose my heaven or hell.

And as the strings sing unearthly arias,
the dancers whirling ever faster
on the slimy penitential stones,

she offers me "One Last Chance"
while seven butchered pigs,
fate's discards, crackle nearby.

But the royalty of the occult,
worn and torn with surfeit of divination,
lies silent on the greasy oilcloth
amid a soiled garden, strewn
with withering crimson blooms.

II

Beware the dark stranger
with eyes that glint red.
He is the loose end of the line,
the untied promise made
by an acolyte of the Tarot.

Polisher of the sacred crystals,
hoarder of occult secrets,
cruising the Near North bus stops at rush hour—
Your "One Last Chance."

He's in your cards,
if you visit a curtained storefront
west on Diversey
where he swims dimly in a shining crystal orb:

All conjure
No class.

SONG OF THE JEWELED BIRD

—Cris Burks

The bird squawked and flew madly around the room, knocking crystal figurines off a wall shelf, fluttering against Manny's waterfall mural with the half-naked nymphs, leaving droppings on the furniture. Her feathers were a blaze of turquoise and fiery coral, her body large like a Toucan's, her eyes, tiny, her face parakeet small. To Neecey, she was a combination of all the exotic South American birds she had seen in *National Geographic*. Yet now she was a whirlwind, streaking toward a plate glass window that offered no exit. She hit it with a thump. Then she wheeled, flew into Neecey's face and squawked. The deep bullhorn screech stirred Neecey's Afro. The bird squawked again. Neecey jumped. The bird's eyes were no longer tiny parakeet eyes, nor were they the baleful orbs of a Toucan. Neecey's own Betty-Boop-round, brown, liquid eyes stared back at her. The bird rose above her head. She fluttered round and round, her wings growing and expanding till they touched the opposing walls of the room, her Toucan body sagging under their weight.

"There's no way out," Neecey cried. "The windows are sealed."

The bird squawked and rose until its back pressed against the ceiling. Jewel-colored feathers floated down, fluffy and colorful, but when they hit the floor they were spiny and bare, the translucent spine glimmered and then dissipated into ash. More and more feathers fell and ashes rose around her stacked heels, around the hem of her elephant-leg pants. The feathers on the bird's wings were thick and lustrous, but its body was as bald as a plucked chicken. Yellow fat oozed from the pores in its body. The fat fell, like big raindrops and mingled with the dust around her feet. The mire rose up to the calves of her legs. The bird squawked and arched its back—whack, whack, whack—it knocked against the ceiling. Plaster, round and crumbly as pie dough, fell and rolled off the bird's back. Whack! Whack! Whack! Squaaawk, Squaaawk, Squaaawk. The sounds twirled around her. A shimmer of light filtered through a pinhole in the ceiling. The light revolved like a searchlight as the opening grew bigger and bigger until Neecey could see the moon and sun in the cobalt sky.

"Yes," she cried. "We are east of the sun and west of the moon."

Whack! Whack! Whack! The ceiling disappeared. The featherless bird swooped and picked Neecey up in its claws—rose, rose, rose from the room. High in the sky Neecey looked down. Now, she saw that the room was only a tiny closet filled with family.

"Good-bye," she cried and with those words the bird opened its claws and Neecey fell, back, back, back through the dark-light sky, back.

"If only I had wings," she cried. "If only…"

In Neecey's dream, the bird soared high above the house, spread its wings and flew away—away—moving beyond the sights and sounds of the family, moving away from the pull of the house. In her dream, she cried, "If only I had wings. If only."

Move became a living, breathing word that emanated from the walls as Neecey moved through the house. Her footsteps caused the floorboards to groan *Move*. Her hand on a switch caused the light to squeal *Move*. The two flights of stairs leading up and down, the nine heavy wooden doors, the two drippy faucets, every window in every room, the cheap prints on the walls, the shag carpeting, the canopy beds and bunk beds, the plates, spoons, dustpan, banister, and even the drain screamed *Move*. The house was a choir, its members from the fixture in the deep bass section of the basement, to the high sopranos in the bedroom, sang out in quick staccato beats: move-move-move-move-move-move, and Neecey studying at the kitchen table, dressing in the cold basement bedroom, ironing in the kitchen, found herself humming: mmm-mmm-mmm-mmm-mmm-mmm, like a hurt child.

The *if only* of Neecey's dream manifested in the Spring of 1973 when Manny's eighteen-wheeler jackknifed, rammed into another eighteen-wheeler, skittered into five cars, and finally rested in a small ravine on I-65, just north of the exit to LaFayette, Indiana. It was considered one of the worst highway accidents in northern Indiana history: eight people were killed, three were traumatically injured, one person slipped into a coma and remained there for two years, before death claimed her, and Manny, her stepfather, was airlifted to the best trauma unit in the Midwest—Cook County Hospital. The doctors wired and set, stitched and pasted Manny back together the best way they could. All the wiring and stitching could not make Manny whole. He was pronounced paralyzed from the neck down.

The first time Neecey stepped into the hospital room with her mother, Marie, she pressed her fist to her mouth and groaned. Tubes twisted around Manny like a mass of snakes: in his arms, up his nose, hooked in his mouth, and snaking from under the sheets into a plastic pouch. A steel bar arched from one side of his head to the other and was bolted, yes, bolted, into his scalp. A long thin wire ran from the steel bar over the edge of the bed, to sandbags on the floor.

This, Neecey later learned, was to keep his neck and head perfectly still. The wire, the tubes, the oxygen tanks, the monitor, the deep hum of the machinery, and Manny's breathing heightened the massive horror of his face. His nose was swollen and black stitches ran along one side. His purple lips were opened, inside were pointy and shattered teeth. A continuous stream of red salvia ran through the tube hooked over his mouth. His jaws, usually fat and puffy, were sunken, ashen. Blood and mucous encrusted his head and face, although Neecey could see parts of his neck and face had been cleaned. Neecey walked around the bed, eyeing Manny from different angles, looking for the big burly guy, the familiar, in this strange convoluted face. In this bed, Manny was helpless, small, dying.

Marie sat in the chair next to the bed. Her pocketbook fell to the floor with a thud. She flopped back in the chair and sobbed, "What am I gonna do?"

The mother, small and crumpled in her blue plaid coat, and the daughter, stern and upright, stared at each other. Marie's eyes darted from Neecey to Manny and back to Neecey, "What I'm gonna do?" she asked Neecey again. "What?"

Neecey watched Marie's eyes dart around the room at the machinery and fixtures, at the oxygen tank, the bed table shoved against the far wall, the green vinyl chair next to the identical one she sat in, at the drab drapes on the suspension wire. She watched Marie's eyes dart around the room, to the oxygen tank and the black bag that pulsated as Manny sucked air, ooo whoo ooo whoo. Marie's eyes looked for a way out through the invisible walls of marital responsibility before she could become fully encapsulated in Manny's physical condition.

"Oh, Lord," Marie cried and dropped her head into her hands. "What am I gonna do?"

"Get a hold of yourself, Marie." Neecey said. "You can't sit in here weeping. What if he wakes up? You want him to think he's dying?"

"Better if he had," Marie snapped.

"Marie!"

"I can't sit here," Marie cried. She leaped out of the chair, kicking her pocketbook over and bolted for the door. "I can't stand hospitals." Marie brushed past the nurse who entered with a fresh IV bag. The nurse leaped out of Marie's way. Neecey watched the tail end of the blue plaid coat disappear.

"Are you his daughter?" a nurse asked as she moved to the head of Manny's bed. She took the used bag off of the IV stand.

Manny's daughter? Neecey thought. "Stepdaughter," she said. "I'm his stepdaughter." She was the stepdaughter who sat in the cinders and watched the ogre terrorize the mother. She was the stepdaughter who spun the straw into gold to supplement the money the ogre threw at the mother. She was the stepdaughter who now watched his body degenerate into her freedom. She thought, *now I can move*, and the moment she thought it, such overwhelming guilt smothered her that she again put her fist to her mouth, sucked in air, and groaned. Tears flooded her face. Neecey looked down at the crumpled man. She wanted to move, to be free, but she had never wished him mangled, dead. Had she?

"Oh, you must be close," the nurse said. She walked over to Neecey and embraced her. "He's getting the best care," the nurse said. "The doctors are doing everything."

The woman's perfume, inexpensive *Heaven Sent* from Walgreens Drugstore, could not mask the cigarette smell that clung to her hair and clothes, nor the smell of death-decaying bodies, or the medicinal stench that held the room, the floor, and the hospital in its grip.

Neecey pulled away from the nurse, hearing her, yet wondering, what would be the best care for Manny, to pull all the tubes out of his body, to let him rot in his own blood, to add one or more stitches to his mangled body? What would be the best care for them all? Manny was, and had been, a thorn. She had never wished him dead. Had she?

She tried to remember one good Manny moment. After ten years, there had to be one good moment that they shared. She thought about holidays and birthdays and other special occasions, and she saw what she never wanted to see—Manny with presents, grumpy ideas for Christmas, the Fourth of July—"Marie, just pack a damn picnic and let's go to Brookfield Zoo, too hot in this apartment for fifty people to be crowded under each other." And that had been the way of all his outings, his suggestions, given almost begrudgingly. Money spent begrudgingly. *Here, gal, go get some Popsicles for y'all. Maybe that'll keep your mouths closed.* Everything, harsh and mean. Everything. She saw it all. Him. Him. Him. Throwing money at them like they were street urchins. "Go get some damn shoes for Jordan and Jeremiah. Those things about to bust." Never a nice word, but always, always on time. Perfect timing.

But he wanted to touch them. Yes. He did. She knew it. And when she looked down at him, at the nurse switching the intravenous bag, she knew what was in her heart was true. He would have touched them. It didn't matter that he had some of their well being in his mind and heart. She saw the predator in him, that beast with claws that haunted her dreams. That thing waiting in dark corners and hallways, that wicked man in him that could not, would not, ever be tamed. Not even now, with a broken body. Yet, she had never wished him dead.

For weeks, Manny could make only guzzling sounds. His teeth were splintered and his tongue, lacerated and swollen. When Manny finally stabilized and consciousness was a regular part of his daily routine, Neecey saw a haunting in his woeful eyes. Beneath all the medication, all the pain, Manny watched Neecey with a foreboding despair and a silent plea as his eyes followed her around the room. Somehow she managed to stay just out of reach. While Marie's long, manicured fingers tapped impatiently against her purse, waiting to flee the hospital, the stench of disinfectant, the drone of machinery, the starched white of uniforms, the drab greens, gurneys, trays, IV's and the always present nurse's button—to escape her broken up husband, who would never walk, never move under his own locomotion, never without her aid. Manny, sensing this desperation in Marie by the way she never really looked at him, or touched him, or cried, or screamed, or raged at the misfortune that had befallen her husband; sensing that Marie was counting up the dollars his accident would bring her; sensing that she would be no comfort, no joy, no friend to him, searched Neecey's eyes. She was smart. She would know what to do. Intuitively, Neecey knew all this was inside Manny's head. Still, she spoke no reassuring words, no promises.

Marie hired a Jewish lawyer and filed for power of authority and guardianship over her incapacitated husband, and then, before Manny got the use of his tongue, she filed a lawsuit against the trucking company. By the time Manny had the use of his voice and was nearing release from the hospital, Marie was his legal legs, eyes, and voice. Visiting Manny in the hospital became a regular thing to do for Neecey, like a notation on a pad: pick up dry cleaning, make appointment for dentist, visit Manny, stop at Walgreens. She would have stopped the visits, if Marie had been diligent in her own visits. Marie, who never took to sickness, visited only enough to keep the hospital staff from calling her a bad wife.

The day Neecey signed the lease for the apartment on Pine Grove and Addison, she walked into Manny's room, expecting to find him flat on his back, but the bolts, rod and sandbag were gone and Manny was propped up in bed with pillows.

"Where's Marie?" he asked. His voice still thick and slurry from months of disuse. His long and thin arms laid useless on the sheet.

"I don't know," she said and placed her knapsack on the chair beside his bed and looked at him. "How are you today?"

She noticed that his arms and fingers had lost their beefiness. After three months in the hospital, loose skin covered his bones. She moved to the end of his bed and looked directly in his face. His nose and lips were normal size again, but both had telltale signs of trauma: scars and ridges. His eyes, sunken like gullies in his wide face, looked up at her. The bar and bolts had been gone for three weeks, but still the indentations and bald spot remained. She knew that hair would never again grow in those spots.

It was always difficult talking to him. He had no interests other than his mangled rig and his pension. Yes, it was true, she told him again and again, there was no way he could have stopped on that rainy highway. The break lines were faulty. And yes, Marie is paying all the bills.

"Could you open those curtains?" he asked.

She walked to the window and pulled the drawstrings. Sunlight, bright afternoon sunlight, flooded the room. Out of the window, she could see people flocking into the main entrance, she saw others walking across the green commons to the Congress-Jefferson Park El. *The things that you take for granted*, she thought. She could run out of the building, across that green expanse to the El, north to her new apartment, south to Manny's home, anywhere she pleased, but he couldn't. He could not do anything but wait for others to help him. When she turned from the window, he was staring at her.

"You grew up to be a nice looking woman," he said lowly. "I thought you were gonna be a fat thing. If it wasn't for those eyes popping out your head, you would be beautiful."

"Like I care what you think," she snapped.

"No sense in getting snippy," he said.

His eyes and brow squinted, making a deep "V" in the center of his head. He watched her tighten her wide mouth until her lips disappeared. While he was flat on his back, she looked taller than five feet four inches. She slowly walked from the window to the edge of his bed. Her bulging eyes never left his face. Her lips sneered and turned down, while her nose squinted up.

"I'm moving," she said.

"Moving?" he said and the frown left his face. His face was blank, empty of emotion.

"Yeah, you finally getting rid of me," she said. She dropped into the second chair. "I found a two-bedroom apartment, up north, far, far away from your house."

"Why now?" he asked.

She said nothing.

"You're happy?"

"Happy?" Neecey asked as she scooted back in the chair.

"About me?"

"About you?" she questioned.

"I can't move. I'm not whole."

"Manny, you were never whole," she said and tucked her legs under the chair.

His face contorted.

"See," she said. "Even now, with all this, you're still evil. Most people would be screaming *why me?*"

"How the hell you know if I don't?"

She said nothing. The rumbling of the dinner cart came through the open doorway, along with the moans of other patients, the cries of some family, and the footsteps of staff rushing back and forth. The bell from a nurse's button sounded. In Manny's room, their breathing filled the space. Neecey looked at him, sitting like a statue with only his head moving from her, to the window, to the door and back to her.

"You picked a bad time to be moving."

"Bad for whom?" she asked.

He said nothing. He thought of Marie, running through his savings, his small pension, and whatever money she would get from the trucking company. He thought of the months and years he would spend in a lonely bedroom. Marie, he knew, would put him there and forget about him, while she traveled the country. Wasn't she always talking about Vegas, Hollywood, always talking about the show business career she could have had? Marie would leave him in the dark room calling for her—for someone to help him.

"We need you," he said flatly. His eyes pleaded, *Forgive me, Neecey, for I have sinned.*

"I'm moving," she said and turned her head. She did not want to cave into his soft, pleading eyes. She would not let him make her forget the years of watching and guarding, of playing soldier.

"Neecey," he called.

She turned back to him. He looked into her eyes and saw the twelve-year-old girl who had stood him down with nothing more than a thunderous look in her eyes. He looked and saw the sixteen-year-old girl who commanded an army of children against him; he looked at the woman before him, svelte and composed. Her eyes wide and fringed with long but sparse eyelashes. There was a hardness in her eyes whenever she visited him but he had seen the softness there—when she talked to her sisters and brothers her face relaxed, her eyes smiled, even the blunt cut of her page boy swung freely, loosely.

"Who hurt you, Neecey?" he asked.

"What?" she asked. Her brow wrinkled into a frown and her jaw tightened. His question traveled down into her heart, past the years, past the place where she knew all the answers, past the empty places, into the dark, slimy hole that was her youth, where she had bottled up the bogeyman, Booker, Keith, extension cords, red screams, red, red, red screams.

"Somebody hurt you."

"You don't know what you're talking about!" she snapped.

"Somebody hurt you and you want to punish me," he said. "You've always wanted to hurt me, kill me."

"You listen. Ever since I was a little girl, I've known men like you."

"Not me."

"Like you."

"I've never done anything to you."

"'Cause I never let you."

"You hate me that much?"

"I've never hated you, Manny," she said. "But I've never trusted you."

"You won't help me."

She looked at the liquid swimming in his eyes. His soulful expression. He was frightened, but there was nothing she could do. She had wings, beautiful jeweled colored wings and she would use them—yes, she would—to fly, fly, fly east of the sun, west of the moon.

THE NOO NOO

──Mary Ruth Clarke

Teletubbies have a Noo Noo
They love him very much
If La La spills the Tubby custard
Noo Noo sucks it up

Noo Noo is a vacuum
As anyone can see
With his elephanty schnozzle
He labors cheerfully

I wish I had a Noo Noo
To follow me behind
Suck up my indiscretions
Efficiently and kind

Spills and doo doos I create
As about I putter
Noo Noo would my best pal be
And slurp up all my clutter

Just think what Noo Noo could erase
Dropped pop stray hair green cheese

Relationships gone loco
Paper trails and pleas

Burnt philosophical inquests
Big turds I shouldn't have spoken
I'd never have a hangover
No matter what I'm tokin'

He'd inhale my niggling nags
My filthy cranky mystery
Loves gone rancid with decay
By God, I could un-history

I'm no angel I admit, and
Can act cruel and hostile
But I'd not feel much remorse
My crap's up Noo Noo's nostril

I'd take Noo Noo to bed with me
He'd sanitize my dreams
I'd drag him to big parties
He'd dispense with all the memes[1]

When I am feeling generous
I'd rent my Noo Noo out
He'd clean up all the oil spills
Dump sites, and men who pout

No longer a self cleaner
I'd have slabs of psychic time
To stew beyond my limits
Reach hemispheres sublime

MARY RUTH CLARKE

Now if Noo Noo should accidentally
Suck some bit essential
Too bad, it's gone, and on
I'd live, nothing's consequential

Alas, I have no Noo Noo
Maybe it's a blessing
Debris defines the who of me
As I continue questing

It speaks of where I've been
It utters I exist
Remnants of my comedy
And that I still persist

[1]Memes: Information patterns that have evolved to a point where people are wont to replicate them. Typical memes include slogans, ideas, melodies, inventions, fashions, etc.

LULLABY FOR TWO

—George Einar Nelson

They say that when you speak of Satan, Satan appears. I wish it were that easy. In the dark I whisper his name and wait. I even try different names—Lucifer, the Dark Lord—but still I wait to see him and feel his breath like wings across my neck.

There are times when I feel him watching me from the shadows of my room. I know he is there. And I know when he is ready he will show himself and then we will go away, the two of us, to some distant liberation far from this sad, old world of shattered dreams. But, until such time, I will heed the advice of Dr. Jaffey and avoid my reflection in the full-length mirror.

Sometimes I wish I were man enough to make the trip alone and leave this hollow life behind me, severed like some useless head. But I have always been alone, and I deserve a strong companion. So I pace the floor until I dare myself once more to whisper his name: Lucifer. All that greets me is my own morbid fear which will have to do for now. But it is my fear, and I love it because it is my fear and because there is nothing left I can count on.

It causes me no shame to admit I love a good scare. When the happy hand of life becomes a bitter fist and that special ungodly fear begins to seep like venom seeking every muscle, thrilling every pore. How quickly, how eagerly I cling to its paralysis. Sometimes like a slave whip it snaps so near my face that for an instant I feel its sting upon my lips and fight the urge to flinch. But, snug in that fear, I can sing arias. The shrill cantata warbles from my throat. I clutch my hairy chest until my knuckles pale and I shiver with the throes of joy. It is a kind of living death, this morbid fear. It is my black death. And within this living death I hope to lose myself in madness. When I dream, I dream of madness. And I do dream. But of late, even as I dream, I find even the madness eludes me. It is a clever thing, like a woman, teasing me, staying ever a dagger's length away from the eager tips of my fingers.

It is late on this warm night and I, Marvin Hackle, am alone again. I am always alone on nights like this. At the corner of Lawrence and Sheridan I stop and pretend to be waiting for someone. But there is no one, save these stumbling faces, pale as gauze, silent lips so tight they can barely breathe. And there is no air to speak of. A car pulls up to the red light. A bare-chested young man at the wheel looks away from me and guns his engine. Unknown leaflets scatter like moths at my feet. I step off the curb as if to hail a cab and realize I am stalling. Somewhere far away a single gallows dances in the breeze. It belongs to me, and it waits patiently in its silent dance for the snap of my neck. I will know it when the time is right. I will give it up freely and take the scratchy hemp on my thin flesh and kick the life out. How much better will it be to go out with a snap, than to starve in that infertile madness these fools call life.

My sister is one of those fools. She lives in the apartment next to mine in this brownstone, and since I am so close, I get to baby-sit Michelle, my niece, so Becky can spend her days at the mall. "I've just got to get out of this house," she shouts, and slaps her man-sized hands on the kitchen table top so hard we all jump. She has been acting this way ever since Andrew left her. They fought for five years, shouting so loud I could hear them through the wall. Then one night he simply did not come home from work. He never called, never even sent for his things. That was almost a year ago, now. Becky says he has started leaving messages on her answering machine and a handful of cashier's checks have shown up in the mail, but so far no Andrew.

To stay focused, Becky invests heavily in her appearance. Her nails have reached an epic red. Her once auburn hair is brittle from frequent home permanents and she has taken to wearing stretch pants and layers of costume jewelry. The sight of her bulging and glittering by the kitchen sink makes me conscious of my own unclipped nails. I rake them in a week's worth of whiskers and wonder if she knows how heavy she looks in tiger stripes.

It baffles me that a grown woman can be so helpless. I zip her up, light her pilot light, tune her guitar. And I do not complain aloud. She is my sister, and now that Andrew has left her, Michelle and I are all she has.

If there is a child in that house it is not Michelle. I say this because, unlike her mother, Michelle prides herself with being grown up. Though she is only four, toys to her spell boredom. She much prefers long hours at her mother's peach ruffled vanity, applying careful streaks of designer eye shadow or glossing her lips. She imitates her mother's gestures like a mime. I sit across the room with a book in my lap and pretend not to notice.

I believe if I love anyone, I love Michelle. I feel so sorry for her, that her father is gone, that she has only Becky to mimic, such a shallow mother to figure out. But I go on wishing, as I must, that someday, through osmosis, Michelle will begin to figure me out as well. I have always been good with children. I have never been good with myself.

It amazes me how she gulps her juice from the jelly jar glass as though this might be her final, dying chance to quench her thirst. At the end she gasps for air, having stopped her breathing in her haste to drink every last drop. I wonder that she can hold her breath so long. How long it would take for her little body to run out of oxygen? And I wonder, too, how time can pass so quickly when we are together. It is always far too soon when Becky returns and I find myself pacing in the dark again on my side of this cold wall.

In the morning I lie perfectly still, flat on my back, and imagine I died in my sleep. I do not think it was a peaceful death. It was definitely not from natural causes. Perhaps I was dreaming. I might have dreamed of riding a magnificent stallion, pure white and unbroken. I surely rode him bareback and with no bridle and he galloped so fiercely that I could scarcely keep from sliding off his back. So I clutched his thick white mane and with my face buried in his neck I closed my eyes against the rushing wind. Perhaps the ground disappeared beneath his pounding hooves and we plunged to our deaths. On impact our bones were crushed. And there below a mighty wall of rock we lay dying, the two of us.

I have heard that when people dream of dying, when they dream to the very end, they die for real. I wonder if it is possible to will myself to die, if just by concentrating I can burst the vessels of blood inside my useless head and release the ghost that is me.

Again, I am lying beneath the cliff among the blood spattered rocks, when I hear a faint but terrible hissing sound coming from behind a great boulder to my left. Gliding slowly toward me is a mammoth, hooded serpent as smooth as glass. Its eyes are half-closed and wary. Something tells me we have met before, that we have an account to settle.

During all this wild imagining I hear a knock at the door. I am sure it is that fool Becky come to borrow a cup of something, or ask me some ridiculous question. I wish I could open my eyes, but I cannot leave the dream. For even as I struggle to, the fiendish creature slips toward me, slithering among the rocks and bobbing its diamond head. Then it crawls no more, but flings itself through the air with a gasp. Instinctively, I try to roll to my side but I am not quick. In horror, I take the piercing, hypodermic fangs in the flesh of my inner thigh. The stab is penetrating the lymph area of my groin. For an eternity we hang together suspended in this strange coupling. The reptile clamps down still harder, jabbing its smooth, angry fangs so they grind against the bone. I twitch. I jerk spasmodically. And then, sweet Jesus, I feel it enter me. White-hot venom spurts deep inside my leg, again and again, until that frothy death once more takes hold of me. I can die now. For at long last I seethe again with that terrible, liberating fear. How well I know these sickening waves throbbing within me. I had forgotten how morbid this is—how deadly sensual. I think that I shall finally now go straight to hell. But instead, by God, I go completely limp. There is a fluid tingling in my fingertips. Perspiration drips from my face like streaming tears. Perhaps I am crying. But, if that is so, it is for joy that I weep. And for this primal simplicity. For I am here at last, fettered in this simple, hypodermic kiss.

But there is something I am forgetting, someone pounding outside my door. She shouts now. She knows I am in here. But for me to stand is to perform miracles. I hesitate as the floor slants in my direction. When I reach my hand to clutch the doorknob, it occurs to me that I do not know what day it is. Becky is drumming her nails on the doorpost, but she gasps at the sight of me. Bangle bracelets jingle at her wrist. She is wearing a banana bathrobe which is partly open, revealing rolls of bare flesh.

"Marvin, what the hell?" she whispers and puts her hands over her mouth. She steps back and tangles her thick fingers in the chains dangling between her breasts. I do not know what has come over her. I imagine I look a bit weary. I feel rather like a ghost. But she cannot know by this fatigue that I have felt the simple kiss, or died the frothy death. She cannot know I may have seen the Dark One this time. But nevertheless, something about me is scaring her. And then, finally, when I look down, I spy it too. It is dripping from my upper lip onto the hardwood floor where a small pool is forming. Even before I touch my face, I realize it is smeared with my blood. I have never bled from my nose before.

Becky helps me wash my face and insists I hold a cold compress against my nose to stop the bleeding. I am ashamed she found me like this. But more than that I am amazed for what I have accomplished. I have read of persons who developed the ability to hemorrhage at will although until now I have considered myself a skeptic. But the proof is there in the crimson pudding my sister is wiping off the floorboards and the stiffening pillowcases we remove for the laundry. She advises me to soak them in cold water first, though they probably will not come clean.

As we fluff the bedclothes I find it necessary to apologize for the gore, but Becky never listens to me. She interrupts me to say why she has come over in the first place. It seems Dr. Jaffey has called again, asking for me, wondering where I was last Tuesday. Anger burns my ears. There are reasons why I have no telephone anymore and Dr. Jaffey is one. I tried twice to explain this to Becky. But I have long since given up on her. After all these years nothing has changed. Nothing ever changes. That is why I have given up on Dr. Jaffey as well.

To keep from showing my anger I quickly change the subject. I ask if she has heard from Andrew. "Oh, that's right," she says. "He called yesterday. Wants to take me to dinner, if you can believe that. He didn't say why, but my gut feeling is that he wants to give our marriage another go." There is a catch in her voice so I hold my tongue. This "fat chance" date is for tonight and she asks me to baby-sit. I agree, though I am surprised she would even ask me, what with my bleeding and all.

When I close the door, I can still hear the clink of her copper bracelets scrambling over her wrists. She must wear those things to bed. I can picture her lying there with those gold plated necklaces up around her face on the soft lacy pillow, earrings flat against her cheeks.

It is certainly a relief to be alone once more. I wonder with my newfound skill if something has changed in me after all. I sit beneath the living room window with my back against the wall. I hear a soft rain outside and the floor feels cold and damp against my legs. The smell of burnt toast means Michelle is finally having breakfast. I remove the cool compress from my nose. The bleeding seems to have stopped for now, and so too, has my dying. But there is a time for every purpose, as they say, and time is all that is left of me to compose the madness. I wonder how I can go so quietly insane without so much as a fanfare. And I wonder how I can greet the Dark Lord with a mind that is so unclear. But he will show himself again. And this time he will ask me to dance. I will say yes, of course. I will gladly do my special jig for him at the end of his short rope.

So I whisper his name and wait. Voices pass my window. I turn around to gaze out at the thin white mist which has settled around the dumpsters, the scattered rags, turning even this simple alleyway into a thing of dreams. He is out there too, crouching over there among the shadows just beyond where I can see. As he watches me, high above his head the scratchy hemp swings back and forth like a clock. I can time my breathing to its gentle sway. The shadow falls across my window as I grind my fists against the sill. Tonight it will cradle my soft neck and rock me to sleep, a lullaby in the dark.

I have it all planned out. I will climb to the platform, and I will take my good old time. I will deliberate. I will make a speech and weave a fine cliché. I will then propose a final toast and dash my cup against the godforsaken ground. And then, at last, by the grace of Satan, I will kick this lousy life of mine right in the teeth, and laugh—and laugh as the toothless thing collapses like sheepskin before the gates of hell. Oh death, where is thy lousy stink? For I tire of life's aroma. Like a tomcat I will spray the scent of my decadence in the corners of my tomb. I will put my things on their hooks where they belong and kick back. It will be good to get away and put my feet up. This life is killing me.

When evening comes I walk down the hall and open Becky's door. I smell her beef stroganoff. She always cooks for us when I am going to be baby-sitting around mealtimes. I guess Becky cannot imagine that a man like me might know his way around a kitchen. I find her at the sink draining egg noodles, all dressed in a smart, leopard print suit. Her hair is up in pink, spongy rollers and one is coming loose. It bounces desperately as it clings to a lock at the nape of her neck.

I wonder how she does it, how she can go on living and living and going God knows where. I want to cling to her and bury my face in her soft rollers. I want to tell her I am sorry for letting her get to me. But we are not the kind of family that shows emotion. She calls to Michelle to come set the table. I can tell that, in spite of her optimism, Becky is worried about going to dinner with Andrew. He probably wants a real divorce. She slams the pots and pans so hard it leaves her breathless.

Michelle bursts in and skips around the kitchen table. I get a quick pinch on the arm. "Hey, there, Uncle Marvin. How do I look?" She puts her fists on her hips and sticks out her chin for emphasis. She is a four-year-old version of Becky. There are curlers falling from her hair too. She has applied her own makeup again. Dark red smudges remain unblended on both cheeks and her eyelids are an electric blue.

"You look beautiful," I say and kiss her on the nose. I laugh at how she carries herself in Becky's dangle earrings. They sound like little chimes as she helps me set the table for the two of us.

When the doorbell rings, Becky runs down the list of house rules as she grabs her coat and purse. "And stay out of mother's bobby pins. I'm tired of picking them out of the carpet." She smacks Michelle on the arm and waves goodbye in a blur of animal hide and a puff of cheap perfume.

After Michelle says grace, I grab her bowl and fill it with noodles. Something tells me she knows I have finally gone mad, but she has the sense not to broach the subject. I do not intend to say goodbye to her. I do not even want her to know I am going away. She will be sad enough in the morning when she learns I have gone. But I cannot protect her from everything. While I butter our slices of bread I find myself staring at her, how she talks with a pout, how she uses big words like "hankering" and "pedicure."

After dinner I read to her from *Glamour* magazine. I am only halfway through some silly article about the new permanent presses, when her pretty blue eyelids begin to flutter. As I carry her into her bedroom it occurs to me that I have nothing to leave behind. Soon there will be nothing left of me except, perhaps, a smudge on the floorboards where I fall when they cut me down. I want to think there might be some part of me to live on in Michelle, but she is really more like her mother.

In the junk drawer beside the sink I find a ball of sturdy twine. It hurts to pull it through my fingers, the fibers coarse and eager for my skin. The shears are in the drawer as well and I cut a length of five feet or so, enough to make a good loop. I have always been great at tying knots. I guess everyone has something they take pride in.

I look in on Michelle one last time. She is sound asleep already. She did not let me remove her curlers and now they frame her face against the soft, lacy pillow. Becky will be home soon, that crazy mother of hers who may never slow down long enough to realize how precious this little girl is. I pull up the flannel blanket so it just covers her chin. I wish I could take her with me—away from this sad, old world of shattered dreams. But I do not know the way. And I just got up the nerve to go it alone. I have always been alone; I should be used to it by now. For even though I spoke his name, the Dark One has left the shadows. I remember how he walked away, shrugging his shoulders, his palms to the sky. I remember how his laughter stung as though tearing my flesh. I have let him go without a fight. But even my fear is gone now, and there is nothing left.

I bend down to kiss Michelle goodbye. "I am sorry, little one." But then, as I pull my face away, I see a drop of blood in her nostril. It is ever so tiny but it is there and it is unmistakably her blood. My hand trembles as I take out my handkerchief and dab it away. Though she does not fully awaken, she opens her eyes for a moment and gives me a knowing wink. I have to grab the bedpost to steady myself. So Dr. Jaffey was right after all. By God, I never dreamed this little mimic would have a few of my traits, too.

Perhaps someday they will bury her next to me and grave by grave we will lie there together. We will let the mosses grow from our silent mouths and let our hair down. I believe, when she comes to me, I will spot her in her pink, spongy curlers and rosy painted cheeks. I will spot her coming from miles away. I will know her anywhere. Until then, I will whisper her name and wait.

CLOSE HARMONY

—Glenna Holloway

Their camera smiles insist nothing will change.
Cracked sepia still holds the lift of her chin
as she sings, her secret pressure
on his shoulder, his long Irish hands
on the old upright Steinway still mellow
with its patina of early Moonlight Sonata
and Gershwin jazz. His nickname was Kip,
hers Betsy. Her untamed red hair and her dress,
back in style, are like mine.
I have the hands he had, the same rhythm
he got from long coils of genetic memory.

A month before their wedding, the desert
claimed their little Cessna winging home
from graduation. His twin brother, her sister,
met at the funerals.
Two years later they became my tone-deaf dad,
my delicate mirthless mother.

Outraged nature hates to lose,
refuses to lose it all. I'm the only red
in the family; I know Betsy

in my static electricity, the low notes
of my range. Kip's my walking bass,
my easy octave reach, my treble sass
and those late night blue chords
always looking for a lyric.

This piano still resonates with their touch,
warming and fizzing beneath my fingers,
telling me how to phrase this passage,
telling me this music composed in my head

is theirs.

LA LOCA

—Deborah Adelman

A sudden hot pain stabbed through Flavia's right side. She caught her breath sharply, steadied herself on the couch, tried to keep reading. She had felt a dull ache all afternoon and ignored it. But when the pain returned a second time, she couldn't keep from crying out.

Hugo heard her. "Hey," he called out from the kitchen. He was preparing the nightly meal for the dogs, measuring exactly to the ounce. "What's going on?"

This was not supposed to happen. She hadn't even considered something like this. But no doubt it was serious.

"Stomachache," she said, and lay down on the couch, turning her face inwards so he couldn't come out of the kitchen and see her tears. Surely the pain would go away, if she was patient enough. She gulped in deep breaths to keep from crying out, until another pain tore into her and she drew her legs into her chest, her body doubled from the hurt.

Hugo was at her side when she fell from the couch, screaming. She tried to turn away from him, but he knelt beside her, his face close to hers. "What is it? Flavia! What's going on?"

The pain burned deeply into her side and chest. She couldn't keep from screaming and she hated herself for losing control. Hated herself, knowing that she was about to lose what she had most hoped for. But even through her shouts and tears she didn't say anything to Hugo. She would lie there on the floor in front of him and die before she would admit the truth.

Die she willed herself, biting her lip to keep quiet, then screaming again. *Go ahead and die.* Her consciousness started to fade. She heard Hugo's voice on the phone through the haze in her brain, heard his terror as he called down to Kingston for an ambulance.

Every part of her body ached. The wound in her abdomen, the row of stitches that closed it, the IV needle in her wrist. Her head ached from the meds and drugs and the awful night that preceded them. Her back hurt, too, but she couldn't turn onto her stomach, not with the hole the surgeons had put in it and stitched back up.

Hugo stood at her side, balding and bulging, dressed in boots and a black sweater. It was the only color he wore since they moved to the mountain and got the Dobermans, as if he wanted to match the dogs' sleek coat. He carried a bouquet of roses, their deep red in stark contrast to his outfit. Flavia winced. The blood that had pooled inside of her, filling her abdomen with a hot stickiness no one could see, the blood that had almost drowned her, was that same deep red.

Hugo knelt at her bedside. He lay the flowers across her belly and buried his head in the bed sheets.

"My God, Flavia," he said.

But Flavia said nothing. She looked at the flowers lying on her flat abdomen. It would stay flat now. It was over. The tube was gone. The ovary was gone. The baby was gone and could not have grown anyhow, not in a tube. The possibilities were gone.

"If I had known," Hugo said. "If I had only known. But you didn't say a word."

No, she hadn't said a word. Hugo didn't want any more children. His three sons and a daughter were already grown and out of the house. Out of his life, really. Things hadn't worked out in that family. His ex-wife badmouthed him to the kids and now they hated him, except when it was time to dish out the cash. One bad experience was enough. No more kids, period.

But she had tricked him, caught him off guard. She made sure they loved at the right moment. Then she had said nothing and noted with grim pleasure the changes in her body, the sore breasts, the exhaustion. She thought she would wait until the fourth month, when even Hugo would not have the heart to say no and make her end the pregnancy. She hid her tiredness and the way suddenly even the smell of coffee revolted her, until last night, when she couldn't hide anymore.

She felt sorry for herself, the poor Flavia of last night who thought that if she could just keep her mouth closed long enough and get rid of the pain without Hugo finding out, she could keep her pregnancy hidden another few weeks. She pitied that poor Flavia of last night, fainting from pain, biting her lip to keep her secret while she started to bleed to death.

She hadn't asked him to call the ambulance from down in Kingston; she hadn't asked him to take her to the hospital; she hadn't asked him for help. She would have stayed there and died right there on the cabin floor without revealing anything. He would have watched, horrified, as she took her leave of life, still unaware that she had tried to create a new one.

"If I had known," Hugo repeated. "If I had only known."

"Known?" she asked. "Known what?" She wanted to hear him say it.

"That you were pregnant."

Flavia stared past Hugo at the hospital wall. She couldn't look at him. She still had another tube and another ovary, but he would never fall for that kind of carelessness again. And she was forty-one. There wasn't much time.

"If only you had known? Then what?" Her heart beat faster; she felt the blood rush to her head, her anger snap. "You said no kids. So what good would it have done if you had known? You'd have held my hand during the abortion, that's what." Her voice rose and cracked. The wound in her abdomen hurt from the effort.

"Go home," she told him. "Go back to your mountain. Get out of here."

The mountain. Their fifty acres of woods. It was winter now, five feet of snow and more still to come. When she got out of the hospital, she'd go back to the cabin, spend weeks without seeing anyone other than Hugo and the dogs. The dogs fighting. That was their life. And she had almost died.

Flavia started walking the property again, once she had her strength back. At first she wore boots and stayed on the paths Hugo and the dogs had already trampled through the woods. After a week she finally put on snowshoes and went as far as she could out onto the mountain. If she kept walking, it would take her half a day through the snow to reach the nearest neighbor, a lot more than that to get down off the mountain and into town. In town there was a coffee shop, a post office, a grocery store and pub.

She walked until she couldn't feel her feet anymore. She imagined sinking into the snow, or throwing herself into the cold dampness. Hugo had driven the three hours to New York City for some errand and wouldn't be back until much later, in the afternoon darkness. He'd never find her in the thick forest. The dogs would, though; they'd lead him right to her, stiff, white, frozen.

The sharp, dry winter air burned her nostrils. Underneath her layers of clothing her wound was healing with little pulls and itches. Instead of a hole in her side, she should have had a daughter. She would have named her Flavia, after herself, and reinvented her own life. She'd grow up tall, beautiful and smart. She'd do anything she wanted. But she wouldn't end up like this, forty-one, no skills, no education, no children, alone on a mountain with a bitter man like Hugo, his guns and Dobermans.

"You need to do something," Hugo said. "Take your mind off what happened. Stop moping around the house."

She stared at him. It wasn't good to think about it, she knew that, but she couldn't stop. The way she had almost died. The way the embryo, that had all the material it needed to grow and develop into her daughter, just hadn't made it to safety, to the place where she could have protected it, and instead had exploded into her abdomen.

He signed her up to deliver Meals on Wheels to the elderly. She had done that for awhile, three years ago.

"Get your mind off yourself," he said. But even when she started driving the mountain roads, navigating her truck loaded with prepared lunches and dinners along the treacherous, snowy curves, she still couldn't stop thinking about herself. Stopping at the dingy worn houses scattered along the back roads, handing over the foil-rimmed plates to hillbillies with no teeth and tired faces depressed her. How had this turned out to be her life? Where had she made the mistake—coming to live on this mountain? Meeting Hugo, agreeing to live with him even then, when they had an apartment in the city and he held a normal job and somehow they managed to look like everybody else, pretend they were like everybody else? It was impossible to pinpoint where she had gone wrong, she had done so many questionable things—left jobs, left husbands, moved from one country to another.

People had always thought she was a little crazy. Her own mother. Her brother, who lived in Chicago, with his young daughter and strict, nervous wife. Hugo too. When she was a little girl, in Caracas, they had called her *la loca. Loquita.* She had a temper. She would throw things, stamp her feet. Her mother would sigh, exasperated. Then one day her mother left, back to the States, leaving her with her father and stepmother. She remembered crying her good-byes at the airport, watching her mother and brother board an airplane and head off to another continent. She stopped screaming after that but her mother and brother didn't return. And even after she stopped screaming, they still called her *loquita.*

But Caracas, what she remembered of it, the mountains, the heat, the crowded bus rides to the beach, were so far behind her, so much a part of another life, that she saw no connection between it and this wooded, snowy mountain, this cabin, this man, the dogs, the angry red scar across her abdomen.

She called her brother in Chicago. Simon was in a meeting, but she had the secretary page him.

"Flavia!" he came to the phone, worried. "Is something wrong?"

She imagined the look on his face, the thick eyebrows drawing together, the little creases under his chin. She drew in her breath, not really knowing why she had called. *La loca.* They were right, of course.

"Do you remember when you left Caracas?" she asked.

"Left Caracas? What are you talking about?"

"Do you remember when you left Caracas?"

"Flavia, that was almost forty years ago. What are you asking?"

"If you remember when you left Caracas. Should I say it a fourth time? Caracas. You and mom. Gone. Bye-bye. Adios."

"Are you okay, Flavia?" He cleared his throat, the way he always did when something made him nervous. "Has something happened up there?"

"You don't remember? I was four-years-old but I do. Everything. Mom was wearing a blue print dress, tight at the waist. You were hanging on to her, frowning. She kissed me, once, on the cheek. She didn't even hug me! She wasn't even crying!"

"She was crying, Flavia. And she cried the whole flight back to the States. You're wrong about that. She didn't talk to me, just wept. We flew over the Caribbean, with her sobbing."

Flavia didn't reply. It was nonsense. Her mother had never cried a tear in her life.

"You know why she left. She had to get away from Dad and his family. She needed to work. To start over. The only support she had was back in the States."

Flavia remained silent.

Simon sighed. "Why are you doing this Flavia?" he asked. "You can't change what happened. No matter how bad it was. That story's been over for a long, long time."

She imagined him sitting in his office, in a plush swivel chair, reclining as he spoke to her, his free hand resting lightly on a solid wooden desk. He wore ties to work, had a secretary to take his calls and bring him coffee.

"I'm writing a book," she said. "The family history. So I need the details."

"A book?" he asked, his voice full of disbelief.

"Yeah, a book. You don't think I can write a book? It's going to be great. I've even got the title. *How Flavia Got Screwed.* By Flavia. How's that? Catchy enough?"

She hung up the phone.

Her truck wouldn't start. She was stranded at the trailer home of Geraldine, the old widow who was the last person on her Meals on Wheels route. There was nothing to do but wait. The tow truck from Kingston would take at least an hour.

Geraldine's trailer was dark and narrow, in bad need of repair, chilly in the late winter afternoon, no doubt too hot in the summer, full of leaks and cracks and old furniture. By now Flavia was used to this desolation, the old homes and buildings left from some other era, the faded signs advertising resorts long since abandoned. Being here was like living in Appalachia in the Depression.

Flavia sat on the living room couch while Geraldine went to the kitchenette to prepare tea. The old woman moved slowly, with pain, the simple act of making tea an effort. She banged the teapot clumsily, had a hard time rummaging through the cabinet for tea bags.

The living room was neat and orderly, but every piece of furniture looked decrepit, the worn sofa, a battered armchair, a coffee table covered with a yellowed lace cloth. There were photos on the table next to her, an old black-and-white of a slender young woman in three-quarter length jeans, standing with her arms around her three young children. Another photo of the same woman, her arms around a man in uniform, smiling. Then the three children, older, standing in smiling poses along a highway in the Southwest, in front of a large, battered saguaro cactus. It was hard to recognize Geraldine, now so withered and stooped, her grey hair cut short, in the young, athletic woman with children, but it had to be her. Flavia stared at the smile, the wide, brimming happiness of mother with children captured in that moment. Her eyes filled with tears. She ran her fingertips across the scarring wound in her side.

"My kids," Geraldine said from across the room, wiping her hands on a dishtowel. "Back in the old days. They're all grown now. Married. Far away. Nashville. San Diego. Portland, Oregon. I hardly see them anymore."

"Is this your husband?" Flavia asked.

"Dead for ten years," Geraldine nodded.

Flavia offered her sympathy. Geraldine dismissed it with a wave of her hand. "Divorced for twenty," she said. "Unhappy for longer than that."

But the man in uniform was handsome, confident, his arm around the young smiling Geraldine. "You didn't look unhappy," Flavia said, pointing to the photo.

Geraldine crossed the room and bent over Flavia's shoulder to peer closely at the photo. Her breath was sharp, a little sour, and she smelled faintly of sweat.

"You're right," she said. She stood up. "That must have been a good day." She laughed. "We were wild then. Before the kids came. I met him in San Francisco during the War, then followed him across country, to Santa Fe. Then Colorado. Then back to New York. Got stuck up here in the mountains and never left. But my kids took off as soon as they could." She paused. "Truthfully, we weren't very good parents."

"I know all about that," Flavia said. "My mother left me with my father. Took my brother and raised him on her own. My mother says my father wouldn't let her keep me. My parents were pretty wild too. And selfish. They shouldn't have even had kids."

"At least my own kids are doing better with my grandchildren. From what I can tell, that is, being so far away." Geraldine crossed back across the room slowly, disappeared in the kitchenette and emerged with two cups of tea.

"You got any children?" she asked.

"A daughter," Flavia said. She hadn't planned on saying this. It was just too hard to say no.

That night, Flavia called Simon. He greeted her tentatively, probably afraid she'd get angry again. But she wasn't going to. She wanted information.

"How's Magda?" she asked. "How old is she now?"

"Three," he said. "She just had her birthday in March."

"She's getting big. My goodness. So what kind of things does a three-year-old do?"

Simon seemed uncomfortable, the way he usually did when he talked to her. "What things does she do?" he asked as if it were an odd question. "Everything. She does everything. She walks, talks, she sings. She loves to sing. She sings by herself, sitting in her room."

"Really? What songs does she know?"

"The usual three-year-old stuff. 'Twinkle, Twinkle.' 'Old MacDonald.' I don't know. Some other songs she's learned in her day care. She learned one in Spanish. About a little worm that gets too hot on a summer day. That's really a cute one. *El pobrecito tenía calor.* She sings it just like that."

Flavia couldn't imagine what her niece looked like. She tried to picture her sitting in a circle with other three-year-olds, their faces pudgy, bellies round, hair in pigtails, wearing flowered outfits.

"Can she pronounce all her letters?" she asked. "Can she get her r's? How does she do in Spanish?"

Simon sounded exasperated. "What is this, Flavia? What's this interrogation? The last time we spoke you hung up on me. You haven't seen Magda since she was a newborn, you never ask about her, and now all of a sudden you want to know the details of her phonetics? If she can pronounce her r's? I don't get it? What is this?"

Flavia laughed. "I need to know more about child development," she said. "And I'm too lazy to open up a textbook. And anyhow there aren't any bookstores around here."

Her brother was silent.

"I'm joking, Simon," she said. "I just want to know more about my niece."

"I hope so," he said.

Geraldine asked her to stay for a cup of tea. They sat together at the small table in the kitchenette.

"How old is your daughter?" asked Geraldine. "Who looks after her?"

"She's in day care," Flavia said. "She's three. She loves to sing."

She looked down at the cup of tea, resting on a saucer, at the blue and white pattern of the cup. I'm not really crazy, she thought. At the same time she remembered the voices that used to call her just that. *La loca.*

"She sings in Spanish too," Flavia said.

Geraldine seemed interested. "I remember when my kids were that age," she said. "I loved it. They just wanted me, all the time. They need you when they're little." Tears welled up suddenly in her eyes, and she brought her hands up to her face to wipe them away. The skin around her eyes sagged into large, swollen bags. Her arms were loose and fleshy in her cotton smock. She was thick waisted and frumpy. Flavia couldn't imagine her as a slender young mother.

"It's nice that you bring me these meals," Geraldine said. "But you shouldn't have your daughter in day care to do this. Keep her close to you while you can."

Flavia reached over and patted Geraldine's arm. "She's got a lot of friends in day care," she said. "It's good for her to socialize."

That sounded like something her brother's wife, Helen, would say. Flavia imagined herself as Helen, tall and thin, strict, her clear sense of what was right and wrong. The last time Flavia had seen Helen was the last visit she had made to Chicago, when Magda was a few months old. Helen had held the baby confidently in one arm while talking on the phone to her office, though she was on maternity leave, instructing a colleague with exact details how to terminate a case she had been working on. *Under no circumstances,* Helen had said, rocking baby Magda on her shoulder, *can we give that child back to her mother. That has to be made clear. Do you understand?* There was no sympathy, no kindness, no hint of emotion on Helen's face.

Helen is the best thing that has happened to me, her brother had once told her.

"It's good for her to socialize," Flavia said again, trying to picture what her daughter would look like—long, dark, wavy hair from her, the black, intense eyes she would have gotten from Hugo. Then she tried to imagine what Helen would say, so she could repeat it. "Children don't have to be with their mothers all the time." In her job, Helen had certainly made sure that some children were never with their mothers at all.

Geraldine shook her head. "Keep her close while you can," she repeated. "You can make a mistake with a husband, choose the wrong one, make a lifetime of unhappiness or maybe, if you're lucky, even start over again. But not with a child. No mistakes there. The child is for keeps."

The dogs had fought again. Hugo had fourteen stitches up his forearm, from trying to intervene. But at least the dogs had left each other intact.

"We've got to get rid of one of the males," Flavia said. They were sitting on the porch steps at night, now that spring was approaching, dressed in wool sweaters, but enjoying the crisp clean air. There were reasons they had moved to this mountain, Flavia reminded herself. Sometimes life seemed almost normal. Almost reasonable. Almost healthy.

"They don't fight often," Hugo said. In seven years on the mountain with the dogs, he had had his arm stitched twice. "I can't get rid of them. I've had them since they were puppies."

"I'm tired of taking care of dogs," Flavia insisted. "What do you want with all these dogs?"

He reached over and put an arm around Flavia. Hugo was solid, muscular, though his midriff was going to paunch. "I need them," he said. "And I need you. All of us, up here. By ourselves. This clean, pure life." He stroked her cheek, her hair, her neck. He dropped his hand to her waist, searching for the bottom of her sweater, pulling it up, his fingers under her shirt, making contact with her bare skin close to the scar from the operation.

When he left his job in the city and they first moved here, he had convinced her it was all right to make love in the open, right on the porch, and they had done it, timidly at first and then boldly, with laughter, realizing that there was truly no one around, ever, to see them.

She thought of Geraldine, chasing her husband across the country. She must have loved him wildly to do that.

She pulled Hugo's hand from her, and moved to the other side of the stairs.

"You're all stitched up," she said. "And I am, too."

She looked at him, made out his features in the dark. She remembered the night she met him, at a bar on the East Side. Hugo was handsome then, a full head of hair, white smile sharp against his olive skin. He dressed well; he had money. Flavia was down to her last ten dollars by then, alone in the city, one more week of rent paid, a step away from the streets, not sure yet to what level her desperation might lead her. She wondered how much he was carrying in his wallet and what she might do to get it. He bought her a beer, then another, and they talked of Venezuela, of the marriage he had just gotten out of, of the way his mother, who had clawed her way out of Europe after the War, still didn't sleep well at night. She went home with him that night, but spent the rest of the week in her rented room in Chelsea, refusing to see him again. She wouldn't give him the number of her dumpy hotel, though when she called him during the week, he begged her for another evening together. At the end of the week, with nothing more than loose change in her pocket, she turned in the key to her room and went to him. He never knew about the room, the ratty block on 14th Street, never knew what had been on her mind when she approached him in that fancy bar.

She couldn't let herself think about what might have been if she hadn't met Hugo.

She stared at him on the porch steps. He was bald, going slack. There was nothing nice to look at in his face anymore. Or maybe there never had been.

Geraldine greeted her with a smile and asked her in. "I've got some things for your daughter," she said. She seemed excited. Flavia waited on the couch while Geraldine rummaged around her bedroom. A plastic bag rustled. Something fell from a drawer or shelf with a muffled thud. Finally Geraldine emerged, a large cardboard box in her arms. She placed it on the floor and sat next to Flavia.

"I've been hanging on to these for years," she said. "It's time someone had them." She pulled out a round packet of old newspaper and unwrapped it. Dust rose from the box. Inside the newspaper, Geraldine discovered an old rag doll. Flavia winced. She'd have to haul off the old woman's treasures and dump them somewhere, pretending to be delighted in the meanwhile. The dust reached her nostrils and burned the back of her throat.

"Raggedy Ann," Geraldine said, holding up the doll. Flavia stared at the doll's wide, smiling face and the two floppy braids. "One of the originals. Hand sewn. I doubt you'd find one of these around anymore. This belonged to my eldest daughter." She turned the doll around, inspected it front to back, peering closely, then held it up at arm's length. "My Katie looked after this doll. Carried it around gently, like a little baby. No stains on it, nothing torn. Katie's always been a careful one."

Geraldine plunged her hand back into the box. Inside another bundle of newspaper she found a long-handled wooden cup, a string attached through a hole in the rim, with a red ball tied to the end. She grabbed the cup handle, jerked her hand around in a stiff, arthritic movement, trying to catch the ball in the cup's hollow. She didn't even come close, but she laughed. "My goodness," she said. "My Danny used to spend hours playing with this."

More toys emerged. A small wooden train, a brown and white stuffed puppy with floppy ears and a long tail. The newspaper packaging was dusty, but the toys were clean and intact.

"I'm sure your daughter will like these," Geraldine said. "I want her to have them. No use sitting on a shelf another twenty years."

Flavia tried to shake her head and form the words *no thanks* but she couldn't. When Geraldine placed Raggedy Ann in her hands, Flavia didn't protest, and rested the stupid, grinning thing in her lap. The train followed, and the wooden cup and ball.

"What's your daughter's name?" Geraldine asked.

Flavia hesitated. "Flavia," she said. Geraldine looked at her quizzically.

"I wanted her to have my name," Flavia explained. Geraldine wouldn't understand what she meant, that she had chosen that name to reinvent her own life. "We call her by her middle name, though, so we won't get confused. Magda. After my grandmother."

"Magda," repeated Geraldine. "What a pretty name. Take these things home and give them to little Magda."

Geraldine pulled out the last package. Buried in all the old newspaper she discovered a black lacquer box, shiny, as if new, with a scene painted on it. A golden horse, a sleigh, swirls of red and green decorated the dark background. It was beautiful, not a child's toy, and Flavia looked at it greedily, hoping Geraldine would offer it to her, the only nice thing in the whole collection, though Flavia knew she shouldn't accept the box.

Geraldine, though, had grown quiet. She held the box on her lap, folded her hands over it, her head lowered. She wiped her eyes with the back of one hand, and gave a low moan.

"This was Katie's. I bought it for her because..." Geraldine wiped her eyes again. "It's a Russian box. Unusual. I found it in a little shop in Kingston. So long ago."

She stood up. She took a deep breath and tried again to explain. "I bought it for her to make up for the worst thing I ever did as a parent. But then I didn't give it to her. Couldn't. I had to make it up to her some other way. Don't know if I ever did." Geraldine shoved the box into Flavia's hands.

"Take this, too," she said. "Be good to your daughter. Little Magda."

Flavia clutched Geraldine's gifts to her chest as she rose and took leave of the old woman. As she drove away, she saw Geraldine, standing in the doorway of her trailer home, her face, sagging and teary, full of regret at the memory of her distant secret sorrow.

Hugo's motorcycle was parked in the driveway, but the cabin was quiet. When Hugo napped, the dogs usually joined him, uncharacteristically peaceful. Even the two males got along then, one sprawled across the foot of the bed, the other on a rag rug on the floor, where Hugo could reach down and pet him if he chose.

Flavia gathered the toys from the truck and headed for the front door. Hand on the knob, she shut her eyes. If only, she thought. If only there were a little girl in there, dark, curly hair, running to the door to greet her, eyes wide in amazement at the treasures in Flavia's arm, the doll, the puppy, the train, exclaiming "Momma!"

She was there, her Magda, her Flavia, her three-year-old, her daughter. Flavia stood at the door, unable to open her eyes, unable to turn the key in the lock, unable to break the moment. There had to be a little girl in there, waiting for her.

But inside, the cabin was quiet and still. Hugo didn't stir from his nap, and the dogs, ever mindful of his needs, came out of the bedroom carefully, offering only a few subdued licks of her hand in greeting.

She picked up her Meals on Wheels at the agency in Kingston. But instead of heading back up the mountain to deliver them, she stopped at a children's clothing store.

"I need an outfit for a three-year-old," she said. "A girl."

She bought a pink flowered jumper with a white blouse. A pair of jeans with ribbons and flowers on the pocket. White sandals. A nightgown with a picture of Barbie on it.

"Sixty-three dollars," the clerk told her.

"How much?" Flavia asked, certain she'd heard wrong. In her wallet she had thirteen dollars in cash, her driver's license, and Hugo's credit card. They had agreed she would use it only for emergencies. Truthfully, she had no idea what his credit limit was.

The girl looked sympathetic. "Sixty-three. It's a lot. The spring stuff is brand new. You know, if you could wait a few weeks, you'd get a better deal."

Flavia waved the credit card in her hand. "That's what the plastic is for," she said. "Buy now, worry later."

"Should I wrap it?" the girl asked. "Is it a gift?"

Flavia thought about Magda, in Chicago, sitting on the floor of Simon and Helen's living room, opening the posted package with delight.

"No, this is for my daughter, now that the weather's changing."

The girl nodded, folded the clothes neatly and placed them into a large brown paper shopping bag. "Enjoy," she said.

Flavia stepped out of the store onto the sidewalk. The day was warm, and pleasant. A group of teenagers loitered at the window of a video shop, looking at posters of the new listings. Two men examined the engine of a car parked at a corner meter, hood open. She walked on the sidewalk, pretending she fit into this picture, that she looked like an everyday kind of person, a normal woman, the kind who might have a three-year-old at home, waiting eagerly for new clothes.

She threw the bag in the back of the truck, together with the foil-wrapped meals to deliver, and headed back up the mountain to do her route.

She brought the clothes into Geraldine's trailer. She unfolded them, placed the dress and blouse on Geraldine's table, and held up the sandals for her inspection.

"Nice," Geraldine said. "The dress is so pretty. Your daughter will love it."

Flavia shook her head. "Really, she doesn't like to dress up much. We live in the woods, up near Tannersville. My little girl hardly ever puts on a dress. Or even fancy jeans like this."

Geraldine looked puzzled. "So why did you buy this kind of clothes?"

"I don't know," said Flavia. "I just felt like seeing her dressed up for a change. The way I used to be, when I was little. I grew up in Caracas. It was hot. And girls wore dresses. I like to see little girls in dresses."

"Caracas?" Geraldine asked, surprised. "You grew up in Caracas? Is that where your mother left you? On another continent?"

Flavia nodded, swallowing hard. "Imagine that," she managed, and then she didn't feel like crying anymore. "Just up and left me."

"Oh, honey," Geraldine said, stepping instinctively towards Flavia and putting her arms around her, but Flavia didn't like the feel of Geraldine's body, too loose and soft, or the way she smelled. She stiffened and pulled away.

"I wore dresses in Caracas," she said. "Pink dresses. Ribbons. Bows in my hair. My father adored me. Dressed me up like a doll. I want my daughter to dress like a girl."

"Well," said Geraldine, "in that case, you better make the changes now." But Geraldine's tone was different, and her expression had changed from sympathy to an uncomfortable recognition, as if she were talking to something broken, someone she should keep away from. *La loca.*

"Make the changes now," Geraldine said, "because whatever your girl is now, she's not going to change later."

La loca. Then and now.

Flavia folded the clothes back into the bag. She stood up and left.

She headed back down the mountain into Kingston. The afternoon was already darkening, and the downtown streets were deserted. By now Hugo would be home, wondering where she was. She rummaged for change, and found a pay phone in the pharmacy.

Geraldine answered.

"It's me, Flavia," she said.

Geraldine waited. Flavia swallowed hard, and spoke.

"I have to tell you something, Geraldine," she said. "I don't have a daughter," she said. "I'll never have children. I made all that up."

She hung up the phone. She had said it. *I do not have a daughter. I will never have a daughter.* She wasn't crazy. She knew what was real.

Flavia walked down the street to the bus station, pulling her sweater tighter around her in the early spring chill. There was a bus leaving in twenty minutes for the airport in Newburgh. She had a credit card, a bag of children's clothes, and thirteen dollars in cash. She didn't know where she was going or why, but she knew that the only thing she really had to take along was herself.

WRITER'S WORKSHOP
for L.S.

──Glenna Holloway

Summer in Aspen: the namesaked trees
investing pale fluff in any opening—
stairwell, window, unguarded yawn,
hired hands filling bags with it. The star,
James Dickey, telling you and me to read
Dryden and Pope and to empty our heads
of metaphor. Slipping into elegant French
rolling down from his heights as easy
as aspen fuzz, easy on his tongue
as old Southern whiskey, he presided
over our premises, our poetic promises.
He didn't believe in beautiful.

Evenings the local jazz was good,
and our Jewish roommate's cheeseless lasagna
at midnight. Afterward, at the dark
bedroom window, the mountain pressed closer,
pleading for lyrics we shunned.

That last angry session you said our poems
had been aborted, dissected to death.
Dickey said they were never conceived,

called them false pregnancies.
I said they'd been artificially inseminated
in glass outside the warm womb—
laboratory entities. What did anyone expect
from altitude so dry and dreamless, swirling
with the white invective of seeds denied?

After all this time on level safe terrain,
each night beneath my lids
the mountain waits.

PROVIDENCE

—Tom Montgomery-Fate

I still don't know if the cat licked my thumb. I'm sure I fed it with my right hand, and that the cut from the machete was fresh, but whether its tongue, its saliva cells, actually came in contact with the open gash at the base of my thumbnail is still unclear. I can't assume that it didn't just because of the way things turned out. I was definitely at risk. Definitely. But I'm writing this more to clarify than justify. We weren't naïve. We knew there were risks in bringing the Word to a remote village like Batac.

Our helper, Rosa, had discouraged us from feeding the stray cats that roamed the banana patch behind our large cinder block house. She said they'd beg all morning on the porch while she cooked, or pester her in the backyard all afternoon while she hung the wash. She didn't force the issue, though. Less than five feet tall and under one hundred pounds, Rosa was so quiet and small that she sometimes seemed to disappear in the house, to evaporate into the humidity. I would notice the delicate, brown curve of her body while she was sweeping or mopping near me in the living room, then I'd get up for coffee, return, and she'd be gone. And I couldn't find her anywhere. She rarely talked to me except in the evening at dinner. Yet, she opened up to my wife, Claire. Sometimes at night I'd hear them gossiping and laughing on the back porch like sisters, as they picked at a coconut and slapped mosquitoes. Claire explained to her why she liked the cats. They reminded her of home, of a quieter life—of Tillich and Bell our huge, grey tabbies, sprawling in the sunlight in our tiny,

63

vintage apartment on Chicago's lakeshore. The local cats didn't stir this kind of nostalgia in me, though. I liked them because they needed us, because we knew how to help them, because no one else would help them, because every evening they gobbled up the fish bones and stale rice that we left scattered on the concrete patio.

One rainy night we let one of the cats come inside, to live with us. The gaunt, yellow bobtail seemed overwhelmed with gratitude as he limped in through the screen door, all wet and bony. We named him Mila, short for *Milagro*. Rosa was bewildered by our decision. After several days her unspoken concern grew into surprisingly direct hints. "Here, in the Philippines, cats carry bugs and things. They are not so clean." Or, "They don't sell litter boxes here because cats don't stay indoors here." Or, "If you put him outside, he'll keep the rats away."

It was a Sunday afternoon. I was gutting a milkfish in the kitchen when the machete slipped, slicing my thumb. While blotting the gash, I thought nothing of letting Mila lick the slimy entrails from my wounded hand. But that same evening he bit Claire. She offered him a piece of boiled egg and he abruptly sunk his front incisors firmly into her palm. His jaw seemed to lock shut. Stunned, Claire gasped, and then stopped breathing.

"Breathe, Claire, *breathe*," I said.

She finally let out a huge puff. "My God, what's wrong with him?" she said.

"Just breathe, honey. I'll get it."

Then, with his teeth still deep in Claire's flesh, the cat rolled his bright green eyes pleadingly up at us, like it was our fault, like he couldn't control his own jaw, and couldn't we please do something. I pried his mouth open with a rice knife and Claire removed her hand. Mila looked as relieved as we were. We locked him up in the kitchen and went back to bed. The next day he went nuts—360 degree flips, one after another, sometimes landing on his head. We tied him up outside to protect Rosa and our neighbors. He nearly strangled himself on the six-foot twine lead.

Batac didn't have a vet. People took their pets and livestock to Dr. Sangre, who was actually trained as a dentist. He could give shots, administer medication, and set broken bones. After I described the cat's behavior, he launched into a long string of sentences in Filipino, followed by one English word, "Soospeeshoos."

"Suspicious? What's suspicious?" I asked.

A smile but no answer.

"Rabies is uh, fatal, right?" I asked.

"Yes. After one week pass, no cure," he said.

He advised us to put Mila in a cage and watch him for two days. If the fits ended, and if he could eat and drink, then everything was fine. So I bought a large bamboo birdcage in the market for two hundred pesos. By the time I got home Mila had worn himself out. He did a kind of drunken cartwheel, hopelessly wrapped himself around a young papaya tree, and collapsed. I asked Rosa if she would help put him in the cage. She agreed. I carefully wrapped each arm up to the elbow in old beach towels for protection. She picked up the panting mass of matted yellow fur and placed it in the cage.

Due to our extensive responsibilities at the school, I felt that Rosa should be the one to feed and carefully monitor Mila's behavior during the quarantine period. Claire wouldn't ask her, so I did. Rosa had no reservations. "Good. I will do that," she said, continually nodding, but not listening. Two days later at dinner she shared the horrific news in her usual reserved monotone. Mila hadn't eaten since we put him in the cage! He hadn't eaten in two days, but Rosa hadn't told us! She said we hadn't told her to tell us, and that she didn't want to bother or worry us.

Claire, working hard to restrain her fear, listened quietly while Rosa explained. Her eyes pardoned Rosa and then shifted to me in a kind of reprimand. She was concerned about Rosa's feelings! I lost it.

"Damn it. This is *rabies*, Claire, not a headcold! If we get it, we'll die!"

Rosa hurried off to her room crying. Claire followed. A few minutes later I peeked in the door. "Look, I'm sorry, Rosa," I said. "I'm just really worried."

I didn't care whose fault it was now. Five days had passed since the bite (and since I had possibly been licked on my wound). Time to panic.

I got out our *Mayo Clinic Medical Encyclopedia:* If the bite was deep and close to the head or heart you had three to four days to get the vaccine. If less severe, and on an extremity, you had six to eight. It didn't mention anything about licking, or other forms of contact. Once the symptoms appeared it was too late. I reviewed them: pain and tingling near the area of the bite, difficulty swallowing, thick, sticky saliva, wild fits of anger, and finally, paralysis and convulsions.

I whirled out of my chair and stumbled off into the dark with my umbrella for Dr. Bueno's office. I didn't trust the dentist on this one. Besides, he kept charging us his "American price," four times what he charged the locals. He assumed we were like the other missionaries. We were and we weren't. Our mission board had developed new policies that year. According to our contract we were now supposed to "live similarly to the international counterparts, sharing the joys and risks of daily life." The hope was to "lessen the historic privilege of missionaries which often insulates them from the host culture"—to prevent missionaries with microwaves, VCRs and new Volvos next door to Filipinos with wood-burning stoves, broken radios, and homemade bicycles. It all sounds good on paper.

I liked Dr. Bueno because he spoke good English and had treated a number of Peace Corps volunteers. He was infinitely patient with my health concerns. I could trust him. But his greeting: "What can I do to you today?" still unnerved me. It also seemed odd that in my six visits to his office that month I only saw him with another patient once. Instead, he was always repairing bicycles; adjusting brake calipers and oiling rusted sprockets. And while he did keep his workshop full of wrenches, dented steel rims, and patched tubes separate from his medical office, I once noticed a cup of ball bearings soaking in kerosene right next to the cotton balls and tongue depressors.

His office was on top of the New Gospel Grocery, so I had to cut through the dried fish section, and a sweaty, moaning Friday night Pentecostal worship service to get to his staircase. He was in but the vaccine wasn't. Manila was the only place that had it. His advice: box the cat and take it on the bus to the university vet school in Manila. Have it beheaded at the lab and examined for rabies. If negative, return to Batac; if positive, proceed to the hospital for vaccine injections. We agreed. It sounded so simple. There was one bus per day. We would leave the next evening.

That night at 2 a.m. I reached over to find Claire missing. In the bathroom, in the hard tiled light, I found her sitting on the closed toilet crying. She looked strange. A red swelling began near the bridge of her nose and consumed nearly half of her eyebrow, puffing it way out like a bee sting.

"I don't know what it is. I think it's starting. What is it? What IS it?" She was in a frenzy. "And look at this. My mucous is yellow…."

"That welt's from a bug—a mosquito or spider or something. Probably a spider," I said, trying to calm her. "We still have several days…."

"You don't know that! I just can't do this. I can't take this not knowing." She began to cry again. I bent down to embrace her.

"We'll get through this," I said. "I'm going to go see if there's any ice."

"Oh God, Martin," she said. "You just don't get it. I don't want to 'get through this.' I want out. OUT! Why did we come here? Do you remember? Why?"

More crying. I held her there in the bathroom until she went back to bed. As I carefully examined my naked body for any abnormalities in the full-length mirror on the back of the bathroom door, I considered Claire's question. I had one answer: providence. We came here because God led us here. We chose to come to the Philippines, but we were also chosen. I take comfort in knowing that. And it wasn't so bad really. The teaching was interesting. The students were respectful. We lived near a beach. We rarely had to cook or clean. There was no snow or ice.

Claire's difficulty in adjusting was due to her inability to believe that God would provide for us. She never had the kind of faith I do (which she defined as "only partially blind"). A year earlier we had both come out of seminary full of raw idealism. But while I came out with an exclamation point in my head, Claire came out with a question mark in hers.

And it just kept growing. She celebrated the human will rather than God's. She thought Jesus was a radical social activist who had been assassinated, rather than God's Son who had died for our sins. She had slowly come to see God as a genderless mystery rather than a benevolent Father.

I admired her analytical approach to things, but her growing lack of faith seemed to leave her defeated. She had profound commitments, immense compassion, but no real grounding, nothing to hold on to, just questions. And her questions never led her to belief, only to more questions. "What exactly do you believe in Claire?" I once asked her after a circuitous discussion. "I believe in believing," she said. The idea of providence made little sense to her. It still doesn't. "Faith and fate are separate entities," she told me. And while I know opposites attract, and remember how much we enjoyed arguing theology, I sometimes wonder how we ever wound up together, how we lasted four years.

At first, she wouldn't consider the mission field. "The conquest is over," she said, only half kidding. But the job market for young married co-pastors was dismal, so when our mission board jumped on the "celebrate diversity" bandwagon and began to change their language, I was finally able to convince her. We weren't missionaries after all; we were "global partners." I think Claire thought we were going to somehow undo the conquest, to compensate for what the Spanish, the U.S., and the Japanese did to the Filipinos. I simply wanted a job, to put what I learned into practice, and maybe to save our marriage.

We *did* have a reason for coming here. Claire just couldn't remember what it was. She was exhausted, her eye was all swollen up, and she was drowning in her own anxiety—going down fast. When I finished inspecting myself I joined her in bed.

"How could this happen to us?" she finally asked.

"I really don't know," I said. "But I think you should at least *try* to give it to God."

The dark, wet, half-ring beneath her puffy eye shimmered eerily in the full moonlight that poured through the window. She looked like someone had punched her.

"I can't, Martin. I just can't. And I'm not blaming you. I just don't have anything left to give—to God or anyone else…."

She flipped the box fan switch to high, and turned on her side, with her back to me. She was crying again. I reached over to rub her shoulders, but she pulled away. So I rolled over on my back, and lay awake imagining new symptoms in the heavy night air.

Finally, the morning sunlight sifted through the rain clouds and banana trees, seeping into our room. Relief. We made it. Claire felt a lot better. And her eye was less swollen, though it itched a lot.

Around 6 p.m., an hour before we would wave down a horse carriage to the Maria de Leon bus terminal, a typhoon arrived, and soon opened to full throttle—a signal three, the worst of the season. A twenty-foot stand of bamboo trees whipped our house, and then the neighbor's. An enormous black limb cracked off an acacia tree across the road and came down on our electric pole. We lost power. And since eight families on the street had hot-wired to this pole, our gravel road was unpassable—a cracking, popping, electric bramble of wires.

I think Claire was worried that she might die. I was worried that we both would. Relative to the pending doom of our illness, the storm didn't seem so serious. With the rain machine-gunning off our corrugated metal roof we packed for the nine-hour trip. I asked Rosa to box the cat. It snarled and swiped at her for a minute or two but then abruptly went limp.

Claire asked Rosa if she'd like to come along. Since they were close, I think Claire wanted the moral support. We were more than willing to spring for her bus fare. I asked her too, but she said "No," and then launched into a hopelessly melded string of Filipino words that I didn't understand. It seemed she talked slower and more deliberately when she wanted us to understand her, and rapidly when she didn't. Claire didn't think so. Claire was better at languages than I, though, so she may have been right. Anyway, I assumed Rosa just wanted some time alone.

We made our way through the downpour, careful to dodge the buzzing wires strung across the road. A *calesa* driver finally stopped his horse at the corner and agreed to take us to the terminal. We climbed into the carriage and rumbled off in the rain. Since the typhoon was headed north, rather than toward Manila, our bus had not been canceled. We heaved and hissed out of Batac, through Pagudpud, to the Marcos highway, and turned south down the coast. This was the sixth day. We wouldn't get to the university or the hospital until the seventh. Claire's hand tingled a bit, and her throat felt thick and scratchy. We both prayed it was her imagination.

At 11:00 we reached San Fernando, a small city which marked the halfway point of our journey. I pushed my window open to have a look. As we drove through the narrow street, the electricity was cut—a brown out. The scattered lights in the tin and cinderblock buildings stacked around us abruptly went black. At a stop sign, I looked through the soft curtain of grey rain to see a young mother with a candle and a crying baby leaning out of her first floor window frame—perhaps twelve feet from the bus. Their round faces flickered above the warm yellow flame. The woman stared at me like she wanted something. But then the wind blew the candle out. I could hear the baby crying but I couldn't see them. I looked away. The bus pulled off with a hot carbonic hiss.

Two miles south of San Fernando a bridge had washed out. We waited all night in the packed bus on the shore of the Rio Coco for an outrigger boat to arrive and take us across. Supposedly, another Maria de Leon bus would then meet us on the other side. Our driver immediately turned off the engine and thus the air conditioning. The windows, dripping with humidity, didn't open. Neither did the bathroom door. There was barely enough oxygen for the sixty-four passengers (I counted) to keep breathing. But at least we had our own seats. The eleven passengers without tickets were stuck in the aisle all night, leaning on each other or hanging from the metal luggage rack bars.

I had almost fallen asleep when the cat escaped. I still don't know how it pushed its frenzied head under the flap and through the yards and yards of masking tape. But the dozing passengers were awakened to a howling, spastic feline gymnastic show in the main aisle. As Claire would later remind me, my yelling, "Rabies!" at that point in the crisis was premature, and had entirely negative consequences. This was one English word that everyone spontaneously understood. Mothers looked in horror at the ripped open box, screamed, and then tried to stuff their babies into their shirts or into their rattan baskets, which were already full. Previously invisible chickens, hens and fighting cocks, took to flight, breaking out of rice sacks and cardboard boxes hidden beneath the seats. They attempted to roost in the racks overhead. Children, sensing the excitement, either laughed and clapped or screamed in terror. Most of the men just watched. Claire looked embarrassed, then worried, then exhausted. "My God, what's next?" she said. She lifted both her hands to cover her face, gently rocked her head for a moment, then slowly spread her fingers open, like a child playing peekaboo—peering through the cracks at the absurd drama in which she, Mila, and I were all starring.

The cat disappeared for a few seconds, reappeared under a rear seat, and then jigged back down the aisle and out the open door, setting off another round of screams. The driver gave me a five-gallon paint can which was wedged behind his seat. I ran after the cat as it began a wild zigzag toward the river. Soaked in the rain, the five or six pounds of slinking disaster looked more like some yet undiscovered rodent than a cat. Desperate to prevent it from being swept away by the current before we could have it beheaded, I proceeded to save its life. I scrambled after him on the slick, jagged rocks until he abruptly stopped, inches from the roiling water. Bewildered, as if contemplating his own end, he turned his head back to look at me for one lucid moment, as if there was something he expected me to recognize. Then his legs buckled and he lay on the rock, barely breathing. I scooped him up in the paint can, returned to the bus, dumped him back into the box, closed the lid, and stuck him under the seat.

The outrigger *banca* arrived at dawn. We crossed ten at a time. Another bus was waiting as promised. After two flats and a broken radiator hose we arrived at the Manila station at noon of the seventh day. I cut a small hole in the box and checked the cat. It wasn't moving. I poked it with my pen. It was dead. We decided to scratch the University lab. It probably didn't matter now, and we'd never get there. A different typhoon had hit Manila from the south. The university would be underwater. But the hospital, still four miles away, was on higher ground and might still be accessible. We got in a taxi. We turned up Quezon Boulevard—past a mile-long squatters' village, a mall, the Hilton, the Holiday Inn, a new sub-division, more squatters, then down a steep hill. The next thing I knew the water was up to the door handles. Realizing his mistake, the driver began swearing. The engine died and we began to drift. Cranking the wheel and using the back wheels as rudders he attempted to steer us toward a curb and ground us. It sort of worked. We rolled up our pants, forced a door open, and got out. The water was fast, but only up to our knees. We could now see the hospital in the distance. The cat smelled. I was nauseous. I opened the lid, pulled out the dead cat, and tossed him in the current. This set Claire off. "What if it *is* infected?" she screamed. I hadn't really thought of that. But it was too late. I was not going to dive into the floodwaters after a dead, diseased cat.

The next sound I heard was Claire thrashing in the putrid water. It was nuts. The carcass, now more grey than yellow, was already twenty yards downstream, swirling under a cement viaduct. She took two steps in, dropped into a hole, and was knocked down by the waist-high torrent. I jumped in, quickly reached out to grab one of her legs from behind, and just barely wrestled her back to the curb. Gagging and crying, she hugged me—more out of relief than gratitude. She looked exhausted leaning on the taxi, but her eyes were still scanning the water for the cat. A blue rubber sandal, three bobbing green coconuts, a hubcap, and a bloated rat drifted by.

"It's gone, Claire," I said. "I'm sorry…really sorry. I was just so sick of that thing that I forgot…"

"I know. I know," she said. "It doesn't matter anymore. Let's just go."

We walked the two miles to the hospital and went straight to the emergency room to avoid waiting with the dozens of other patients slumping and squatting outside the main clinic and in the hallways. This was an emergency after all. But the nurse behaved as if we were stopping in for our annual physicals. "Could you take a seat, please." She actually said this! She then handed me clipboards and new patient intake forms. I pushed the clipboards and her out of the way, bolted through the swinging metal doors marked "staff only," and headed straight toward the doctor's office. "Stop, Martin!" Claire shouted at me down the hallway. "An extra half hour isn't going to matter!" she screamed. I paused at the door, turned and looked at her. She knew I couldn't stop. I was going to get the treatment we deserved. I walked in on a vaginal exam. When I opened the door the doctor looked up at me and then dropped a shiny, metal instrument which went pinging across the linoleum floor. The young pregnant woman, with her bare feet in the metal stirrups, her short brown legs bent to ninety degrees, was oddly beautiful—and terrified. She rolled herself into the sheet, off the exam table, and out the door in one remarkably fluid motion.

The doctor was angry, then restrained. He wanted to get rid of me. That's probably why he tolerated my explanation. He prescribed the equine vaccine for Claire, but nothing for me. This was when Claire quietly slipped in his office. I tried to explain again, in my slowest and clearest English, about the gash and my feeding it with an open hand. He listened to about half of it, lost patience, then interrupted me.

"Listen. You are really not at risk if the cat didn't bite you. You can get the shots if you insist, but I don't recommend it. Some have a bad reaction. They're very, very expensive. And you don't need them."

I detected a note of sarcasm in his voice. Restraining my anger, I rushed to the pharmacy to check on the cost of the vaccine. The equine series cost five hundred U.S. dollars per person—a suspiciously round number. I ordered two rounds anyway. Thankfully, they took Visa.

Even though there was still an outside possibility we had waited too long, that we would die, I pretended that we wouldn't. Claire wouldn't talk about it, or anything else. We went to a Pizza Hut and a movie at the Manila Mega Mall that night to unwind—a Jackie Chan kickboxer movie—but I didn't care. Two hours in the air-conditioned darkness was well worth the admission price. After an extra day in Manila to get caught up on our rest, we returned to Batac the next evening on the overnight bus.

Rosa cooked us an enormous grouper stuffed with onions and garlic for dinner the day we returned. Afterwards, we played three games of Yahtzee. Rosa won them all. The next day she came down with a sore throat. We sent her straight to Dr. Bueno. (We always encouraged Rosa to go to the doctor whenever she felt the least bit ill, and we always paid.) She took amoxycillin for a week. It didn't help so she tried another series. Still no relief. Then Bueno figured it out. The tender, itchy inflammation on her forearm wasn't from a spider. She had it. The cat had bitten her. More than once. She had thought the bites so insignificant that she hadn't said anything. Her friend had given her an herbal compress that she believed would prevent infection. Rosa, dear Rosa, our beloved cook and friend, had rabies. After Bueno's diagnosis she went straight to Claire's study to tell her. She asked Claire what we wanted for dinner and then broke down. They cried for hours. First, I heard Rosa's soft, shaking sobs, then Claire's, which were louder, more regular. When I walked up to ask Claire if she wanted me to go to the market to get the groceries, I saw them through the narrow crack in the door. Claire was curled into a soft S behind Rosa on the cot. She was stroking her hair. "I'll take care of you," she purred over and over in her ear. And she did.

Except for her throat and some minor joint pain, Rosa felt pretty well for the next week. But then she went wild. She threw a knife into the floor and a rice pot at me. I got four stitches in my temple. She screamed she was going to bite me so I'd die. I, of course, avoided her. But Claire still insisted that she stay on with us. She even invited Rosa's mother and sister to come down from their place in the Cordillera Mountains to live with us. During that last month Claire did most of the cooking for us by herself along with maintaining her substantial teaching load and other responsibilities at the chapel. I guess you could say we did everything we could for Rosa and then some. She died in April, the hottest month of the year, the day before her twenty-third birthday. Claire gave a nice eulogy at the graveside service—thanking God for the gift of Rosa's life. (Rather than reprimanding Him for her death, which I had feared.) We covered all of the funeral and burial costs.

After Rosa died, Claire lost whatever remnants of faith she had left. She blamed our "failure to acculturate" on me. I really don't know what she expected. She even blamed Rosa's death on me. She said she'd found out "more than she wanted to know" about me.

"My God, Martin," she finally said. "Are you blind? These people don't need us to teach them anything. They don't need the English language or fax machines or computers or motorcycles or cell phones or any of that other crap you keep trying to order from the Mission Board. We're not helping anyone. They can read the Bible without you! They can run the school without you! For God's sake, if we'd leave, most of the faculty could live in our house, instead of those tin shacks down the street."

I tried to avoid her guilt trip. How could I know if or how much the school "needed" me? That wasn't the point. I told her that I simply thought God wanted us to persevere, not to abandon His plan due to fear. "Give your pain to God," I told her. "Give it to Jesus. He can heal you. Jesus may still be your answer."

She looked astonished and then said it.

"Yeah, but what's the *question*? What's the fucking question?"

After four years of marriage, that was the last thing she said to me—an accusatory tirade punctuated by the "F" word. She left on the overnight bus for Manila. I haven't heard from her since. That was three months ago. I've already forgiven her. And though I'd be lying if I said I didn't miss her, Marta, my new helper, has made the transition easier. She's much taller, more talkative, and younger than Rosa—seventeen I think. She's a good cook and takes care of my needs. I do wish Claire well. But we simply weren't meant to be. And she was just too spiritually exhausted to endure the risks of daily life here.

Speaking of which, I'm still battling some health problems as a result of the rabies vaccine. My body couldn't handle the horse serum. It's my lymph nodes. They're swollen. Five in my groin, two under each arm, and one in my neck—most about the size of navy beans, except the one in my neck. It's more like a peach pit. They call it generalized adenopathy. All of the doctors I've seen have ruled out AIDS and lymphoma. However, I did eventually find several doctors who recognized the need for further testing. One suggested allergy tests, another a complete analysis and profile of my thyroid output, and a specialist at the medical school suggested I have one of my nodes cut out for a biopsy, just to be sure. I've scheduled the allergy and thyroid tests for next week. But George, a missionary friend in Baguio, says to forget about the biopsy. "No way. Don't ever let them cut on you," he says. "Go home for that." He suggested taking a leave and getting it thoroughly checked out back at the Mayo Clinic's pathology center. So I've written the Mission Board, requesting that they fund a one-month emergency health leave in the U.S. I still haven't heard from them. But that's not surprising. The mail here is completely unreliable. And to think, Claire thought we'd have no need for a fax machine.

MILES FROM HOME

—Ellen Zalewski

Transplanted to an afternoon
Sitting on the stoop
The grass painted white
Drifts and hollows
Against a hybrid
Robin's sky
Fades
Into velvet night
Three-quarter ivory moon
Closing the day
Opulent and lovely.

GABRIEL AND THE BOSS MAN

—E. Donald Two-Rivers

The thing about second chances is that you never know how or when one is going to hit you. Take, for instance, the day that Gabriel Peoples, a Lakota boy from Chicago, was released from the prison downstate. At first glance, you might assume that it was he who was getting a second chance, and in many ways you would be right; but consider the circumstances of the assistant warden in this story, too.

"Peoples. Jones. Walters. Let's go," said the assistant warden. "Grab your stuff and follow me."

"Where are we going?" Jones asked, a grin lighting his black shiny face.

"To hell if you don't change your ways."

"I just been there, Boss Man."

"I'll drive you men to the bus station. You'll board and that's the last I'll see of any of you…at least for awhile. Now let's go."

After serving ten years, Gabriel Peoples was finally walking out of the Illinois State Penitentiary. Although he wouldn't, or maybe couldn't admit it, he was scared. Scared about what changes he might find. He wondered if he'd become institutionalized or something. He shook his head to erase that thought. No way, he whispered to himself. In the dank concrete hall leading out, he listened to the assistant warden's footsteps. They seemed to say last chance, last chance, last chance. It won't be long now, he thought. Sure, he was scared, but he was also ecstatic. In his head a band played, pretty women danced, and the whole world jumped for joy. His face, however, remained stoic, like it was chiseled from the granite that layered his homeland in Canada. In this place it was best to keep your emotions hidden. Over the years he had gotten good at it.

He would spend his twenty-ninth birthday on the streets. He tried to imagine what that would be like. Things had changed drastically in the old neighborhood, his aunt told him during her last visit, before she died.

"It isn't hardly worth living there anymore," she had said. "A woman can't even go to the store without getting hassled by sidewalk Romeos."

She stopped talking for a moment, looked around carefully, then leaned closer to confide in him.

"I just had a black girl threaten to kill me because she thought I was Spanish. I'm afraid to take out the garbage because I caught a young black boy taking a piss by our garbage can. He didn't care if anybody seen him. The neighborhood's changed, Gabriel. I think it would be best if you went somewhere else when you get out. You won't like it around there."

The assistant warden kept up a happy chatter on the ten-minute ride to the bus station. Gabriel could tell this was the one aspect of his job that the assistant warden really liked. He always insisted on driving the released prisoners to the bus station. He told jokes that none of them really wanted to hear, but Walters and Jones laughed and shucked with him.

"Yeah, Boss Man, you be telling some mean jokes all right. You should have been a comedian on TV. That's how good you is," Jones said as he slapped the assistant warden playfully on the arm.

"You're a goddamn ass kisser, Jones. If you ever come back here I'm going to set you up real pretty. Make you my runner. You can kiss my ass all day long."

Jones laughed. Gabriel stared out the window.

"What's wrong with *you*, Peoples?" the assistant warden asked.

"I bet he's all spaced out on getting him a woman tonight," said Jones. "Ain't that right, Chief?"

"I was just thinking, that's all," said Gabriel. He cleared his throat.

Walters, a thirty-year-old car thief from Peoria, turned to the assistant warden and asked what the papers were.

"Boy, those are our walking papers," said Jones. "Ain't that right, Boss Man?"

"So how many times does this make it for you, Jones?"

"What you mean, Boss Man?" Jones was tall and loud—two things, thought Gabriel, that usually didn't go together.

"How many times you been back here?"

"This be my second trip down here."

"You just turned twenty-five, too. Next time you come back, you're going straight to the coal yard."

"Aw, Boss Man, you wouldn't do me that way, would you?"

"Three times, it's the coal yard. Don't come back."

The assistant warden looked in the rear view mirror.

"What about you, Peoples? Where are you headed?"

"Chicago."

"With your life, I mean. You don't say much, do you?" The assistant warden's eyes narrowed. "You don't like me. Is that it?"

"What gives you that idea?"

"In ten years, you ain't said ten words to me." He paused to let that sink in. "What did you get busted for?"

"Armed robbery."

"Armed robbery, *Boss Man*," said the assistant warden.

"That's what I said," said Gabriel.

"You didn't say *Boss Man*."

"Is it necessary I do?"

"If you want to get along with me, it is."

Gabriel turned and looked out of the window. What does it matter if I want to get along with him or not, he wondered. What does he care anyway? To hell with him. I'm out of here.

The station wagon turned into the driveway of the Greyhound Bus Station and lurched to a stop. Situated on the west side of town, the station was not much more than a garage with a converted office. The assistant warden swiveled around to look at Gabriel and Jones in the back seat, an irritated glint in his eyes. "I guess you could give a shit, right Peoples?"

He handed Jones his release papers and an envelope.

"There's a bus ticket and twenty-five dollars in there," he said. "Don't miss the bus."

"Yes, Boss Man." Jones reached across the seat to shake hands with the man, then quickly opened the door and slid out. Gabriel watched him breathe in very deeply as he stuffed the papers into his jacket pocket. He thinks he's free now, Gabriel thought.

"Walters. Here you go. Behave yourself up there in Peoria, hear?"

"You got it, Boss Man. I'll be a model citizen."

The warden pulled the lever that let the car seat move back and looked hard at the Indian.

"Stick-up man, huh?"

"That's what I was accused of."

"I see you did every day of your sentence."

"I maxed out."

"Why do you think that is?"

"The parole board maxed me. I don't know why."

"Well, I do. In fact, I recommended it. I don't think you're reformed at all. I'll bet you do it again."

"Everyone's entitled to their opinion."

"That's right, Peoples, and do you know what? It's also my 'opinion' that you'll be back. And when you do come back, I'll personally teach you to address me in the proper way."

Gabriel watched the two other men go into the station.

"I could have looked out for you, Peoples. I'm part Indian myself, you know. Cherokee from way back."

"I heard something like that."

"Your bus leaves in twenty-five minutes. Here's your ticket." He extended the envelope.

"Do you want these walking papers?"

"Yeah, I do."

"Yeah, you do…what?" The car jounced when he raised his voice.

"Why? Why do you want me to say that?"

"Because it'll make me feel better. Like you were reformed. It's simple, Peoples, really simple. Now say it."

"I'm sorry."

"Is it a goddamn Indian thing, Peoples? I told you I'm part Indian, too. Give me the respect that I deserve."

"I always have."

"You're not doing it now. You are not giving respect to your superior."

"I thought you were Indian."

"I am your superior," the warden shouted. "I'm the goddamn assistant warden of a state penitentiary. Not everybody gets to be that, Peoples. It took a lot of hard work. Don't you think that makes me your superior? I have the power. People with power get respect. It's simple, Peoples."

"I don't have to grovel to respect you."

"Look, Peoples, I had to practically claw my way to the top. Do you understand? I worked hard to become the assistant warden, and I'll continue to work hard to become warden. Do you have any idea what I have to do to keep my job?"

"No, I don't."

"I got your freedom in my hand, Peoples." He waved the release papers in Gabriel's face. "Now the least you can do is say Boss Man."

"Freedom doesn't come on paper."

"You son of a bitch. You hate me, don't you? You hate everything I represent."

"Freedom doesn't come on paper. Neither does honesty nor respect. Indians like me learned that long ago. We were born with that knowledge. Treaties? Didn't you learn that?"

"You bastard. Get out of this car." He threw the papers at Gabriel. "And if you ever come back to my prison, you know what's waiting for you."

"I won't be back."

"Yeah, well, some Indian will."

Gabriel stooped to pick up the papers. He knew what he had to do. Ten years of stifling his emotions had taught him a discipline that survival demanded.

"I don't deny that you worked hard. I've watched you."

The assistant warden eyed Gabriel, waiting for an insult.

"And you know what? I admired you. You are 'the man,' all right. You know what the other prisoners say about you?"

The assistant warden stared apprehensively.

"They say you're rough, tough, but fair. Hell, I remember that kid, what was his name? Blair. You remember him? When his mother died and you had to tell him. I was sitting close enough to hear you. Remember that?"

"The kid committed suicide."

"You told him she was in a better place. And that she'd want him to make her proud—to make it out and do her proud. They were goods words. He just didn't listen."

The assistant warden looked away.

"Things could have been easier for you," the assistant warden said. "I wanted to put you on the farm as a truck driver. Do you know that these guys would practically kill for that job? All you had to do was show me respect."

"Groveling isn't respect."

"You think I sold out?" said the assistant warden,

"Those are your words. I think you were in a hostile environment everyday and still survived. That takes guts."

"You got some guts, too, Peoples. Now go on. Get on that bus and don't look back."

He reached out his hand and Gabriel shook it.

"You take it easy," said Gabriel. He pumped his hand one more time and then added, "Boss Man."

Gabriel turned away to walk toward the depot.

83

"Hey, Peoples," called the assistant warden. "I mean it: don't come back. The Boss Man will be waiting on you. My tomahawk will be aimed at the side of your head. You come back and you're mine."

"You wish."

"Have a good life, Peoples."

"You too, Boss Man."

The assistant warden put the car in gear and went back to work. He whistled on the way, an Indian tune that he hardly remembered.

Gabriel lowered his eyes under the glare of the sun and took a deep breath. The dank smell of the prison was still on his clothes.

THE PILOT STUDY
(a pastiche)*

——Deborah E. Ryel

Tired perhaps of
the smell of
fried chicken, once
a delight, 30,000 Americans
took their own lives.

Readers in Zurich had the same
emergent dread.

He watched carefully
where he set
each foot. With deathly
suddenness he had become wed
to a diplomatic dance.

What we need, he said,
is a strategy, we need
data. Let us agree
at the outset, the brain
was not molded for joy
preponderant. The fact of
death, however, may not be

tragic. Certainly 200,000 people
died of famine, joining
others in an ambitious
experiment. One million
Afghans murdered by Russians
may provide clues to
the crucial mystery
of minimum critical size.

Transfixed by
the preeminent velvet
rope, though death's edge
prove so abrupt
so near

no one observed

the great leap forward
for instance, when twenty
(or forty?) million died.

Regarding Hitler, he adds,
estimated to have executed
the deliberate
starvation, for an example,
as a matter of policy.
For what, I would
ask you to consider
is the numerical relation between
insularization and
doom?

THE PILOT STUDY

I must warn you, he
concludes. The millions
and millions upon millions

we ourselves, a speck
in the sky, the incandescent
dazzle of twirling
multilingual
signs.

*This poem is composed of sentences and parts of sentences from several magazine articles.

THE JONQUILS

——Michael Burke

Kenneth Collins is doing what Kenneth Collins always does when Kenneth Collins is anxious: repeating a silent prayer, the "Hail Mary," again and again until the boredom of repetition subdues his nerves. Of course, boredom is not the point of prayer, but boredom is what Kenneth Collins desires. Dull, plain, safe boredom.

As he recites the prayer, Kenneth Collins watches his ex-wife take a seat at the dining room table as his new wife ushers one of his dead son's friends to the smaller table that showcases all of the memorial photographs.

When Kenneth Collins sees Vince—his dead son's lover, his dead son's boyfriend, his dead son's partner, that is—Kenneth Collins finds himself wanting to pray again. "Hail Mary, full of grace," he says to himself. "The Lord is with thee."

Roy gets a glimpse of himself

Words, words, nothing but fucking words and no words at all about fucking. And that was the great thing about Jordan, though you wouldn't know it by anything that was said at the memorial this afternoon. Jordan was a great lay, one of the all-time best lays, one of those dark-haired, make-you-sweat, break-your-back boys who aren't supposed to exist in real life.

But Jordan did exist in real life.

And I loved him.

And I miss him.

To tell the truth, there hasn't been one fucking morning or one fucking night this whole past year when I haven't thought about Jordan. And that surprises me. That surprises me because I knew I loved Jordan—but I didn't know I loved him *this* much.

Gretchen celebrates a success

Still upset about the artichoke dip. Turned out much too runny. But, the rest of the table—the spinach dip and the garbanzo spread, the cucumber fingers and the carrot sticks, the cauliflower buds and the green pepper rings, the cheeses, the mushroom paté, the red onion potato salad and so on—why, it was all just splendid. And the house looked wonderful, too, for once. Since Ken finally listened to me and fired Gabriella and hired Gracie, this old place has never looked better. The floors. The oak staircase. And, yes, the flowers were perfect, too. Jonquils! Muted yellow in crystal vases. Not at all morose and certainly not overly chipper. Just right—just perfect, surrounded by all of the framed photographs of Jordie.

Bonnie finds more time for disappointment

Mom held up so much better than I ever expected and she looks great now that she's losing all that weight. When she gets way down, Dad's going to be sorry and not just sorry about Gretchen or leaving us, but sorry about everything—*every*thing.

I can't believe he didn't even cry—all afternoon and not a single tear. The house is shoulder-to-shoulder with people blubbering away—Mom, me, family friends, Vince, Jordie's other friends—all of us, weeping, and Dad just stands there, hands in his pockets, eyes to the floor. Like he's waiting for a bus. Some big, white bus to pick him up and whisk him away from all of us and himself and Jordie and God only knows what other ghosts who haunt him.

And what about when it was his turn to talk?

"My name is Kenneth Collins and I want to start by thanking you all for coming"—like he was opening one of his sales meetings. "There's somebody named Jordan Collins who means something very important to each of us"—like Jordie was this month's top seller.

Dad even had his wide, sales smile, too, and he held his head back, chin up, in that way he always does when he's really only talking about himself. Everyone else had something sweet to remember about Jordie, the time he did this, the time he said that. But all Dad could muster was his usual crap, his typical Dad b.s., his—

Is that the baby crying?

Vince is trying not to laugh. He recalls a variety of feelings from these past few months—the hollowness, the sorrow, the loneliness, the choking anger, the relief, the guilt over feeling relieved, the numbing fear—and suddenly, now, he feels like guffawing. Of course, laughing is not a sin.

Vince is standing in the big kitchen, asking Bonnie and Gracie if they need help. They say no, explaining how they prepared each and every dish, how they changed their minds, how Gretchen had the final say.

But all Vince is thinking about is Jordie: How Jordie must be looking down from Heaven and loving this party because Jordie, once again, is the very center of attention.

"Vince?" Bonnie says. "Why are you smiling?"

Roy sings a song

I tell the cab driver to hop on Lake Shore Drive, to take the long way home, and I ask myself this question: How come Jordan and I never really got together? "Dated," I mean. "Lived together." As boyfriends.

We'd known each other for almost seven years, since I moved up from Maple Park. We'd had pretty much the same life early on: a series of those fast, hard, three or four month relationships; but always with somebody else, never each other. We'd always been friends and, sometimes, hell, a lot of times, we'd slept together. But we never spent even two nights in a row together. It was always wake up, get out of bed quick, tell each other how great the sex was (the truth, but let's not even glance at one another) and then make some mostly-serious joke about never messing around again because it would someday, certainly, without doubt, ruin our friendship (a lie, but let's exchange meaningful looks and knowing nods). Christ. I suppose—no, in fact, I know for a fact—that Jordan was far better off with Vincent than he ever would've been with me. Vincent stuck it out through the end with Jordan—hell, Vincent is still sticking it out with Jordan—and, let's face it, that's more than I can say for myself.

I don't think I would've stuck it out. I don't have the sort of guts you need for the Stand-By-His-Side routine. *This*—friendship—is tough enough.

But who knows? Who the fuck ever knows?

To think of all the shit Vincent had to put up with—and I don't just mean all the sick shit, all the hospital shit, all the dying shit: I mean the family shit, the Collins shit. None of them ever really warmed to Vincent, made him feel welcomed. Vince used to say it probably had more to do with Mr. and Mrs. Collins divorcing than with him and Jordan getting together, but I doubt it. And Bonnie was no help, with her blockheaded banker husband and the way they kept the twins and the baby away from Jordan after Vincent moved in—and particularly after Jordan got sick.

Fuck that. Just look at this afternoon: The kids? Nowhere in sight. Probably home with Papa Beancounter. And Mr. Collins? He sulked in one corner while Vince lingered in another, both looking like they were mostly worried about getting arrested for loitering.

Vincent has always done his best to smooth over the family distance—"They're all very nice people, really.... Every family has its quirks"—but when I brought my little plate over to him this afternoon, he whispered, "Do you see them? Do you see the way they all stare at me like I'm the other shoe waiting to drop?"

This was still early, so I tried smiling instead of frowning. "'We—Are—Fam-i-ly,'" I pretended to sing and that at least got Vincent to laugh.

He laughed so hard, some red came to his cheeks.
"Now," he said, "you sound like Jordie."

Gretchen considers an act of generosity

Have to tell Ken—if he ever gets himself out of that bathroom—that I'm more than happy with Gracie's work. Almost couldn't have pulled off today without her. Maybe we can slip her a little extra something.

The day just went so well.

. . .All things considered.

Bonnie could have told you

Vince looked good. Healthy. I wonder how he's doing, how he's feeling, how he's holding up. He certainly seemed fine and he had so many funny, funny stories about Jordie. He's always had so many funny stories about Jordie: The time they went to that party on that yacht and Jordan—wearing his black tuxedo, juggling three bottles of champagne—slipped off the gangplank and went ass over tea cups into Belmont Harbor.... The time Jordie insisted that they give a lift to that hitchhiking nun near Montreal.... The time Jordan invented his Three Rules for a Happy Life: "One: Always tip the bartender. Two: Never say no to a man named Marcello. And three: Live—and let live already."

Everyone laughed when Vince recalled the rules, but I looked around. Dad was fake laughing and Gretchen's eyebrows were arched high enough to spell, "My, my!"

Kenneth Collins is fumbling with his eyeglasses, taking them off, putting them on. Kenneth Collins walks over to Vince and clears his throat to speak, but Gretchen taps his shoulder.

Of course, Gretchen doesn't know any better.

"Dear," she says to Kenneth Collins. "The bean salad. Be a lamb."

Roy turns red

I don't know why today pissed me off. I've been to other memorials—countless other memorials, for Christ's sake—and I've never been bothered like this before. Maybe, today, the memories just echoed with too much hypocrisy. According to Vincent, there had been so little remembering for so long. I don't know. Maybe I just shouldn't have been there. Maybe I'm just tired of people still getting sick and people still dying. Maybe I'm just tired of always having to remember. Maybe—maybe maybe maybe, always a thousand fucking maybes.

At the very least, I shouldn't have spent so much time talking to Vincent. He reminds me too much of Jordan. The way they both stand, relaxed, all the weight on one foot. The way they both laser beam their blue eyes right into yours when they're talking. At the very least, one minute less with Vincent and I wouldn't have asked that stupid fucking question: "Do you miss the sex?"

The way Vincent looked at me, I couldn't blame him.

"I'm sorry," I started to mumble. "I didn't mean—"

But by then Vincent was smiling again, touching my elbow, telling me not to apologize.

"Sex with Jordan was the best sex I ever had," he explained, broadening his smile.

Right then, Jordan's real Mom walked past and the three of us shared polite, wordless nods. She's a big woman and she's always been kind of pleasantly batty, but she was his Mother for Christ's sake and I could feel myself turning red—something, you can bet your ass, which hasn't happened in a long fucking time.

Then Vincent leaned closer toward me, lowered his voice. "But you know what Jordan liked doing the most?"

I couldn't help it. My mind flipped back to three years and before, shuffling through a catalog of blowjobs, handjobs, and late nights filled with squeezed muscles, jabbing boners and wet tongues.

"What?" I asked.

Tears slipped into Vincent's eyes. "Kissing," he said. "Jordan loved kissing the most."

I couldn't help thinking how little Jordan and I had ever actually pressed our lips together.

"Kissing?" I said.

"Yeah," Vincent said. He nodded, still smiling, still leaning close. "Jordan used to say that everything else was just foreplay to an orgasm—and an orgasm was something you could always give yourself. But a kiss, he said, a kiss means you need someone else there with you. Someone to hold."

Gretchen gets miffed

Can't believe he's asleep already.

"G'night," he says and climbs under the covers, turns his back to me.

Yes, the party was his idea. Yes, I, at first, did object. But once I was on board, Ken turned it all over to me—today was my baby—and, may I say, today was my triumph!

But now he gives me this: his back and his silence. No "thank-you." No "the-place-looked-beautiful-today-darling." No "you-were-simply-fantastic-this-afternoon."

Just a "G'night"—and this: his back.

Bonnie weeps

The thing that irks me the most about Gretchen is the way she refers to Jordie as Jordie. Like she ever really knew him. Like she was his "Mother," like they were close. She has no right calling Jordie Jordie.

The other thing that really gets me is the way she managed to make herself busy just when Mom arrived. "Bonnie" she had said, in that way of hers, that way that just makes my shoulders pinch together. "Be a dear and see who's at the door. Gracie and I must finish chopping our carrots."

She smiled then, like she and Gracie were best and dearest friends, like she's not constantly picking on that poor old woman, telling her the "right" way to do this and do that.

I should've said something.

Why didn't I say something?

Gretchen knew very well who was at the damn door. She had seen Mom's car pull up the drive just as I had.

And she knew very well who was ringing the bell when Vince arrived, too. She wasted no time swooping to the door to greet him—"Vince, sweet, poor Vince! Come inside, quick, before you catch cold!"

She made sure to say it loud enough so we all could hear, even back in the kitchen.

And then, before she's even got the door closed, she's badgering him—"Did you remember to bring a picture? Can you believe how cold it's gotten again? Did you forget your photograph of Jordie for the table? I thought winter was over."

Vince tugged a photograph out of his gray overcoat pocket—a large, gold-framed shot of Jordie grinning, looking back over his right shoulder, standing barefoot in jeans on a sunny Michigan beach.

"It's a little out of focus," he said.

"Nonsense," Gretchen said.

"But it was Jordie's favorite picture of himself," Vince said.

"It's perfect!" Gretchen said, flashing her witch's smile, getting her claws around the frame and scampering off to the narrow table beneath the picture window with all of the flowers. "Just perfect!"

I was out of the kitchen by then, so I walked around and took Vince's coat to hang up.

"Hi, Bonnie," he said, stooping to give me a hug. I had forgotten how tall Vince is. We pressed our cheeks together and then he went over to hug that spooky Roy and all those other guys.

For a minute, I stood there holding onto Vince's coat, and when I turned to hang it up, it hit me: This is the coat of my dead brother's lover, I thought. This is the coat of another dying young man. And then I started to cry. Silent tears. The first of my many tears today. And I thank God the kids weren't there to catch me crying. God knows I saw my mother crying way too often, way too much.

Vince is standing at the door, putting on his coat, calling thanks to Gracie, telling Bonnie how good it was to see her again, how he really must see the twins and the new baby sometime soon.

Bonnie nods.

"Thank you for everything," Vince tells Jordan's Mom and she smiles, hugging him without saying a word.

"And thanks for all of your hard work," Vince tells Gretchen.

"Oh, it was nothing," Gretchen says, "nothing—nothing at all."

Kenneth Collins hands Vince a pair of grey gloves that had slipped from Vince's coat pocket. The two men pause for a moment, their hands almost touching.

"You know," Kenneth Collins says, his voice nearly a whisper, his eyes on the gloves. "I guess I never imagined that Jordan would die before me."

Vince bites his lower lip and finds himself looking at the gloves, as well. "I know," he says, taking the gloves into his hands, allowing his eyes to lift and meet Kenneth Collins' for just a moment. Of course, both men want to say so much, but both men feel the lateness of the day.

"I know," Vince says again.

"Yes," Kenneth Collins says.

"I know."

Roy makes a decision

When my time comes, I'm going to insist on no memorials. I'm going to leave orders: burn my body, flush the ashes down the toilet and get on with your fucking little lives.

No Collins shit for me, with people whispering, with everyone muttering about the "dearly departed" but only really thinking of themselves, with the drapes half-drawn as if the fucking house was still half-hiding some big secret, with everyone but Vincent afraid to even speak aloud the scarlet letters.

No sir. No memorial. Not for me.

No way. No more chances to fuck-up a good-bye. No.

I'll die and that'll be it.

I'll die—and it'll all just be over.

Over and out.

Gretchen holds her ground

Bones to him, is what I say. Bones to him—and his lack of gratitude.

Bonnie tells a story about her mother

Earlier, after we had listened to all of the speeches and nibbled all of the desserts, Gretchen herded us around the photo table and we eventually began swapping more stories about Jordan. But a few minutes into it, Gretchen starts fondling this one picture of Jordie pretending to pout. She sighs, dramatically, and then, trying to be witty, I guess, she says, "He was such a good looking boy. Speaking as a woman, it's too bad he was gay!"

I could feel my stomach knot and I could see Vince come this close to a scream. Dad didn't say a word, of course. And the rest of us stayed quiet, too.

But then we heard Mom say, "Narcissus."

We all turned to look at her.

She was sitting apart from all of us, in a straight-back dining room chair near the kitchen door. She was wearing her new, dark purple dress. She was balancing a tea cup and saucer on her lap. She was smiling brightly.

"Why I mean the flowers, of course," she said. "The Jonquils. Their family name." Still smiling, she looked directly at us, taking her time with each and every one of us. I remembered a late night from childhood in this very house, hours of bickering in the deepening darkness that finally ended when Dad shouted that Mom's "big-eyed smile" was driving him nuts.

Mom was smiling that smile now. She nodded toward the flowers. "They're beautiful, no?"

HAIKU

—Connie Scanlon

At the tea table
a spider crawls near my bowl
I take it outside

ON A CERTAIN MORNING

―Edward Underhill

CAST OF CHARACTERS (in order of appearance)

Ellen Hennesy Denby
Mrs. Zemke
K.J. Hennesy Larson
Maximillian Yarrow
Jack Hennesy
MaryAnn Carson
Karl Golian

TIME AND PLACE

September 2000: In the Chicago apartment of the recently deceased Anna Feld Hennesy.

ACT I

The Curtain Rises: In the large living room of a city apartment, ELLEN HENNESY DENBY stands in a closet (to stage left), humming—only her back is visible. ELLEN is wearing khakis and a casual sweater. She is forty years old.

ON A CERTAIN MORNING

A pile of old coats rests on an easy chair just to the front of stage left, and a fully-decorated, four-foot artificial Christmas tree rests against a sofa which occupies the center of the stage. A small, Sixties-style coffee table is in front of the sofa. To stage right of the sofa is a cardboard box on which is written in thick, black marker, "Christmas stuff." Several other large cardboard boxes are scattered across the floor. One is marked, "winter clothes;" another is marked, "Good China." A mahogany china cabinet vintage early 1960s, stands against the rear stage wall; its glass doors open; its shelves empty.

Next to the china cabinet is a mahogany server. There is a phone on the server and an old box-style, portable record player.

On the stage right wall is a fireplace; on its painted mantel are small stacks of books, plates, a hammer and cleaning supplies. The wall over the mantel is faded, except for an area about three-foot square, where it seems a painting or picture hung.

The phone rings.

(ELLEN *steps into the living room carrying a cardboard box on top of which lie three old coats.* ELLEN *picks up the phone. As she talks,* ELLEN *puts the box on the server, and begins to go through the pockets of the uppermost coat.*)

ELLEN Hello? Oh, honey, I'm so glad you called. Where are you? California!? I thought you were coming home today. No, I understand—your work is… Yes, yes. No, I'm not complaining. Really I'm not. I'm just exhausted that's all, and this apartment is so hot. I don't think Mom's air conditioning works. Anyway, I got a call from Max this morning. Max Yarrow, the art dealer from New York. I call him Max because he told me to. Don't worry, I am being careful—I know we shouldn't trust him. *(pause)* That's why I wish you were here to…you know…help. No I'm not starting. I'm not. I understand. I do. I do. Anyway, Max… Mr. Yarrow… is coming over in a little while to discuss some important news about the painting. I thought it would be nice for him to see Mother's apartment—see where the painting hung for the past nine years. No, I won't be alone. I called Jack and K.J. They're supposed to be here in a little while. I want them to hear what Max...Mr. Yarrow has to say.

(ELLEN *puts the coat down.*)

ELLEN Gary, I think Max has confirmed that the painting is real. He didn't tell me that in exact words, but...he was very enthusiastic, and said he had to meet with me; that it was important.

(Pause)

(ELLEN *opens the box she had set on the server. She pulls out some 78 r.p.m. records. She starts to sort through them as she briefly listens to her husband*)

ELLEN *(after several seconds)* I called Jack and K.J. just in case the painting is real... we'll have some important decisions to make. *(pause)* I know I'm the executor, but I want all of us to agree... as a family. I don't want any bad blood from this. Gary, can you believe what's happening? It's like we won the lottery. Okay, I know you've got to get going. Call the kids before it gets too late. They're staying at your sister's. They're fine with her. They really are. And Gary, if this painting is what we think it is—it could change our lives. If we sell it, well... maybe you'd be able to take some time to find a new job. Something closer. I'm not criticizing. No, I'm not. I'm not, really. I just want us to be. Right. Okay. Goodnight, and I...

(ELLEN *slowly hangs up the phone. She goes back to the box of records. She reads the label on one—which is written in German—aloud*).

ELLEN *(struggling)* Zu-Amsterdam, Bin Ich Geboren.

(ELLEN *goes over to the server and opens the portable record player. She adjusts the player for a 78 r.p.m. record, and puts the record on. The record plays. It is a scratchy recording of a woman who sings in German. For the first thirty seconds or so,* ELLEN *pays close attention to the song, but then absent-mindedly returns to checking the pockets of the coats she has piled onto the chair. Until… A knock at the door.*

ELLEN *walks over, opens the door. There stands* MRS. ZEMKE. *Age, glasses and a shiny wig are the most prominent aspects of this seventy-ish woman. She has no strong ethnic features. Her voice is old and concerned; there is only a slight Polish speech pattern and accent.*)

ELLEN *(surprised, but not surprised)* Hello, Mrs. Zemke! How are you?

MRS. ZEMKE Hello, Ellen. Sorry to disturb you, but I heard the music.

ELLEN Oh; was it too loud? I apologize.

(ELLEN *hurries to the record player. She turns down the volume, though the song can still be heard.* MRS. ZEMKE *steps into the apartment.*)

MRS. ZEMKE Oh, the music is fine. Lovely in a way. I've been trying to figure out for months where it's been coming from.

ELLEN Look; I found these old 78s among my mother's things. I've never seen them before. See; they're all in German.

(MRS. ZEMKE *peers at the records through the bottom of her bifocals.*)

MRS. ZEMKE Yes, that's why I knocked. About three or four months ago, I began to hear these old German songs. Late at night. I had no idea of where they were coming from. It even took me a few days to remember I knew these songs. But one night—as the music drifted into my apartment at the very stillest hour, I began to sing a few of the lyrics of the song that was playing. And the song and the singer all started to come back—just as if I were a young girl again, listening to *The Amusierkaborett.*

ELLEN What?

MRS. ZEMKE *Amusierkaborett.* That's the German word for these songs.

ELLEN Oh, cabaret music?

MRS. ZEMKE Not quite. This is more serious music, more respected. Cabaret music—*entartete musik,* the Nazis called it, which means degenerate—was different. What we're listening to now is Claire Waldoff. Even the Nazis thought she was acceptable. And, of course, in the 1920s and '30s—she was so marvelous. The most famous singer in Europe. Bigger than this Celine girl is today. Of course, I never saw Claire Waldoff in person; I just heard her voice over the radio and on the records.

ELLEN What's the song about?

MRS. ZEMKE This? I can't remember German anymore. I barely recall my Polish. In this whole building, there's only two women who speak Polish besides me—one of them is an imbecile, and the other is her younger sister. I can only recognize a few words—the song is about a poor prostitute—Claire Waldoff was forever singing about being a prostitute. And this prostitute is in Amsterdam, which is not unusual. The rest has something to do with an umbrella she lent to some man and he never gave back.

ELLEN An umbrella?

MRS. ZEMKE It's all double-meaning, my dear. After the Nazis took over, they restricted what could be sung. And even who was allowed to perform. So those they let sing would hide what they were really singing about in harmless, deceiving lyrics. Everybody understood what the song was really about. Only the Nazis didn't know, or pretended not to know. That was the rule everybody in Europe followed for a long time. Hide what you're doing, and pretend not to know anything. To tell you the truth, until I started hearing these old songs through the walls, I'd completely forgotten about these things. I never remembered there was such a person as Claire Waldoff. I'm very surprised to finally discover the music is coming from your mother's apartment.

ELLEN I didn't know my mother listened to any records except *The Sound of Music*.

MRS. ZEMKE No one who lived on this floor would deny she loved *The Sound of Music*. Sometimes twice a day. But I never guessed she knew these old Berlin singers. You know, these 78s are very rare. The Nazis chased all of the popular musicians and artists out of Europe in the '30s and most of them just disappeared.

ELLEN It's funny Mom would have brought up my grandmother's old phonograph and started listening to these recordings. I didn't know she had saved them.

MRS. ZEMKE Oh, she probably kept them in her storage locker. After Doctor Mellon told her the cancer had returned, she started going through all the old boxes in the basement. Everyday she'd come by, asking me if I wanted this thing or that.

ELLEN I can see she started labeling boxes and garment bags. She didn't throw anything away, it seems.

MRS. ZEMKE She gave me a Pyrex measuring cup. You're welcome to…

ELLEN No. No. It's yours. There are more things if you'd like. Plates, pots, clothing.

MRS. ZEMKE Thank you, but no thank you. To tell you the truth, I already had a measuring cup. Two, in fact. But when a friend who knows she's dying offers you something…

ELLEN I understand. We appreciate all you did for our mother. When she was in the hospital, and toward the end.

MRS. ZEMKE Your mother was a fine woman. Everyone in the building liked her. Except Mrs. Kitteridge. She doesn't like anybody; the busybody, that she is. Your mother was also a good bridge player. Made a wonderful cheesecake; light as air, and not too sweet.

ELLEN She didn't really talk much…about herself, her family….

MRS. ZEMKE Talk about you? And your brother and sister? Of course! She talked about you all the time. And her grandchildren. Why wouldn't a woman talk about her family? She was proud of all of you. But she didn't brag; she wasn't like that.

ELLEN I mean, about her own family. She was born in Austria, in a city called *(slowly, as if not sure of the pronunciation)* Kitzbükel. She came here as a little girl. Mom never really talked about those days.

MRS. ZEMKE Those days hardly seem to have been real. You know, I came from Poland in 1950. I was twenty-five at the time. But none of my experiences in Poland seem like they actually happened. The world in which I lived as a child was so strange. First, there was the war and then all the devastation. There was no food, no clothes, no houses. Imagine. No phones. No toilets. I lived in Lublin, in a cold-water flat with all my aunts and uncles. Somehow, my father got the money together to bring us here. I never knew how—I'm not sure I want to know. Once we arrived, we lived in an apartment all by ourselves. Just the six of us. And soon we got a television and then eventually a car. And there was so much food. I was embarrassed to even think about my relatives living in Lublin. Believe me, there was nothing to be nostalgic about. The Europe I left in 1950 held no attraction for a young girl. Just fear and rubble and stench. And everyone was so grey and tired. *(pause)* Your mother was about my age—a little older, maybe.

ELLEN No; you're the same age, I think.

(MRS. ZEMKE *gives* ELLEN *a look, which* ELLEN *doesn't see or understand.*)

MRS. ZEMKE So, if we're the same age, then I'm sure she felt the same way I did about the old country. Did she ever go back to Austria?

ELLEN No. I think she wanted to…but my parents…well, my father was sick a lot when we were kids—he died when I was about ten. After that, well, my mother just seemed to never look back at things.

MRS. ZEMKE It's too bad she never returned to Austria. I traveled to Poland with my husband—he was born here in Chicago—in 1977. I saw all my cousins and a few surviving aunts. I felt so much better seeing them alive and fat and smiling. In my mind, you see, I'd always pictured them the way they were in 1950; thin, and dusty, and waiting for something terrible to happen. It's strange to say, but when I went back, I could sleep better afterward. Going back to where you came from helps you understand things. Helps you accept things.

ELLEN I think my mom may have realized that too late.

(The building door buzzer rings. ELLEN *goes to the intercom.)*

ELLEN Who is it?

(From the intercom comes the voice of K.J. LARSON.)

K.J. *(offstage)* It's me. Open up.

(ELLEN *presses the buzzer.*)

ELLEN That's my sister—K.J. We're going to sell…a few things. Go through the apartment once more—all of us together. My brother, Jack, is driving in from Dubuque. Would you like to stay a bit longer? Have some tea, perhaps?

MRS. ZEMKE No thank you, dear. I can't eat or drink anything after four o'clock or I'm up all night with the Home Shopping station. Anyway, good luck to you…and thanks for solving the mystery.

ELLEN What mystery?

MRS. ZEMKE The mystery of who was playing the old records.

ELLEN Oh, yes. I almost forgot.

MRS. ZEMKE Goodbye, dear.

ELLEN Goodbye, Mrs. Zemke.

(MRS. ZEMKE *exits, but* ELLEN *does not close the door. She returns to the record player, takes the record that was playing off the machine, and puts it back in the box. She places some old kitchen towels inside the box, before closing the flaps. She puts the box back in the closet.*

K.J. HENNESY LARSON, Ellen's *sister, enters the apartment.* K.J. *is dressed in a skirt and a casual blouse. She carries a summer-weight sweater. She is about forty-three years old. Upon seeing* ELLEN, *she lets out a squeal of delight.)*

K.J. Yeahhhhh! We're rich!

(K.J. *gives* ELLEN *a big twirling hug. They both laugh.)*

ELLEN *(pulling back a bit)* Well, there's nothing definite yet and we still have to decide…

K.J. Oh, my dear sister, for once I think that good fortune is smiling on the Hennesy family. Smiling the enigmatic smile of the contented rich. Rich from the sale of a previously unknown masterpiece. A masterpiece, Ellen. Our lovely Monet. Our lovely, ignored, almost forgotten, Monet—and thanks to you, Ellen, it was not accidentally thrown away—Oh, God, it makes me sick to realize how close we came to…

ELLEN I can't even think about it.

K.J. Thank God Mother made you the executor, Ellen, and not your older sister. I would have just pitched everything in the place. (K.J. *looks around*) But you, Ellen; you who sees the value in everything, saw grandmother's old "morning" painting and realized what Jack and I would have overlooked.

ELLEN I still can't believe it—a Monet. Our mother—our grandmother—owned a painting by Monet. It has to be a mistake.

K.J. Don't even think it. Until the old thing is sold, we have to think only positive thoughts —positive. And profitable.

ELLEN Assuming it's real, and assuming we all decide—as a family—to sell it.

K.J. Oh, I know it's real. There was always something about that painting. The way Grandmother Feld always kept it near her. Her "morning painting," she called it. I'd forgotten that until last week. As dirty and grimy as it got, and even in that old pine frame, there was always something....

ELLEN Why do you think Mom didn't tell us about the painting? Why didn't she tell us it was a Monet?

K.J. I'm sure she didn't know. You said yourself, the way it was framed, the signature was covered.

ELLEN But the antiques dealer—the first one, said that the painting wasn't in its original frame. That this frame was probably put on in the '40s, so Mom...

K.J. So Mom was only a teenager then. And, let's face it, our mother was never a patron of the arts; she grew up in a little town in Austria. She didn't go to college. How would she know anything about art?

ELLEN But it was her mother's painting. So I'm sure Granma Feld told her what it was.

K.J. Why would she? Our mother didn't tell us...and we almost threw it away.

ELLEN Well, I'm surprised then Dad didn't recognize it. He was always interested in art. After he got sick, he started to draw...

K.J. We've been through this a dozen times already. Our father never saw past his law books or his scotch. And like you said, the painting was hidden behind decades of dirt; the signature was covered by the frame.

ELLEN Somehow, I think Mom knew....

K.J. Look, what does it matter? The important thing is that it's ours. Now, we just need to prove it's really by Claude Monet.

ELLEN *(suddenly excited)* I think that's why Max wants to see us! *(pause)* I think he's confirmed it's real.

K.J. Did Max say what it's worth?

ELLEN No; I don't think he wants to get us too excited until he can prove it's really by Monet.

K.J. Who is this guy—Max? How did you find him?

ELLEN Well, you remember I called you last week when I started looking at the painting, and wondering if it might be valuable?

K.J. Yes, I remember. You know, Ellen, you don't have to start every story at the beginning.

ELLEN Yes. I do. Anyway, I took the painting over to Ben Decker. He's an antiques dealer I know. Ben got very excited as soon as he saw it, and he called Fred Phillips who owns Phillips Gallery on Michigan Avenue. I thought Phillips was going to have a heart attack when he saw the painting—he was the one who took it out of the frame. As soon as he unfolded the bottom of the canvas and saw the signature, his face turned bright red. Thirty seconds later, he was on the phone to Max.

K.J. But who is Max?

ELLEN His name is Maximilian Yarrow. Fred Phillips told me that Max is a very famous art dealer in New York City. That he specializes in this sort of thing.

K.J. What sort of thing?

ELLEN I'm not exactly sure. Paintings that are...unknown, I guess. Art people talk in a completely different language. I'm not sure I understand everything they say.

K.J. Now, don't take this the wrong way, Ellen. But you were smart to call me and Jack. Things may get complicated, and I don't want this New York art dealer thinking we're just hicks from the Midwest. It's important he knows we're in charge—not him.

ELLEN Max is a good person, I think. He seems very knowledgeable.

K.J. What's he like? Is he gay? Or is he Jewish? All of the art dealers I've ever known were either gay or Jewish. But never both.

ELLEN I...don't know. I don't think he's gay. Or Jewish. He's not...anything. He asks a lot of questions. But he doesn't say a lot.

K.J. He's quiet, then?

ELLEN No. Not at all. He's very talkative. But after he leaves, it's hard to remember what he's said exactly.

K.J. Well, if he thinks the Hennesys are pushovers, he's in for a surprise. Oh, Ellen, I still can't believe... Let's have a drink to celebrate our good fortune. And put some music on. Something fun.

ELLEN You're not going to believe what I found. In one of the old boxes. Why don't you get some glasses? In the kitchen cabinet over the sink.

And there's about two glasses worth of some white wine in the fridge.

K.J. God, how old is it?

ELLEN *(from the closet)* Just a couple of days. I bought it at the White Hen along with some cleaning supplies.

K.J. Wine from the White Hen. I bet *that's* good.

ELLEN I have a glass every afternoon—after I've finished cleaning and packing.

(K.J. *goes into the kitchen.* ELLEN *brings out a cardboard box. This one is marked, "Girls' Things." She sorts through some 45 r.p.m. records for a few seconds before finding the one she wants.* ELLEN *places the record on the phonograph, but does not turn it on.* K.J. *returns to the room, holding the bottle of wine and two glasses.*)

K.J. What were you listening to when I arrived? I heard some strange music over the intercom.

ELLEN Oh…just the radio. I wasn't really listening to it. Just noise. *(quickly)* Anyway, I was actually talking to Mrs. Zemke.

K.J. Who?

ELLEN Mrs. Zemke. Mom's neighbor. She was at the funeral.

K.J. Oh—the old Polish woman.

ELLEN I hope it wasn't a problem coming into the city on such short notice. I know how involved you are with Donald's business, and Tim's probably busy with swim team….

K.J. My husband and son can fend for themselves. Not that they have any domestic skills. Still, they know how to order a pizza. And they had some "golf highlights" tape on the big screen television when I left, so I think they're probably surviving all right. It's the country club I'm abandoning. There's a director's meeting tonight, and I promised to give a report on new membership. Fortunately, there isn't much to report this month.

(K.J. *struggles to uncork the wine.*)

ELLEN Oh, your club is so beautiful. I'm sure you have no trouble bringing in new members.

K.J. Ellen, darling, my task is not to bring people in, but to keep them out. Our standards are rigorous—higher every year. Do you remember Penny Franklin?

ELLEN Tina Franklin's sister? The one with the overbite?

K.J. Yes, that's her. Except, the overbite's gone. So is the straight brown hair that every Franklin girl had. Now she's blonde, chesty and waxed as regularly as her black BMW convertible. And she's married to a trader.

ELLEN When people say somebody's a trader, what do they mean exactly? I'm always too embarrassed to ask.

K.J. Well, in the case of Penny's husband, I'd say he trades ten-dollar bills for hundreds. At least, that's what I understand. They knocked down a million-dollar house in Wauconda to build one for two-million dollars. Anyway, they've applied for membership in Rosewood.

(K.J. *pours the wine.*)

ELLEN That's great! Penny was always funny, and a good tennis player in high school. She made the state finals.

K.J. She won't make our finals. She and her husband just reek of new money, and the membership committee has had enough of these people who think cash is the same thing as class.

ELLEN But couldn't you convince them? The Franklins were such a nice family. I dated Larry Franklin in high school. He was one of those guys who was always shaking his leg.

K.J. Rosewood does not want leg shakers or any other kind of shaker for that matter. We want people who arrived at least a generation ago. Their wealth has to be a bit dusty.

ELLEN But you and Donald...

K.J. I know what you're going to say—that Donald is "new money."

ELLEN Yes, but he...

K.J. Well, Donald Larson's money may be recent, but my name—the Hennesy name—is vintage enough. The Hennesys have been pillars of the community for five generations. Our father was a prominent lawyer. Our grandfather, a bank president—and a member of Rosewood. And our great-grandfather was a Presbyterian minister.

ELLEN I was going to say I think it's much more impressive that Donald started his own company from scratch. Without any connections. Just the two of you.

K.J. To a certain extent, I agree. But the working rich seldom show the grace that those who grow up with money possess. Especially the people who make their money as traders and investment bankers; all they're interested in are toys. And monstrous houses and breaking traditions. They don't know how to honor the old ways.

ELLEN But we didn't grow up with any money. We certainly didn't inherit any.

K.J. No, Father saw to it that the Hennesy fortune fell away long before it could reach us. But we still felt the glow of it. From Dad's parents. When we were growing up…

(K.J. *hands* ELLEN *a glass.*)

K.J. Cheers! To our Monet!

(ELLEN *takes a sip of wine; walks over to the record player. She puts the arm onto the record.*)

ELLEN Wait till you hear this!

RECORD ON PLAYER IS HEARD:
"Honey…
Oh, Sugar, Sugar…
You are my candy girl…
And I can't stop wanting you!"

K.J. Oh, my God! The Archies!

ELLEN Isn't it great? Mom saved all our old 45s. Remember the dance we made up?

(ELLEN *and* K.J. *begin a synchronized, go-go-girl dance. The front buzzer rings.* ELLEN *keeps dancing, but* K.J. *stops to listen. The buzzer sounds again.*)

K.J. *(over the music)* Somebody's here! Maybe it's Jack.

ELLEN So much for the Archies!

(ELLEN *turns off the music, presses the intercom, shouts "C'mon up," and sounds the buzzer.*)

ELLEN It's like the old days, isn't it, K.J.? When we were just kids—before husbands, children. Before money.

K.J. Well, life after money is pretty good, too.

ELLEN What I mean is, it's nice to get together. You and me. And Jack. We used to talk a lot more when Mom was still alive.

K.J. That was just six weeks ago, Ellen.

ELLEN I know, but…

(MAXIMILIAN YARROW *enters the apartment.* MAX *is in his late forties; he is tall, in good but not athletic shape. He wears an expensive shirt with cuff links, black slacks and a grey sport coat. His hair was cut yesterday, and is nicely groomed.* MAX *has a healthy, light tan.*)

MAX Ellen, I have wonderful news….

(MAX *looks around, sees* ELLEN, *then* K.J.)

MAX But first; introductions, I think.

ELLEN Max, this is my sister, K.J. K.J. Larson. I called her and my brother—I thought we should decide what to do about the painting as a family.

MAX A splendid idea. Really, the only way to make a decision like this. All as one. It's a pleasure to meet you, Ms. Larson.

K.J. Please, call me K.J. No point standing on formality.

MAX Formality? Hideous thing. I abhor it. Here's my card. Please call me Max.

(MAX *hands* K.J. *his card.*)

MAX I believe Ellen told me you live in Lake Forest. Do you know the Bennetts? Cameron and Mary?

K.J. Yes. They belong to our country club.

MAX Well, the next time you're in their home, ask to view the Degas they acquired from me last year. It's magnificent. Just a small charcoal sketch, but really unforgettable. Perhaps you've seen it?

K.J. I can't say we're that close to the Bennetts. Still, it's reassuring to know we have mutual acquaintances.

MAX Yes. Yes. Mutual acquaintances are much better than references, don't you think? A reference always smacks of a blind date with somebody's stuttering cousin.

K.J. *(through an appreciative smile)* Do we have any other mutual acquaintances? When engaging the services of a stranger, I always think it's helpful to get three mutual acquaintances.

MAX That's good, K.J. Three mutual acquaintances. I'll have to remember that. Seriously, I'm sure I've assisted many people you know or know *of* with their art transactions. But, I'm not at liberty to discuss my clients without their consent. For obvious reasons—discretion is an essential element of my business.

ELLEN What do you mean, Max?

MAX Let's just say, there are those who don't want it known that they have *bought* something extraordinary, and there are those who don't want it known that they have *sold* something extraordinary.

K.J. And you find our mother's painting extraordinary?

MAX Yes, yes! One never gets blasé about representing great art. Makes you a part of history, really. But of course when I consider a great canvas, I must balance my enthusiasm for the work with, shall we say, a concern for its monetary aspects.

K.J. Getting the best price, in other words.

MAX The precise other words.

ELLEN That's if it's real, and if we decide to sell.

K.J. So you have handled other Monet canvases before, Max?

ELLEN Don't insult Max, K.J.

MAX No insult taken, Ellen. Your sister is right to make inquiries. The commercial aspects of art are very much concerned with investigation. And identity. Sometimes gaps in a painting's heritage can be bridged by a confidence in its owner's reputation. And the dealer's rep, as well. And with a painting like this, reputation is everything. Reputation and confidence.

ELLEN What do you mean, confidence?

MAX Confidence that the painting is what it purports to be. And in the case of a painting that appears out of nowhere, confidence is what we must establish.

K.J. Well, I don't think of our mother's home as nowhere. Is it so unusual for a painting like ours to just appear?

MAX Everything is unusual in the art world, K.J. But to be specific, I'd say it's not uncommon for a painting to appear like this one has—seemingly from heaven. By this, I mean that the painting does not originate from a museum or a renowned collection. Instead, it arrives from a dusty living room or parlor, kept by its owner for decades. Its true value—and more significantly, its monetary value, a secret from all. Maybe even from its owner. Then, as in the case of your mother—death betrays the secret. At first, the heirs are merely curious, perhaps mildly expectant. The idea seems incredible. "Things like this don't happen to me," you think. And, sadly, you're right. Most of the time the expectations are not met. The canvas is an admirable imitation. But its only monetary value is found in an antique frame. Even the sentimental value of the work is lost at that point—since the painting seems to have played a nasty trick on its new owners, and who wants to keep a deceitful painting?

ELLEN But ours is real; right, Max?

MAX Of course it's real. It's a real canvas stretched across a real wood frame. Oil paint has been applied to the surface of the canvas. That's all physical evidence of the painting's existence. The essential question is this: was the painting created by Claude Monet? *(pause)* On that question—no final verdict has been rendered. The evidence in favor of its genuineness is merely this: a study of the canvas itself strongly suggests that the painting was created about the time when its alleged artist, Monsieur

Monet, is known to have worked. The signature on the painting, "Monet" appears genuine. Strangely, no date is shown. However, based on the style it appears to have been painted in the twentieth century, probably sometime after 1905, but before 1915. Also, the physical elements of the painting—the canvas itself and the paint have been tested, and they date from the early twentieth century. Moreover, the technique, character, feel and, shall I say, supreme power and beauty of the painting are also consistent with Monet's many other known paintings. It is a fact that Monet is not often "faked," inasmuch as his use of light and color were quite unique and are difficult to imitate. Those few experts—assuming—there is such a thing—who have briefly studied the painting, have tentatively—oh so tentatively—concluded it is genuine. *(pause)* On the other hand, we have found no record that Claude Monet ever painted such a canvas and significantly, we don't know the painting's name or date, which handicaps us considerably. No mention of the work appears in any of the major catalogues. The experts—assuming there is such a thing—can find no evidence that such a painting was ever exhibited, which is very strange since by 1900, Monet was a critical and popular success. Consequently, it is remarkably…curious that a painting by Monet made after that time has no provenance; no bibliography, no exhibition list. *(pause)* So there you have it. The evidence in favor and against.

K.J. All art mumbo jumbo aside, Max? Is the painting by Monet or not?

MAX I think that this is an instance where a painting's history and its authenticity cannot be seen as separate issues. Tell me, K.J., what do you know about the canvas?

K.J. Didn't Ellen tell you about it?

MAX Yes. Her report was quite useful. But—and I apologize in advance for the slander —you are the oldest child, and so it's possible you can recall something further back.

K.J. Well, I don't know what more I can say. It was my grandmother's painting—Grandmother Feld. My mother's mother. Her name was Anna Katherine Feld.

ELLEN That's who K.J.'s named after. Her first name's really Katherine. After Granma Feld, and her middle name is JoAnne after my father's mother. My brother gave her the nickname K.J. when they were kids. Jack couldn't pronounce Katie, for some reason, so he called her K.J.

K.J. I don't think Mr. Yarrow is interested in learning the origin of my name, Ellen.

MAX Oh, but I am. Your lives are now an essential part of the painting, and the painting a part of your lives. Who knows what will prove relevant? You mentioned your Grandmother Feld; I understand she owned the painting?

K.J. Yes, that's right. She brought it with her from Austria. I mean, I assume she did. As long as I can remember, the painting was in her apartment.

ELLEN The one on Berdeux.

K.J. Before that even. The one on Lowell; it was just a few blocks from here. Grandmother and Grandfather lived in their Lowell apartment until he died....

ELLEN I don't remember that.

K.J. Well, he died in 1960...*(trying to think)* well, 1960 something. Maybe 1960 or '61; anyway, I remember Grandmother Feld moved in with us after Grandfather died, and I had to move into your room, Ellen. You were still in your crib, so it must have been when you were about a year old.

MAX K.J., when did your grandmother come to America?

K.J. In the 1940s. I'm not sure when exactly, but after the War. World War II, I mean.

MAX How did your grandmother acquire the painting? Did your grandfather purchase it for her?

K.J. I can't be certain, but somehow I always felt that the painting always belonged to Grandmother. I mean, nobody ever said as much, I just felt it. She used to call it her "morning painting." She had it over her dressing table in her apartment. Then, when she moved in with us…

MAX After your grandfather died?

K.J. Yes. After Grandfather Feld died, Grandmother moved in with us for almost a year. Our house in Arlington Heights—my parents' first house—only had three bedrooms. Grandmother Feld took my room, and I moved into the baby's room—Ellen's room. Jack slept in the basement. I remember that Grandmother hung the painting over her bed. The painting and an old cedar chest were the only things she brought with her. Everything else was put into storage until she took the apartment on Berdeux. Mother wanted her to find a place near us in the suburbs, but Grandmother insisted on living in the city.

MAX We still haven't determined how your grandmother acquired the painting. Was her family wealthy?

K.J. No. I don't think so. It was our father's family—the Hennesys—who had money.

MAX What about your Grandfather Feld? Did he have any wealth?

K.J. No. He was a baker, I think. Back in Austria. Though he didn't seem like one. He always wore a suit—Well, he died when I was only four or five, so I don't remember much about him. He didn't speak much English. My grandmother was not any better. She didn't talk much, actually. She was very…distant; not mean or anything. Just…anachronistic.

ELLEN Anna—what?

K.J. You know—like she was left over from another time. To be honest, we didn't really like going to Grandmother Feld's apartment—Jack and I, I mean. Ellen was really too little to remember any of this. Grandmother Feld—Granma, we called her, used to serve us things like radish sandwiches. She was constantly pickling things. Watermelon rinds and cucumbers. Her apartment always smelled like vinegar. She would put out these plates of cucumbers in vinegar. To make us eat them, she would add sugar. They were still hideous. And she had all these old German records. She used to play them. On that.

(K.J. *points to the old box phonograph on the server.* ELLEN *turns away.*)

K.J. To tell you the truth, Granma Feld was a little frightening. Father's family was completely different. The Hennesys had a huge house in Arlington Heights. And when we visited Pop-pop, that's what Jack called Grandfather Hennesy—we ate at McDonald's—I think it was the first one. In Des Plaines. And they had a color television. And Granpa Hennesy had this big Chevy. And we would go to their country club—Rosewood Country Club—for brunch on Easter. They were like dream grandparents. Well anyway, we never wanted to go to Granma Feld's apartment.

MAX So you never heard anyone talk about the painting?

K.J. No. Sometimes Grandmother Feld would say, "See my 'morning painting,' Katrina? It's lovely, isn't it?"

ELLEN Granma called you, Katrina?

K.J. Yes. She was the only one. I never liked it.

MAX So you never heard anyone say the painting was valuable or famous, or anything like that?

K.J. No. Not that I can recall.

ELLEN Is it possible Granma Feld just bought the painting herself? Would it have been so expensive back then?

MAX It's unlikely she purchased the painting. Even in the 1930s or '40s when your grandmother was a young woman, a Monet would have cost around ten thousand dollars, a significant amount of money for the time. And if she had purchased it from an art dealer, a record of the painting's existence would have been generated.

K.J. What's the alternative?

MAX Oh, there are many alternatives. Most likely, your grandmother— or possibly even your grandfather, inherited the painting from another relative, perhaps one of their parents.

ELLEN So, maybe even Granma Feld didn't know it was a Monet.

MAX Possibly. It's possible that none of its owners ever knew of its value. The replacement of the original frame, though, raises some interesting questions. The frame now on the painting is from the 1950s. It was made here in the United States. A very common, inexpensive frame; it tells us nothing. Of more interest is that sometime earlier, in the late '30s, perhaps, your grandmother, or somebody, had a new stretcher put on the canvas so that the bottom of the painting—where the signature appeared—was folded under, hidden from view. The painting was then reframed, but that frame as well as the original, are long gone.

ELLEN Why would somebody intentionally cover up the signature?

K.J. Because they didn't want anyone to know who the painter was?

MAX And why would they want to keep the identity of the painter a secret?

(MAX's *cellular phone rings. He takes the call.*)

MAX Hello? *(pause)* Oh, yes. Hello, Ben. I'm glad you called back. One moment, please. (MAX *places his hand over the phone and addresses the sisters.*) It's Ben Decker, the antiques dealer to whom you first showed the painting. I found out he's telling everyone on the North Shore of Chicago about the painting; he's even called the local newspaper. I've got to stop him before he turns a nuisance into a problem.

ELLEN What nuisance?

MAX Ben himself is the nuisance. He wants the whole world to know about the Monet. Is there a room I can talk in?

ELLEN Back that way. Mom's bedroom. There's a desk and chair.

K.J. Why is the whole world knowing about the Monet a problem?

MAX Because the whole world isn't going to buy it. Most people will just want to attack the work; spoil our fun; diminish the painting's value. Jealousy and envy, K.J. They are not a pretty thing to watch in the art world. Now, excuse me, while I instruct our friend to cool it.

(MAX *exits toward the hallway.*)

MAX *(offstage)* Yes, Ben, I'm back. Glad to hear from you. Ben, I want to talk to you about some of the stories I've been…

ELLEN I didn't realize you had so many memories of Granma Feld.

K.J. I didn't realize it myself until I started talking. God, what a difference between Dad's family and Mom's. I don't think Dad's mother could stand to be in the same room with Mother's parents.

ELLEN Dad liked Granma Feld, though.

K.J. Dad liked everybody—when he had a drink in him. And since he always had a drink in him…

ELLEN You remember all those things so much better than me. All I can remember from my childhood is listening to the Osmonds, watching the *Dean Martin Show* with our parents. Adoring Haley Mills in all those old Disney movies. Eating Captain Crunch…

K.J. Washing with Dial soap; wearing hip-huggers…

ELLEN Don't forget, Midnight Plan "A."

K.J. What was that?

ELLEN Remember? You and I and Patty O'Brien and Carol Oreal were all going to sneak out of our houses at midnight and steal cherries from the Hansen's backyard.

K.J. Oh, yeah. I remember that. Did we ever do it?

ELLEN No. Of course not. But we talked about it a lot. Remember? You used to have that pink phone.

K.J. *(squealing)* Oh, my God. I thought it was just the best thing. I have never loved anything in my life like I loved that phone.

ELLEN Then I have a surprise for you.

(ELLEN *rummages through the same box from which she removed the 45s; she extracts a pink, rotary-dial phone like a magician pulling a rabbit from a hat.*)

ELLEN Ta-daa!

K.J. Oh, my God! My phone!

(K.J. *takes it from* ELLEN. *Holds the receiver to her ear.*)

K.J. My first born!!!

SOUND: *The building buzzer.*

(ELLEN *goes to the intercom and presses the button.*)

ELLEN Hello?

JACK *(over intercom)* It's me, Jack.

ELLEN C'mon up!

(ELLEN *buzzes* JACK *in, then opens the front door a crack.*)

ELLEN Now, remember, K.J., Jack hasn't made up his mind yet on whether we should sell the painting—assuming it's real. So, let's take it easy.

K.J. Nonsense. Jack has to go along with us. It's two-to-one. Majority rules.

ELLEN I'm sure we can convince him, but let's not push. I'm hoping we can decide what to do as a family. Maybe we can use this as an opportunity to get to know each other again.

K.J. We already know each other, Ellen. We're family.

ELLEN Maybe you could say that with some enthusiasm.

K.J. Ellen, before Jack comes up, I... There's something I need to tell you.

(ELLEN *approaches* K.J.)

K.J. It's extremely important to me that we sell the painting right away. Donald's in some trouble. Financial trouble. Maybe even legal trouble. It's nothing he did wrong; except maybe trust his partner a little too much. Anyway, everything we have is gone.

ELLEN What do you mean, "everything?"

K.J. I mean the...the generally-accepted definition of everything—which is, everything; our savings, the business, our Michigan house, maybe even our home.

ELLEN How can that be? You spent two weeks in Hawaii in May and then you chaired that big cancer society ball at the Art Institute....

K.J. Yes; but I had to do those things. To keep people believing everything was fine; rumors are beginning to circulate about Donald's company, and if people knew how bad things are, his problems would only get worse.

ELLEN What problems? What happened?

K.J. It's very complicated. But essentially Donald's company got overextended at the bank, and then there was an allegation that the company made some misrepresentations in its financial statements in order to increase a line of credit. Anyway, the bank's chairman called the feds. It makes no sense. We've known the man for fifteen years; Donald's brought him more business than that shitty bank could handle.

ELLEN How much does he owe?

K.J. It depends on who you ask. Maybe three or four million dollars. It's the company's debt; not Donald's. But it's important we keep the company going, it's the only way; and to do that we need money. Money to pay the subcontractors; money to pay the lawyers —anyway, we might not get a chance to talk alone again—and I wanted you to understand—you're the only one I can confide in.

ELLEN Yes. Of course. I wish I'd known. I mean, I'm not sure I could have helped, but I could have listened.

K.J. I wanted to tell you. I really did, but everything happened so fast. Besides, I know you and Gary have been having problems, and I didn't want to bother you. Anyway, that's my secret. I'm embarrassed about it, but…. That's why we have to convince Jack to go along with us on selling the painting. Even if it's only worth a few thousand dollars.

(ELLEN *says nothing; just nods slowly.* JACK HENNESY *knocks and enters, dropping a duffel bag on the floor as he comes in.* JACK *is dressed in jeans, a sweater and black sport coat. He is forty-two years old. K.J. stands by the server, looking through the box of 45s.)*

JACK (*toward* ELLEN) Hello, beautiful! How you doin'?

ELLEN Great, Jack. I'm so glad to see you. You're right on time.

JACK Fortunately, there's nothing between Chicago and Dubuque but corn and a dozen bad AM radio stations.

JACK (*friendly, but not warm*) Hello, K.J. And how are you?

K.J. Fine, Jack. You're looking well. Still the "boy professor." It's a good look for you.

JACK Kind of you to say. Too kind, actually. I take it something's up.

ELLEN Now, Jack. Let's not start. Max is in Mom's bedroom….

JACK Max? Who's Max? And why's he in the bedroom? K.J. send him there without his supper?

ELLEN Max is the art dealer I told you about. The one from New York.

JACK Yes! Yes! And where is the painting? I want to make sure we're all talking about the same picture I remember.

ELLEN It's at a gallery in the city. Max has some experts examining it.

JACK Not too closely I hope.

K.J. What's that supposed to mean?

JACK Just that I enjoy being the owner of a painting by Claude Monet—or a one-third owner, anyway. And I don't want the fantasy to end too soon.

ELLEN It's no fantasy, Jack. It's real. We're sure of it.

JACK Sure the way Dad was always sure that his family descended from Vikings?

K.J. You always have to turn a parade into a funeral march, Jack. Or are you just so accustomed to being a loser that you can't accept that something good has happened to you—albeit completely by accident?

JACK Okay, you win. We had a Monet hanging in our living room for fifty years. And what was in the bathroom? The *Mona Lisa*?

K.J. If you're so certain the painting's not real, then why not sell me your third right now? I'll give you a hundred dollars for it.

JACK It's tempting, K.J. But I couldn't take advantage of you that way.

ELLEN How long will you stay, Jack? I was thinking we could have a barbeque on Saturday.

JACK Sorry, Ellen. I have to be back tomorrow afternoon. I could only cancel my morning classes on such short notice. I figured I'd stay here at Mom's tonight; then drive back first thing in the morning.

K.J. What do you expect, Ellen? He barely made it in for his mother's funeral, so nothing as mundane as money could hold him here for more than a day.

ELLEN Please, let's try to get along, if only for...

(MAX *enters the living room.*)

MAX I apologize for the interruption. Oh, so sorry, didn't realize the last of the family had arrived.

K.J. He's only last in our hearts, Max. Otherwise, he's the middle child.

JACK How do you do, I'm Jack Hennesy.

(JACK *and* MAX *approach each other, shake hands.*)

MAX A pleasure, Jack. I'm Maximilian Yarrow—like the river in Scotland. But my friends call me Max.

JACK Then Max it is. Ellen told me you own an art gallery in Manhattan.

MAX Well, gallery is not precisely correct. I have a studio where buyers can examine the art I represent. I'm on 57th Street.

JACK I looked you up on the Internet, but couldn't find any information.

MAX Oh, my studio is not open to the public. I show my works by appointment only. I have a select clientele, and a select catalogue of art.

(MAX *pulls a business card from a silver cardholder he carries in his jacket; he offers it to* JACK.)

MAX Here's my card. Call anytime. My assistant, Rose, is usually there until seven or eight, most weekday nights. I'd love to show you some of the works I represent anytime you're in New York. I just acquired two very lovely DeKoonings from the 1960s. When his powers were at their zenith. You may have read about them in last month's *ARTnews*, though

I never said I thought the Met was trying to acquire them. I merely said the director was interested.

JACK All right, Max, I'm convinced—you're really an art dealer.

MAX I apologize if I come on a bit strong. But I do like my clients to have complete confidence in my experience and abilities. And you, Jack; I understand you teach history?

JACK That's right. At Grant College. It's a small, private school.

MAX In Dubuque. Its reputation reaches New York. A solid, Midwest college. Are you a full professor?

JACK Associate. You have to be given tenure before appointment to full professorship. And the tenure committee and I don't see eye-to-eye on some things.

MAX For instance?

JACK Well, Grant College—it's named for an oil baron, not the president—has a rather conservative culture.

K.J. And Jack's politics always favor the underdog, even when the dog's just bitten the hand that's fed him.

JACK It takes a bitch to know something about dog bites.

ELLEN Jack, please don't...

MAX (*trying to relieve the tension*) And your wife? Did she drive up with you?

ELLEN Oh, Jack's not married.

K.J. No, after all, Joan of Arc is dead.

MAX *(moving on)* What do you teach? Something fun, I hope. Like, the growth of Roman Catholicism in medieval Alsace.

JACK Nothing so rarefied. I teach basic American history. The Revolution to the Civil War.

MAX Of course. The essential facts. After all, those who don't know their history…

JACK Seem to do enormously well as business majors.

MAX *(chuckling)* Have you had anything published?

JACK A few things. I just had an article published in *American History Quarterly:* "The Trail of Tears—New Perspectives; Old Prejudices."

MAX Our treatment of the Native Americans is evidence that in a capitalist society there are only two classes of people—the exploited and the exploiters. No other labels really amount to anything when push comes to shove. Wouldn't you agree, Jack?

JACK If you're correct, then which are we, Max? The exploiters or the exploited?

MAX You're both, of course. By virtue of having been born Americans. But it's my job to now make you all exploiters extraordinaire.

JACK I've never felt so patriotic.

K.J. Don't take Jack too seriously, Max. Our dear brother has our father's high ideals, and his low opinion of the world. The living world, that is; Jack gets along much better with people who've been dead for a while than he ever has with the people he's forced to live and work with. I'm afraid Jack's forever disappointed that people often have no choice but to act in their own best interest.

ELLEN Now, let's not...

JACK Welcome to our family, Max. Don't expect us to get along this well all the time—we're on our best behavior when meeting strangers.

MAX I hope you won't think of me as a stranger for long, Jack. Not after I give you my good news.

ELLEN You've confirmed that the painting's real...authentic I mean.

K.J. Let the man talk, Ellen.

MAX Quite all right, K.J. No, Ellen, as I explained earlier, I've not yet confirmed its authenticity. We're getting close, but we're not quite there. My news though is not unrelated to that issue—I've found a buyer for the painting.

ELLEN But how? If the painting hasn't been authenticated...?

K.J. How much?

JACK Who said we wanted to sell it?

MAX Now, now, everyone. Listen to me for a moment. *(pause)* I've been studying this painting for almost a week now—I've had it cleaned; ever so delicately, and at my own expense, of course. I've also had it restretched so that the whole canvas is now visible. And I've had two art historians, whose judgment and discretion I trust, examine the canvas. Based on their reports, and my own examinations, I believe the painting to be authentic. But what is of greater importance is that we find a *buyer* who believes that the painting is genuine. Nobody will pay a million dollars *or more (pause)* for a painting unless their belief in the work is deep and unshakable. In that sense, the painting's authenticity is ultimately a question of money.

JACK Martin Luther said that for a leap of faith to occur there must be a conversion of the heart, the mind and…the pocket book.

MAX Exactly, Jack. Martin Luther and I are in complete agreement on this point. And assuming for the moment that we're interested in selling the painting—how does a buyer acquire this religion? For example, is there a record somewhere of Monet painting this particular canvas? *(pause)* A canvas whose title is unknown, and whose subject appears to be a fog engulfed bridge spanning a narrow river. Unfortunately, thus far, the answer is no. This painting has no provenance.

ELLEN What's that?

MAX A provenance? It's the painting's history. The record of its life, from birth to this morning. Our Monet—your Monet—was probably born a hundred years ago, and yet we can only account for the last fifty-or-so-years of its life. But it is the painting's first fifty years that matter most.

ELLEN Perhaps this is silly of me to say, but I assume paintings don't come with something like a birth certificate?

MAX Not exactly. But Claude Monet was a hugely successful painter. Even an early work by Monet would have been immediately published in one manner or another. Either shown in an exhibition or described in one of the leading art magazines of the day. But the *Catalogue Raisonnes de Monet*, which contains every canvas he is known to have created, does not reveal any record of this painting.

JACK Then it's a fake?

MAX No, I don't think it's fake. It wouldn't make sense. Why fake a painting that has no provenance? Why not create a fake *Grain Stack*, or a fake *Water Lilies*? Something people are familiar with, a subject Monet is known to have painted many times over. And if you're creating a fake, then why leave the date off? Besides, Monet is difficult to fake. His use of colors and light was magnificently subtle. Nearly impossible to copy.

K.J. Then how do you establish authenticity if there isn't a…provenance?

MAX By selling the painting to a knowledgeable collector. The purchase itself vests the work with credibility. And we may have found such a person. A party with whom I've dealt in the past. A wealthy patron. He has seen the painting. Briefly. Yesterday afternoon. He's very excited about it.

JACK Does he think the thing's real?

MAX Let's not call it a thing, Jack. It is a work by one of the greatest painters of his time; a work which will outlive us all. Besides, if I'm correct, it's worth millions. So let's show the lady some respect.

(long pause)

K.J. What do you mean, "millions?"

MAX I didn't want to say anything too soon. But if the painting's genuine, and we can prove it, then I estimate the painting's worth five to six million dollars; at least.

ELLEN   Oh, my God!

JACK   And you say, you've found a buyer—somebody willing to pay that amount?

MAX   It is perhaps more accurate to say our potential buyer found me. His name is Toshino Kawamura—he is the principal owner of the leading steel company in Japan. His private art collection rivals those of the world's leading museums. I sold him a painting by Caravaggio about two years ago. He heard about the Monet and called my office.

JACK   How did he hear about the Monet so fast? I just heard about it myself a week ago.

MAX   Word travels quickly in the art community. Especially now that everybody has these goddamned computers. I've already gotten a dozen calls from dealers and friends asking if the rumors are true—that we've discovered a new Monet. I haven't confirmed anything to anybody yet—except Kawamura. He's the only one I thought would be useful. He's in the U.S. on business. He asked to look at the painting. Of course, I consented. He examined it for half-an-hour late last night. He'd like to see the painting again, this evening. At seven o'clock. He's bringing his own expert with him. A former curator from the Museé d'Orsay. If his expert confirms my findings, I expect he'll make an offer.

K.J.   How much?

MAX   As I said, if the painting is by Monet and we can somehow confirm it, then it's worth at least five million. However, if Kawamura wants it now—before we can offer it at auction, then he has to pay a premium. But we are getting slightly ahead of ourselves. For now, I merely wanted to report to you this unexpected development. It is welcome news, certainly. But we've not discussed sale of the painting before. So I thought it appropriate to let you know somebody is interested.

ELLEN You mean, if Kawa…

MAX Kawamura.

ELLEN If Kawamura's interested…he'll just make us an offer? For five million dollars? Just like that?

MAX Yes. Just like that. Either he believes in the painting, or he doesn't. Your canvas is either worth a hundred dollars or it's worth several million.

JACK This is ridiculous. You don't really believe…?

MAX Yes, Jack. I do believe. But the offer could even be higher. And whatever is offered is certainly negotiable.

K.J. Just as an exercise, mind you, what would we receive if the painting sold for five million dollars?

JACK Oh, K.J. stop it! That old painting's not worth five…

K.J. Shut up, Jack. I'm asking a question. Max?

MAX Well, my agreement with Ellen provides that I receive a twenty percent commission on a private sale of the painting. From my commission, I take care of Ben the talkative antiques dealer and my friend, Paul Phillips, as well as the other experts who've assisted me. But that's not your concern. Simply put, you get eighty percent of five million dollars. Or, four million dollars. The estate would then pay inheritance taxes of about a million dollars, leaving a balance for distribution of three million dollars. Or, about one million dollars for each of you.

ELLEN *(quietly)* A million dollars a piece.

MAX At least. Probably a million two. And that's tax-free.

JACK Tax-free? But you said…

MAX The estate pays a tax. But the money distributed to you is tax-free. Figure, at least one million dollars each, free and clear.

K.J. What if the painting's worth more?

MAX That's possible. If we could firmly establish the painting's provenance—authenticity—the price would be significantly higher. Or, if we put the painting up for auction, the bids may exceed six million dollars. But auctioning the painting raises a whole new set of problems. We don't have time to discuss them all right now. It is enough to say that people like Mr. Kawamura never buy at auction. It's too public. They prefer to come in early. Determine the market price; offer ten percent more. Some negotiation ensues. A price is reached. And then, they whisk the painting away to some remote mansion where it becomes a private treasure.

JACK But Mr. Kawamura has not offered us six million dollars for the painting, has he?

MAX No. Not yet.

JACK And he hasn't said he thinks the painting is real, has he?

MAX No.

JACK Well, for now, I'll keep my day job.

MAX You're right to be cautious, Jack. But you have to be ready—all of you—to act in the event Kawamura makes an offer. You may have to decide tonight.

ELLEN Tonight?

MAX Yes, my dear. Tonight. As I said, Mr. Kawamura is bringing his expert to look at the painting. I'll have one of my experts there, as well. If Mr. Kawamura is interested in making an offer, he'll do it tonight. Once he puts the matter into play, we have to move with all deliberate speed.

JACK What's the hurry? The painting's been in the family for fifty, sixty years. What's the harm in holding onto it for a few more months? We have time.

MAX Time! Time, Jack! I could write a book on how time plays its games with a painting's monetary value. The longer people study something, the more unsure they become. Doubts begin to fill their heads. Can they afford it? Might the money be better spent on the wing of a hospital? Do they really like the artist? Do their friends like him? Isn't it the wrong color for the library? These are all the concerns that diminish a buyer's resolve. Faith is what you called it, Jack. Faith and resolve. Other forces come into play, as well. Influences which work to dissuade a potential buyer from making the commitment.

JACK Sounds like we're trying to sell a used car.

MAX My motto is, "Sell in haste, retire in leisure."

JACK You may want to consult your Bartlett's on that, Max.

K.J. Never mind my brother, Max. Go see your Japanese industrialist. We'll wait here for the good news.

MAX Excellent. A fine plan. And while I'm gone, rack your collective brains. See if there's anything else you can remember about the painting. Anything at all that might help establish its authenticity. Ellen, you're sure there's nothing in your mother's papers that relate to the canvas?

ELLEN I've looked through everything, Max. There's nothing.

MAX Nothing left from your grandmother? Letters, or birth certificates, photo albums; family Bibles?

ELLEN I've searched through everything.

MAX Look again. As a favor to me. Remember, since we presume your grandmother acquired the painting in Austria sometime before 1946, the bill of sale or other documents recording the purchase will be written in German. If we can prove the painting's by Monet, the asking price goes up. So, if you find anything in German, put it aside, and I'll look at it later.

ELLEN I will, Max. But, as I said, my mother didn't keep anything from her childhood...and I've looked.

MAX Yes. Exactly. Exactly. Well, I'm off to do war. I'll call sometime after seven o'clock. Let's keep our fingers crossed. *Adieu*, for now.

(MAX *exits.* ELLEN *moves the box that contains the old 45s into the closet.* JACK *walks over to the bookshelf, and pulls out an old volume, starts to flip through it.*)

JACK I get the feeling Max is not telling us something. Which, by the way, he's quite gifted at.

K.J. He's said all I need to hear. In a few hours we'll be millionaires.

JACK Who said we were going to sell the Monet? Assuming it's real, *and* worth what Yarrow says it is…

K.J. Damn right we're going to sell it, Jack. Ellen and I both agree—the painting will be sold.

ELLEN Well, we haven't really decided—not finally, and not all of us.

K.J. Then let's decide. Right now. Like Max said, time is of the essence. Let's agree to sell, then decide on our price.

JACK We can't just sell the painting as if it meant nothing to us; nothing to our family.

K.J. It does mean nothing to us—except for the money it can bring.

JACK C'mon. It was Granma's painting. She owned it for thirty, forty years. And Mom had it for another twenty-five.

K.J. Yes, and neither one told us what it was, or what to do with it after they died; so now the decision is ours.

JACK Why do we have to make a decision tonight?

K.J. Weren't you listening to Max? There's a Japanese billionaire who's ready to buy. I would think even a history professor could understand that opportunities like this come along once in a lifetime. And ours is arriving in just a few hours. So, let's take a vote.

JACK Can't we at least spend a little time looking for…something that will explain how Granma acquired the painting? Or try to figure out why she didn't tell anyone she owned a canvas by Claude Monet?

ELLEN Jack, I've already explained—there's nothing of Granma's left. Mom must have gotten rid of everything.

K.J. I'm surprised mother didn't save any of Granma Feld's belongings. When we were children, there were all these old German do-dads around, tea cups and candle sticks; a yellowed linen tablecloth; mother always put it out for Christmas dinners and Granma's birthday. I remember there was this old leather photo album—it had a painted postcard of Vienna framed on the cover....

JACK I remember that. It was Granma Feld's album. With pictures of Granma's family from Austria. There was one picture of a teenage boy and a girl taken on the steps of this government building; you could see the Nazi flag in the background. And there were policemen on the steps with swastika arm bands and stone faces. They were like something from a movie. It's hard to believe our own mother grew up in that world.

K.J. Ellen, when you were going through the storage lockers did you come across that old pine trunk that mother used to keep in the spare bedroom?

JACK Yeah—that was Granma's.

ELLEN Yes, I looked. But there was only some old blankets and sheets in there.

(JACK *nods, thinks to himself.*)

ELLEN Believe me, I've gone through everything.

(*There is a knock on the door.* ELLEN *goes over to it.*)

ELLEN It must be Mrs. Zemke again.

(ELLEN *opens the door.* MARYANN CARSON *stands at the doorway.* MARYANN *is a plain-looking woman, professionally dressed, about forty-five-years-old. She is carrying a shoulder bag.* ELLEN *is taken aback a moment by the unexpected appearance of the woman.*)

ELLEN Can I help you?

MARYANN Are you Mrs. Hennesy?

ELLEN No. I'm her daughter, Ellen. Ellen Denby. Mrs. Hennesy—my mother—passed away a few weeks ago.

MARYANN Yes, that's… I'm very sorry to disturb you. I know this must be a difficult time.

(JACK, *hearing the conversation, looks up from his book, studies the woman.*)

ELLEN Do you live here in the building?

MARYANN *(slowly)* No, I…I'm from California. I just flew into Chicago yesterday. When I heard about the painting.

ELLEN The painting? You mean, the…? What do you mean?

(JACK *takes a step closer to the two women. K.J. also looks alert at this mention of the painting.*)

MARYANN I mean, the Monet. *Le Matin au Pont de Rialto.*

ELLEN What?

MARYANN *Le Matin au Pont de Rialto.* That's the name of the painting. *Morning at the Rialto Bridge.* It's a bridge that crosses the Grand Canal. In Venice.

JACK You know about the painting?

MARYANN Yes—I've been investigating it for many years.

K.J. Do you know who painted it?

MARYANN *(somewhat surprised by the question)* Yes—it's by Claude Monet.

ELLEN Are you sure?

MARYANN Quite sure. It was painted in 1908. In Venice. Or at least it was begun in Venice. Monet didn't complete the painting until 1912.

JACK How do you know all this? We were told the painting has no provenance.

MARYANN No official provenance, but I have records that establish the painting is by Monet and that it belongs to me; belongs to my family.

JACK What are you talking about?

MARYANN I'm here to recover what was stolen from my grandfather. Stolen many years ago.

JACK Stolen? From who?

MARYANN Stolen from my grandfather. You see, my great uncle, Ernest Bloomstein, purchased the painting in 1920 from a physician friend of

Monet's. Bloomstein was a wealthy banker in Vienna. He was also a Jew. He died in 1936, and the Monet, along with some other works, passed to his brother, Joseph. Joseph Bloomstein was my grandfather. Two years after Joseph Bloomstein inherited the painting, it was stolen from him by the German government. The painting was one of thousands of artworks plundered by the Nazis after the *Anschluss*—the takeover of Austria.

JACK So, you're saying, you think that we have a painting, and that painting belongs to you?

MARYANN Yes. To my family. It was stolen from my grandfather by the Nazis in 1938. I'm sure what I'm telling you comes as a shock. I wish there was a less abrupt way to give you this news. I don't know how much you know about the Monet; but I've been searching for it for almost ten years. I've brought information with me—records, photos, letters, which prove what I'm telling you.

K.J. Wait a minute, Miss…?

MARYANN Carson. My name is MaryAnn Carson. As I said, I live in Sacramento. I'm an interior designer. Here's my card.

(MARYANN *offers her card to* K.J., *who does not take it.*)

K.J. Well, Miss whoever-you-are, you couldn't be more wrong. Our painting—our Monet—has been in our family for years.

JACK How did you learn we had… a painting?

MARYANN An art dealer in Los Angeles I've been working with informed me. A friend of his here in Chicago called him earlier this week to say that a previously unknown Monet had surfaced. I flew out as soon as he confirmed that the painting which had appeared was similar to

Bloomstein's Monet. Once I see it, I'll know for sure. I'll know I've finally found my grandfather's painting.

JACK Well, I'm not sure you've found anything yet.

MARYANN Then your painting is not *Le Matin au Pont de Rialto*? It should be about twenty-eight inches tall, thirty-six inches wide...

JACK Excuse me, Ms. Carson, but we obviously just can't start talking to you—a complete stranger—about matters that are private... and personal to us. I suppose there's no harm in our looking at whatever pro... information you have. Compare it with our records...

(MARYANN *removes a large envelope from her purse. She hands it to* JACK.)

MARYANN I've made copies of the relevant documents—with translations. Some of the documents are in French; most are in German. I ask only that you not sell or transfer the painting until I've had a chance to examine...

K.J. We won't make any such promise. We have every right to do as we please with our property.

MARYANN But the painting you have is *Le Matin au Pont de Realto*, isn't it? You can at least tell me that much.

JACK To be honest...we don't know.

K.J. Jack, be quiet. We have no obligation to tell this woman anything.

MARYANN If the painting you have is *Le Matin au Pont de Rialto*, then it isn't yours. It was stolen from my family. You can't have proper ownership.

JACK What happened to your grandfather's Monet after it was taken by the government? Do you have records showing that?

MARYANN No. *(hesitantly)* No, of course not. The Nazis didn't keep accounts of their art thefts. In most instances, they gave or sold the paintings they plundered to high-ranking Nazi officials or valuable friends in industry. How did your family acquire the painting? Do you know?

K.J. Well, our records certainly don't show that our grandparents were Nazis. You really have enormous nerve to just barge into our mother's house like this, and make these accusations. I have never been so insulted.

MARYANN Please—I understand that what I'm saying is a shock. I'm sure you had no idea how the painting was acquired by your...

K.J. Enough! I've listened to all I'm going to. I don't know what you're trying to pull, but to come into somebody's home and accuse them—accuse their family—of being Nazis and thieves is slander. I have a good mind to call my lawyer.

MARYANN But what I'm telling you is the truth. The evidence is in that envelope.

JACK I think we've heard enough...for now, anyway. Is there someplace we can contact you?

MARYANN I'm staying at the Chicago Hilton. On Michigan Avenue. I've written the number on the envelope. Will you promise me you won't sell the painting until you...?

K.J. We've told you—we won't make any promises.

MARYANN Believe me, I'm just trying to avoid a lot of grief for everyone. Maybe we can reach an understanding of some kind. Otherwise, I'll have to take legal action to protect my family's interest.

JACK I tell you what—we'll look through the papers you've provided. All I can promise is that we'll contact you when we're through.

MARYANN I'll wait to hear from you—but it must be soon. Noon, tomorrow should be enough time. Call your lawyer if you want. Better still, call an art dealer. Someone knowledgeable. I hope you realize that I'm not trying to hurt you. Any of you. But I've searched for this painting for a long time. I owe it to my grandfather....

ELLEN And we owe it to our mother to protect what was hers. I hate to be rude...

MARYANN Just one more thing—when I first told you the name of the painting—*Le Matin au Pont de Rialto*—you looked surprised. But there may be another name by which you know the work. As I said, my grandfather inherited the canvas in 1936 when his brother died. By then it was apparent what would happen to Jews who found themselves under German control. Realizing that the Nazis would confiscate the painting if they knew its real value, my grandfather tried to hide the most obvious evidence that it was a painting by Monet; he had the canvas reframed; so that the signature of Monet could not be seen. He also referred to it by a different title. For many years, it was called, *On a Certain Morning*. *(pause)* Perhaps this information will help convince you that the painting is not yours. I look forward to hearing from you.

(MARYANN CARSON *turns and walks out.*)

Curtain
End of Act I

Act II—Scene I

(ELLEN *and* K.J. *are in the living room.* ELLEN *is taping a box closed.* K.J. *is reclining on the sofa.*)

K.J. Tell me again; what did Max say?

ELLEN He wanted to know if she gave us any court papers. When I told him "no," he seemed very relieved.

K.J. But what did he say? About the Japanese man? Does he want to buy the painting?

ELLEN I didn't ask him—I—I just told him about the woman, and how she said the painting belongs to her. And then Max asked if she tried to serve us with a lawsuit. I told him "no." He said, "Then not to worry. Max will explain everything when he returns."

K.J. That woman wouldn't have the nerve to sue us—we'd counter-sue for libel and for trespassing. *(pause)* Did Max say when he'll be back?

ELLEN No, just soon. Anyway, that was half-an-hour ago. He should be here any minute now.

K.J. I still can't believe that woman just snuck into the building. If Mother were alive, I'd move her right out of here. I never understood why she moved into the city in the first place. To leave that wonderful house on Kennecut, where all her friends were, and take this crummy apartment away from everybody.

ELLEN Do you believe her?

K.J. Believe her? Who? Ms. MaryAnn Carson? No. Of course not. She's either delusional, or else a crook. This is how con-artists operate, Ellen. They prey on the elderly and on families of the recent dead.

(K.J. *stands; walks over to the server. She examines some glass candlesticks.*)

ELLEN But she seemed to know so much about the painting. Like its title. I told Max what she called it, *Le Matin-au*-something-something. He didn't seem surprised or anything.

K.J. I'm sure nothing surprises Max. Remember he said that when news of the painting spread, there'd be crazies coming out of the woodwork.

ELLEN But what if she's right? What if her family does own the painting?

K.J. Don't be ridiculous, Ellen. We own the painting. You know that. It's been in our mother's and grandmother's home for more than fifty years. Nobody ever asked about it before. Don't you think that if the painting had been stolen, somebody would have come looking for it sooner?

ELLEN But Jack says…

K.J. I don't give a good goddamn what Jack says. Ellen—listen to me—I'm not going to let Jack bring his whole "trail of tears" guilt trip into our mother's house. The painting is ours. And we agreed, majority rules. As long as you and I vote to sell the painting, Jack can't stop us. Right?

ELLEN I'm…

K.J. Right?

ELLEN I. I don't want us to fight about this.

K.J. We're not fighting. We're agreeing. You and I agree on this. And in his heart, so does Jack. Believe me, he wants to sell the painting, too; but of course it would be too crass, too…honest for Jack to say that money is important to him. That's why he's in the bedroom playing on his computer. Ever since he was a little boy, whenever there was trouble, Jack would go and hide. He'd let everyone else make the hard decisions. And when the dirty work was done, in would walk Jack, all ready to pronounce on how morally corrupt the rest of us are.

ELLEN I'm not sure that's fair to Jack. He just said he wanted to do some research. See if he could find anything on the Internet about the painting.

K.J. Jack's research always confirms the worst. Nowadays, history is written by the losers.

(The phone rings. ELLEN picks it up.)

ELLEN Hello? Max! Where are you? *(pause)* Yes, there is. Park on Bowie. Then come in through the alley. I'll meet you down there in two minutes.

(ELLEN *hangs up the phone.*)

ELLEN That was Max. He's in his car. He's got the painting with him, and he doesn't want to come in through the front door. I'm going downstairs to let him in through the delivery entrance.

(ELLEN *runs into the kitchen, returns with some keys, which she sorts through.*)

K.J. Ellen—please don't forget what we talked about earlier—about the financial situation I'm in—if this painting's worth anywhere near as much as Max thinks—well, it's like a gift from God—a second chance for me.

A chance to avoid personal embarrassment, financial ruin....

ELLEN You know, whatever happens, I'll be there for you. For you and Donald. Regardless of what happens with the painting.

K.J. That's sweet of you, Ellen. And I know you mean it—but my problems can't be solved by talking them out over the phone. A sympathetic ear is not enough. Money is what I need. And I need it now. I'm willing to admit that I'm a selfish bitch, a greedy...monster, if that's what you want.

ELLEN No. No, I've never said that—I'd never think it.

K.J. *(controlled)* But you *can* think it —you can think anything you want, as long as you give me the chance to save my family.

ELLEN It's just... Look, I know you're different from me, K.J. I've always known it. You're a very special...

K.J. No. No. I'm not trying to...

ELLEN Let me finish. What I'm trying to say is that for your whole life people have thought of you as someone who's almost...perfect; someone who always knows what to say; what to wear; someone who gets things done. You were the cheerleader captain in high school; you went to that private college in Lake Forest, and you graduated at the top of your class. Mom was so proud of you, but she didn't treat you the way she treated Jack and me. I mean, she loved you, but...but she was also...a little frightened, I think.

K.J. Frightened? What are you talking about?

ELLEN Do you remember when you were about ten, you started taking piano lessons with Mr. Kent?

K.J. Yes, I remember.

ELLEN You loved that piano; you played for hours every day; even in the summer. Dad would sit in the living room and listen to you practice; sometimes just scales. Over and over. When you turned thirteen, I think, Mr. Kent suggested that you apply for some music scholarship to that private school in the city. What was the name of it?

K.J. The Mishton Music Academy.

ELLEN Yes; that's right. I knew you'd remember. Anyway, you practiced the piano and studied music for months before the competition. Every morning before school; every afternoon after school, even Mr. Kent thought you were too...dedicated. Not Dad, though; he just listened to you practice. I still remember how you taped scales to the mirror in our bathroom and to the closet door; every second of your life was devoted to winning that scholarship.

K.J. Yes, yes. I was there, Ellen—why bring it up now?

ELLEN Well, do you recall what happened just before the competition— you slipped on the stairs one morning, and sprained your wrist?

K.J. Of course, I remember.

ELLEN You weren't able to play the piano for weeks, and you missed the competition, and the scholarship. So you went to Arlington Heights High School instead. And eventually you became captain of the cheerleaders; prom queen, class president and all that.

K.J. Ellen—is there a point to your recalling this tired bit of biography?

ELLEN Yes—my point is that except for the piano competition you never failed at anything else you tried at again. You went to the college you wanted; were accepted by the best sorority; married the man you fell in love with. Helped him build a big construction company.

K.J. So?

ELLEN But you never played the piano again. Not once. After your wrist got better, you had Dad move the piano to the basement. You said you wanted to practice in private—away from everyone. But I know—you never played it again; everyone knew it.

K.J. I was disappointed at the time; so what?

ELLEN Well, Mom and Dad waited for you to react to what happened; they waited for you to cry, or get angry, or something. But you never said anything to anybody. You just stopped talking about the piano; the scales came down from the walls; the lessons stopped; the books of music went into the closet. For three years, that piano was your whole life, and then— it was gone, and so was everything associated with it. Things changed between you and Dad, too. I could tell. In some way, his listening to you practice every day was the only link you had with him, and when you quit playing—quit practicing—it was as if you had moved away. No one said anything, but everyone felt it. I think Mom and Dad were sort of scared of you after that.

K.J. Scared? Don't be ridiculous.

ELLEN No—they were; they saw you could just turn off a part of yourself if you had to. I once heard Mom say you were stronger than they were. Stronger than anyone she'd ever met except Granma. After you stopped playing the piano, Mom and Dad started to…defer to you more; to give you more space; if that's the right word—there was a recognition that you were special; that you were gifted and absolutely determined to succeed.

K.J. What does any of this have to do with the painting?

ELLEN I'm not sure—but I think maybe now you think you don't have the right to fail; that it's your job to get Donald through whatever trouble he's in.

K.J. It is my job, Ellen; he's my husband. Even if he's been an idiot—or worse. It's still my obligation to make sure he—we—get out of this.

ELLEN Maybe. But people are allowed to make mistakes; to fail at things. You can't always make things go your way just by the sheer force of your desire. Accidents happen; people fail. Sometimes there's nothing you can do to stop the inevitable.

K.J. You're wrong, Ellen. If there's one thing I know in life, it's that you can make things happen just by wanting them badly enough; more than someone else wants it; by not letting anything stop you; not logic, not common sense...

ELLEN Not even family?

(ELLEN *and* K.J. *look at each other for a few seconds.*)

K.J. This is not about family, Ellen. It's about money. That's all. However Grandmother acquired the painting, it's ours now. Ms. Jewish-Interior-Designer-from-California can say that she's fighting about the principle of the thing. But the truth is, she wants the painting because she knows how valuable it is. Believe me, nobody starts a legal battle over principle—it's always about money. And that's what this has to be about for me—the money.

ELLEN I... I better get Max.

(ELLEN *leaves. K.J. takes a deep breath. From the shadows of the hallway,* JACK's *voice emerges.*)

JACK *(barely visible in the hallway)* That was quite a performance; very persuasive. (JACK *enters the living room*) Someone once said that behind every great fortune is a crime. Aren't you even a little bit concerned that there's a crime buried deep in the history of our good fortune?

K.J. *(coldly)* I didn't know you were listening, Jack. Eavesdropping's a crime, as long as we're on the subject.

JACK I didn't hear all of your conversation. Just your closing. I take it Don's company is in some sort of financial difficulty. I noticed that he didn't sponsor that obscenely expensive golf tournament in June like he usually does. And he didn't send the carton of steaks in July. How bad is it?

K.J. What do you care?

JACK I'd get no pleasure from watching your company fail if that's what you're suggesting.

K.J. But you're not willing to do the one thing that will save it?

JACK I'll do anything I can—as long as I can live with myself afterward. Anyway, I haven't made up my mind.

K.J. Ellen and I have made up ours, which means your opinion, like your overall involvement with this family, is irrelevant.

JACK Assuming Ellen votes to sell the painting.

(The voices of ELLEN *and* MAX *rise from the hall as they approach.* MAX *enters first;* ELLEN *is right behind him.* MAX *carries a pine box, about three inches deep, and roughly thirty-by-forty inches square;* ELLEN *carries a small folding easel.)*

MAX *(as he approaches the sofa)* And you're sure she didn't place a summons and complaint in the envelope? *(suddenly)* Jack, Ellen says the woman didn't serve any summons or complaint. Is that true?

JACK Not that I saw.

K.J. We should have thrown her out the minute she started talking.

(MAX *places the box onto the sofa.*)

MAX On the contrary; she brings us good news.

(MAX *smiles at all three; then he takes the easel from* ELLEN. MAX *looks around the room, considering the light. He walks over to the far left wall, and there sets up the easel. He returns to the sofa and gently removes the top of the pine box.*)

MAX Ellen, make sure the door is locked.

(ELLEN *runs over to the front door, locks and dead bolts it.*)

MAX We must take every precaution....

(MAX *pulls apart some towels and plastic which are wrapped around the unframed canvas. He picks up the canvas and carries it—so that its back is to the audience—over to the easel. MAX places the painting on the easel. He stands back.*

ON A CERTAIN MORNING

The painting is illuminated from an overhead stage light. JACK *and* ELLEN *and* MAX *study it. K.J. remains on the other side of the room, purposely nonchalant about viewing the work.)*

JACK That's it, all right. Though it looks a little different.

ELLEN Brighter.

MAX I had it cleaned—just enough to show its true colors.

JACK It's so small.

MAX In fact the painting is larger now than it's been in a long time. See—I had new stretchers put on the canvas, it's taller by almost three inches—you can see the signature now.

(JACK *approaches, nods his head.*)

MAX "Beauty is truth; truth beauty. That is all ye know on earth, and all ye need to know." *(pause)* Keats.

(MAX *looks at* JACK, *who continues to study the painting.*)

JACK "Beauty provoketh thieves sooner than gold." *(short pause)* Shakespeare.

(MAX *looks over to* K.J., *who has remained at the other end of the room.*)

MAX I recommend that you come over and observe your painting, K.J. You might not have another opportunity.

ELLEN What do you mean?

MAX I'm pleased to report that Mr. Kawamura has made us an offer.

(ELLEN *gasps;* JACK *steps back slightly, his back stiffens. Even* K.J. *is too anxious to speak; she moves toward* MAX.)

MAX Mr. Kawamura examined the painting for about twenty minutes. With his expert, Monsieur Bendall, formerly of the Museé D' Orsay. Monsieur Bendall does not have the best credentials, but the Japanese are always so impressed by the French and the French are always impressed by Japanese money. *(pause)* Anyway, Monsieur Bendall was non-committal at first. Yet I could see he was intrigued; quietly hopeful. You see, if he declares the painting to be authentic, then he gets credit for helping discover a lost Monet. After examining the canvas for a few minutes, Mr. Kawamura said he thought the painting looked familiar. Monsieur Bendall diplomatically but firmly dismissed his client's observation—but I was surprised to find myself agreeing with Kawamura; it did look familiar, like when you unexpectedly meet the brother of someone you know. And then it occurred to me where I'd seen this painting—well, not this painting exactly, but its siblings.

JACK The Venetian Series?

MAX Precisely, Jack. You've been doing some research, I see.

K.J. What's the Venetian Series?

MAX A group of paintings begun by Monet in Venice in 1908, but which he did not complete until 1912. I consulted Wildenstein's catalog, and there we found the better-known kin to your canvas. More than three dozen Venetian scenes, mostly of buildings and sights along the Grand Canal. All of the paintings shown in the catalog were of an appropriate dimension to yours, and in style and substance, there is no question. We spent fifteen minutes comparing various catalog plates to your canvas.

Overwhelmed by our discovery; Mr. Kawamura and Monsieur Bendall reacted like small children in their enthusiasm. Still, the catalog identified only thirty-nine paintings from the series, and our lovely was not among those shown or described. *(pause)* Was it possible?—Monsieur Bendall wondered aloud —that the painting was a very clever fake? Perhaps done in the 1920s or '30s? Could we provide no provenance? Not even a single bit of evidence establishing that Claude Monet actually painted this canvas?

(MAX *sighs, pauses*)

MAX I then explained all that we knew of the painting. I could see they wanted to believe; that they did believe. Even so, they needed something more, just a small push…. *(pause)* And then, like manna from Heaven, Ellen called.

ELLEN You didn't tell them about Ms. Carson, did you?

MAX Of course I did. I told them the whole story.

K.J. What? Are you crazy; he'll never buy…

(MAX *puts up his hand to silence* K.J.)

MAX *(calmly)* Mr. Kawamura offered us six million dollars in cash for the painting; one million is available tonight in a combination of U.S. dollars, Japanese *yen* and U.S. traveler's checks. The rest can be wire-transferred tomorrow morning. He imposed only two conditions—the first is that he must be able to take the painting back to Japan with him tomorrow morning.

K.J. You can't be serious. He wants to buy the painting? Even though there's a claim out there that it was stolen?

MAX Not despite the claim, but because of it. Don't you see? Your woman established a provenance for the painting. She also provides us with a name for it. *Le Matin au Pont de Rialto; Morning at the Rialto Bridge.* There is no longer any doubt as to the painting's authenticity. Did Ms. Carson say how the painting was acquired by her family?

JACK She said her great uncle bought it from Monet's doctor in 1920. There was a letter—or a copy of a letter—in the envelope she left. The letter's from the doctor to the great uncle. It's written in French. There's also a translation. Assuming the translation is accurate, the letter explains that the doctor is selling the painting to Ernest Bloomstein on the condition that the canvas not be displayed publicly for ten years and that the sale not be disclosed for the same time period. Bloomstein paid twenty thousand French *francs* for it.

MAX That would explain why the painting's initial sale was not published. I suspect that the old doctor received the canvas from Monet in lieu of a fee—probably just after the painting was completed—obviously, he didn't want Monet to learn he was selling it.

JACK That's my guess. There's another letter from the doctor explaining that he received the painting from Monet as a gift. There's also a photo of Monet with the doctor…

MAX Let me see!

(JACK *hands* MAX *the photograph.*)

MAX Wonderful! Your claimant has given us all we need.

K.J. Then you don't think this woman is just some crackpot?

MAX Not likely. Let's hope not, anyway.

ELLEN But what about her claim? Her accusations?

MAX *(distractedly)* What else did you find on the computer, Jack?

JACK Well, I found out that in 1908 Monet spent several months in Venice, painting the city. His wife became seriously ill, and together they returned to France. The wife died soon after, and Monet didn't finish any of his Venice canvases for four years. He hated all of the paintings; in part because he thought they were bad and in part because he associated them with his wife's death.

MAX So, based on your research, do you now believe the painting is a genuine Monet?

JACK *(reluctantly)* Yes…I guess I do.

MAX If you're convinced, Jack, then so am I. But, as I explained earlier, what matters is Kawamura's opinion. That's the second condition—he wants to see Miss Carson's documentation. We'll give the papers to Mr. Kawamura when he arrives…his conversion will be absolute then, and we can finalize the sale.

ELLEN Kawamura's coming here? Tonight?

MAX Yes. In order to avoid any unwelcome or messy complications, we have to complete the transaction tonight. Before Miss Carson can prevent the sale of your painting with a lawsuit. That's why I brought the canvas back here, so Mr. Kawamura and his expert can review the evidence that will "seal the deal," as it were.

JACK Don't you think that's a little deceitful—using Ms. Carson's documents to deprive her of the painting?

MAX There's no deceit involved, Jack. We've done nothing illegal; nothing immoral.

JACK Except arrange to sell a painting that may not belong to us under the nose of the woman who may really own it.

(JACK *puts the envelope into* MAX's *hands.*)

JACK Here, take a look yourself.

(MAX *places the envelope on the coffee table.*)

MAX Miss Carson's papers do not absolutely and unquestionably establish her ownership, do they, Jack?

JACK Nothing in this world is absolute, Max. But for argument's sake, I agree that there's nothing in what she gave us which directly shows that the painting was stolen from her grandfather by the Nazi government. However, there are records which show that Joseph Bloomstein was sent to a labor camp in Germany in 1938, and that he died there two years later. Now that's about the time our grandmother seems to have acquired the painting. Which, in my opinion, is enough of a connection to make our acquisition of the painting suspect.

MAX *(almost indifferently)* Suspect? Maybe. But nothing can be proven now. So who should own the painting? You and your sisters, or Miss Carson and her brother? Maybe she's right. If so, why didn't her parents pursue the painting years earlier? Why didn't they file a police report at the end of the war?

JACK *(certain and suspicious)* They may have. I'm sure they had more immediate problems to deal with. I… Wait a moment—you know about

Ms. Carson don't you? You know her name; you know she has a brother. Somehow you even know that no police report was ever filed.

MAX Of course, I know about Miss Carson, Jack. It's my job to know these things. I heard she was making inquiries earlier this week. The possibility that the painting had been stolen at some point in its long life was not so remote. After all, the painting had been reframed some time in the late '30s to hide Monet's signature. As I said before, the business of art can be embarrassing at times. So, in light of the painting's known history, I looked into Miss Carson's story. But after consideration, I concluded that there is no evidence to establish that the painting was stolen from her grandfather by the Nazis. Nor is there any evidence that your family acquired the painting from Nazi sources.

JACK Why didn't you tell us about her then?

MAX Because it was not relevant. And because I knew you might get caught up in the emotions of her story. I checked out her allegations, and was satisfied that her claim could not be proved. When paintings like your Monet surface, there is always some pesky claimant who comes forward, with little bits of information which they weave into tales of theft and claims of unjust enrichment. The real question is this: What could Miss Carson prove in a court of law? Her belief, no matter how fervent, does not constitute ownership.

ELLEN But her family did own the painting at one time?

MAX Yes; if we accept Jack's weighing of the evidence, which I certainly do. I've not reviewed any of the documents myself. I merely heard the report of her story from an art dealer she hired in Los Angeles. But just because her family once owned the painting, doesn't mean it was stolen from them by Nazis.

JACK Doesn't it strike you as odd that our grandmother used to call this canvas her "morning" painting, when its actual name is *On a Certain Morning*? Clearly, our Granma knew its title, and if she knew its name, she must have known who painted it, and what it was worth.

K.J. Well, maybe the Bloomsteins gave her the painting.

JACK They just gave her a million dollar painting?

K.J. Maybe they sold it to her.

JACK Then where's the receipt?

MAX You have the right idea, Jack. But the wrong perspective. We have possession of the painting. Possession presupposes ownership. Again, I say it is Miss Carson's burden to prove it was stolen.

JACK Oh, she's supposed to prove the painting was stolen by Nazis fifty years ago—how? By a signed confession?

MAX Under international law, her grandfather's family had an obligation to report the painting stolen after the war, and to pursue its return. Even under American law, the Bloom family—they dropped the "Stein" when they arrived here—had a legal obligation to conduct a good faith search for the painting, which they did not do. Nobody looked for the painting until MaryAnn Bloom, now Carson, started making inquiries about five years ago.

JACK She said it was ten years ago.

MAX That's what she *says*. But there's no record the family made any claim for the painting until five years ago. That's when Miss Carson contacted the Austrian government.

ELLEN Five years. Ten years. What difference does it make? Either the painting belongs to us, or it doesn't. Is there any way we can find out? Right away, I mean.

MAX In a way we have. The fact that she has produced no proof that the painting was stolen means that the painting belongs to you. Unless Miss Carson produces evidence—solid evidence—that you are not the owners, then the law presumes your grandmother acquired the canvas legally.

ELLEN Is that what you believe, Max?

MAX What I believe doesn't matter—but since you've asked: yes, it's what I believe.

JACK Of course, you stand to earn a million dollars yourself—if we sell the painting. So your judgment is…

K.J. Jesus Christ—I've listened to all the nonsense I'm going to. Max has done nothing but represent this family in the most effective way possible. In one week, he's taken what we all believed was a worthless old painting, and brought us a six million dollar cash offer. We should be congratulating him; not attacking him. I, for one, say thank you, Max; thank you for the very competent way you have guided us through this. Now, let's get down to business—I vote that we sell the painting tonight; let Max negotiate with his Japanese industrialist the best deal he can. But let's sell the painting, and be done with this.

JACK I'd hate to sell the painting so quickly and find out later that it was given to our family by the Nazis as a reward for…some job well done.

K.J. What in the hell do the Nazis have to do with us? That was all a million years ago. I'm not a Nazi; you're not; Ellen's not; we grew up in

Arlington Heights, Illinois, for Christ's sake—we're Americans. However our grandmother got that painting has nothing to do with us. But it's ours now, and I'm not going to start feeling guilty for what happened to…some people I never heard of fifty years before I was born.

JACK Not fifty years, K.J. Less than twenty. If you want the painting, you'll have to accept responsibility for its history. There's no way you can avoid it—I'm not saying our grandparents were Nazis—I'm just saying we need to figure out how Granma Feld acquired the painting.

(JACK *looks toward* ELLEN.)

JACK Maybe we'll never know. But if we send that painting off to Japan—before we've investigated it further, we'll regret it.

MAX And yet a delay of any kind will create additional problems. Looted artwork is a very hot issue right now for Jewish organizations. More and more families are coming forward, as Miss Carson has. Making claims for works which are alleged to have been looted by the Nazis during the Second World War. In most cases, there is no way to determine how or why a particular work changed owners. A large amount of art was sold by desperate people in the late '30s to raise money to escape Europe; some was stolen outright by the Nazis; some was simply lost. Even the most respectable art museums in the world— The Metropolitan Museum of Art and The Art Institute, to name just two—have become embroiled in fights over looted art. And they've been attacked for directly and indirectly depriving Jewish families of their rightful property. Property taken from family members who were killed in death camps and work camps. The media love these stories; love the controversy, the side-taking. Regardless of what a court of law decides five years from now, you will first have to deal with the court of public opinion.

K.J. The hell with public opinion. Let people think what they want.

MAX As long as you're prepared for what lies ahead. As you can imagine, the stories are always sympathetic to the long-dead owners. Everyone thinks you're anti-Semitic no matter what the evidence shows. You'll get nasty phone calls and letters. Even your children will be harassed. You can't win—it's you against six million dead Jews. The entire Holocaust is laid at your feet. And then there's the lawyers. They're worse than Nazis. Allowing yourselves to be sucked into the fight means that, at a minimum, you'll have to concede something. At best, you'll have to sell the painting to a museum for the amount of the estate taxes and the attorney's fees. And still some people will always wonder, "Were they Nazis, or weren't they? How did the Hennesys get that painting?" *(pause)* I know all of this because this is what I do; this is my—I hesitate to say, "specialty." I represent many so-called "looted" art pieces. So I have seen what happens. And before you say anything, or even think it—permit me a further confession; I, myself, am a Jew; I'm more Jewish than Miss Carson. Her paternal grandparents, the Bloomsteins, were Jews, but her mother's family are all Catholics. For Jews, it's the mother's side that matters—if your mother was a Jew, then you're a Jew.

JACK And if your grandparents were Nazis, then what does that make us, Max?

K.J. Fuck off, Jack! I can't listen to this anymore.

MAX What I'm trying to say, Jack, is this: I'm quite sympathetic to Miss Carson's claim. But sympathy is all that she deserves. She hasn't proven anything. From a legal or historical perspective. And she knows it. Otherwise, we'd have already been served with a lawsuit. But if you give her enough time....

K.J. Max is right. We need to decide what we're going to do here and now.

MAX I think it best if I leave you alone for a few minutes. I have to make some calls. Decide your course of action: Shall I call Mr. Kawamura and tell him not to come? Tell him the family has decided not to sell. If so, I have to do it soon. He'll be here in an hour. Talk among yourselves. Just the family. Think about what's involved. If you can't reach a decision… Well, that itself is a decision. But decide as a family.

(MAX *exits toward the bedroom.*)

K.J. Let's vote on it. Right now. There's no point discussing it further: Do we sell the painting, or don't we? I vote yes, and so does Ellen.

JACK Wait a goddamned second, will you? Can't we take a few minutes to talk about this? Consider—I mean really consider—the consequences of selling the painting; or not selling it. Don't you think I'd like to be rich? Be a millionaire?

K.J. No. As a matter of fact, I don't think you do. I think you're afraid that if you had money, you'd realize how small your life has been up to now. If you had a million dollars, you know you wouldn't be able to work for that shitty college anymore. You'd realize that teaching history to horny, money-struck kids is a stupid waste of your life. *(suddenly imploring)* But, Jack—think about it—with some serious money, you could write full time. Do all the research you want. You'd be free. That's what this money would be. Freedom.

JACK This is not about freedom. It's about conscience. It's about correcting past sins. Look, I know you need the money, but we can't pretend that the history of this painting is irrelevant to our decision. I'm not saying we can't ever sell it—but I think we need to satisfy ourselves that it was acquired legitimately.

ELLEN But Max says that the woman can't prove anything. That her family didn't report it stolen right away.

JACK I'm not talking about the law. The law never helped anybody who really needed it. I'm talking about satisfying ourselves. Who knows? Maybe we'll discover that the painting wasn't stolen by Nazis; maybe it was simply sold to our grandmother by this Bloomstein man. I just think we need time to look into it.

ELLEN But Max says that there will be publicity, and that we'll be attacked, and there'll be attorneys, and everything.

JACK We'll just have to deal with it.

K.J. Oh, now I see. You want the publicity. You want to be Jack Hennesy, the great benefactor. The historian who offered the Jews some redress. The peacemaker who gave up his chance for wealth to correct history. That would make you famous, Jack, wouldn't it? God, I can't believe I didn't see it immediately. Well, wearing a hair shirt for all time may work for you, Jack. But it has zero appeal to me. Or to Ellen. Let's vote. Now. Let's not kid ourselves. How we vote will be motivated by self-interest. And that's as it should be. I vote we sell the painting.

JACK I still vote no.

ELLEN What if there was a way for us to find out more about the painting without waiting? I mean, what if there was somebody who could tell us something about Granma and the painting? Someone we could talk to tonight?

JACK What are you talking about?

ELLEN I guess I should have told you both sooner—there was a man at Mom's wake. An old man. He knows about the painting. He knew that

Granma Feld owned it. He told me so. He saw it at Granma's apartment in Austria. He was a neighbor—a friend of Mom's. They went to school together.

JACK *(hesitantly)* You talked to someone at Mom's wake about the painting? Why didn't you tell us?

ELLEN Because I wanted...I wanted you both to think that it was my idea to have the painting appraised...to see what it was worth.

K.J. Did the man know it was a Monet?

ELLEN No. No—he didn't say that. He just started talking to me at the wake; about how he grew up in Kitzbükel, and was friends with Mom. He mentioned some other neighbors; then he started talking about the painting. He asked me if our family still owned it. He remembered that it was a painting of a bridge. He said he knew how valuable it was to Granma. He said that Kitzbükel was very wealthy in the '30s. And that a lot of the paintings and books and jewelry people had were valuable. He had a name for it.

JACK Portable wealth?

ELLEN Yes, that's right. He said that people who'd grown up in Europe during the First World War and after the Depression kept all their wealth in portable things. And if a woman had a diamond necklace, for instance...

K.J. You could assume it was real. Why didn't you mention this man to us before, Ellen? He's very important.

ELLEN I...I know I should have. But I didn't think it would matter so much.

K.J. It wouldn't matter? Don't you have a brain? Don't you see this man might help us slam the door on the Blooms, and their bullshit claim? Why didn't you tell us this before?

JACK She already said why she didn't.

K.J. Fine. She wanted us to think she was a brilliant art historian. But when Max started asking us all those questions about the painting's history, you could have told us then... It's almost a certainty that Mother knew....

ELLEN I don't think she knew—or understood what the painting was really worth. I went through all of her papers; there's nothing in there.

JACK Ellen, who was this man you talked to? What was his name? Do you remember?

ELLEN No. He was the tall old man who wore the mismatched brown pants and brown sports coat. He had white hair that went all over the place.

K.J. I remember him. He looked like he just got off the boat. And he smelled like a fish market.

JACK But what was his name?

ELLEN It was Sam something or Karl, I think.

JACK Where's the book? The sign-in book from the funeral home?

K.J. Yes! Yes!

(ELLEN *goes over to a box near the table. She starts to sort through it. After several seconds,* ELLEN *withdraws a small register from the box.*)

ELLEN Here it is.

(ELLEN *hands the register to* JACK.)

JACK No—you look through it. For the name.

(ELLEN *takes a seat on the couch, and begins to thumb through the register.* MAX *reenters.*)

MAX Have we reached a decision? Tell me we have, and make your Uncle Max a happy man.

K.J. Ellen's been holding back on us, Max. She didn't discover the painting on her own. An old man told her about it at our Mother's wake. He lived in Granma's town in Austria.

MAX *(anxiously)* You're kidding? What did he tell her? Ellen, what did he tell you?

(The phone rings. K.J. picks it up.)

K.J. Hello? Hello? *(pause)* They hung up.

MAX Uh-oh.

K.J. What's that mean?

MAX Maybe nothing. But it might mean our friend, Miss Carson, wants to confirm we're still here. She may have discovered we moved the painting, and now she's preparing to serve papers.

ELLEN Here it is. Karl Golian. He has a Chicago address. 1410 Rosemont. That's about fifteen minutes from here.

K.J. Call information. See if he's listed.

MAX May I ask what we're doing?

JACK We just told you—Ellen says there was a man at the wake who knew about the painting; we're trying to reach him to see if he can tell us something about it... Tell us how the family acquired a painting by Claude Monet.

(ELLEN *goes to the phone, dials directory assistance.*)

MAX Do you think that's such a good idea?

JACK What are you talking about? You were the one who told us to look for records.

MAX Records; yes. Witnesses; no.

JACK Are you serious?

MAX Listen to me for a moment. Records don't have a mind of their own. If you discover something in a book or a document...inconsistent with your own records, you can evaluate its place privately. But once you involve people in a matter, it is often difficult to get them to keep quiet again. And sometimes, they say things you rather they not say.

K.J. I see Max's point. What if this Karl man says Grandmother didn't own the painting?

JACK Then we don't own the painting. At least we'll know the truth. Which, Max, I don't believe you have the slightest interest in hearing.

MAX I'm not suggesting you refrain from contacting this man. I'm merely pointing out that there are risks involved.

JACK Max, if you'd been an officer on the Titanic, passengers would still be trying to decide if it was in their best interest to get into the lifeboats.

ELLEN He's listed? I have his number!

MAX Again, you should decide whether you really…

JACK Fuck off, Max. We're going to call him. I'm going to call him.

(JACK *walks over to the phone; takes the number from* ELLEN; *dials the phone.*)

JACK (*after a pause*) Hello; I'm trying to reach a Karl Golian. I (*pause*) (*to* ELLEN) the woman who answered the phone is going to get him. (*pause*) Hello, Mr. Golian, my name is Jack Hennesy; I'm Anna Hennesy's son…that's right. Yes. Thank you; we appreciate your thoughts. Mr. Golian, I understand you spoke with my sister, Ellen, at my mother's wake. (*pause*). Yes, that's her. I have two sisters. Ellen and K.J. You spoke to Ellen. She tells me that you knew our grandmother, Katherine Feld; that you grew up in Kitzbükel. (*pause*) Yes, that was a long time…. Um, the reason I'm calling is…the painting; yes that's right. We're wondering if you had some time to talk to us about it. You see, we've only just discovered that it may have some value, and we'd like to know more. Thank you, I appreciate your offer, but I wonder if we could talk to you tonight. (*nervous laugh*) You see, I've driven up from Iowa, and I have to leave first thing in the morning. I know it's getting late (*pause*). (JACK *nods his head at* ELLEN) That's fine—thank you, so much.

(MAX *rushes to* JACK.)

MAX Tell him he has to come here.

JACK *puts the phone to his chest.*

JACK What? I can't ask...

MAX As long as we're doing this, we might as well have him look at the painting—confirm it's the same one as in Kitzbükel. And we can't move it; not now. Tell him we'll send a car for him.

JACK What do I tell him is the reason?

MAX Tell him the truth, Jack—that we need him to look at the painting, confirm it's the same one. Tell him, it will be faster if we send a car.

JACK (*to* MAX) People in Chicago do not send cars... (*into the phone*) Mr. Golian, I wonder if I could ask you to come to my mother's apartment—I'll pick you up myself. If it's not too much of an imposition, we'd like you to look at the painting for us, and we can't really move it right now. *(pause)* We're at the Golden Oaks Apartments. It's at.... Yes, that's right. On Argento and Loftus. We're apartment 708. We'll have someone... Oh, that's great, but we don't want to put anybody out.... We appreciate your help. Thank you. See you in half-an-hour. Right. Bye.

(JACK *hangs up phone.*)

JACK His daughter's bringing him over. He knows the building. I think he's very intrigued by the painting. He said—and I quote—"I'm relieved you understand its value."

MAX Alright, I'll call Kawamura and ask him to put back our meeting to nine o'clock.

ELLEN Max, I'm confused. Is this man coming here good or bad?

MAX It depends, my dear, on what he says. That is one of the thrills of art history. Its goddamned unpredictability.

ELLEN Maybe I should get some crackers and wine for people—I can go out the delivery entrance, just to be safe.

MAX Not a bad idea. Is there a decent liquor store nearby?

ELLEN There's a White Hen...

MAX *(condescendingly)* We can't serve one of the wealthiest men in the world a wine from a convenience store! What will you serve with it? Hostess cupcakes? *(pause)* I'm sorry, Ellen, I didn't mean to be short with you. *(pause)* I guess we're all a little anxious. *(pause)* K.J., why don't you help your sister find a liquor store in the area? A good Bordeaux may be worth an extra hundred thousand dollars when all is said and done.

K.J. That's fine, Max. But before we go anywhere; Ellen, where's the radio?

ELLEN What radio?

K.J. When I arrived, you said you were listening to the radio. But I don't see one.

ELLEN I... I... There is no radio. I was listening to the record player. To some old records that Mom had. German records. *(quietly)*. They're in a box in the closet.

K.J. Why in the world did you say you were listening to a radio then? Why didn't you just tell me what you were listening to?

ELLEN Because... I don't know why. I was confused and nervous. Please, please don't get any madder at me than you already are. I just want us...

I just want us to be a family. Together. Like we were when we were kids. I thought if we could just come together this once, to do something all together, then maybe it would make us closer. I didn't mean to conceal anything. Not really.

K.J. But why lie about phonograph records? Do they have something to do with the painting?

ELLEN No. No. I don't...I just thought it was something you wouldn't want to know about.

K.J. Well, is there anything else you're not telling us? Anything else you've discovered that you think we wouldn't want to know about?

ELLEN No... No. The old records are all I found. Nothing else.

JACK What about Granma's photo album?

ELLEN No, no. I told you the records are all I've come across.

K.J. Ellen, I can't tell you how surprised I am by what you've done. Surprised and disappointed.

JACK Oh, please! Don't pay any attention to her, Ellen. She just wants you to feel guilty, so you'll go along with her plan to sell the painting.

K.J. You know, Jack, you're not the only person in this family entitled to take a moral stand. Of course, I forgive Ellen. *(slight pause)* Provided we sell the painting.

MAX Jack, K.J. Let's concentrate on our immediate goal: establishing how the painting came into your grandmother's hands. Your mother's old friend will be here soon, followed by Mr. Kawamura.

K.J. All right, all right. Ellen and I will find a liquor store.

JACK Ellen, where are the keys to the storage locker? I'd like to poke around a little.

ELLEN They're in the kitchen. On the hook next to the fridge. There's a white tag attached to the key.

JACK And Ellen—it's okay. You've done everything fine. Better than I could have.

(ELLEN *smiles weakly.*)

ELLEN Here. Let me show you where the key is.

(JACK *and* ELLEN *walk into the kitchen.* K.J. *picks up her purse and sweater.*)

K.J. What kind of wine do the Japanese like, Max?

MAX Something that sounds very French. Even if it's really very American.

K.J. Then a French sounding wine it is. *(pause)* I hope we're not making a mistake bringing that old man here.

MAX Whatever happens, K.J., it won't be a mistake. That much I know.

(K.J. *gives* MAX *a penetrating stare, finally nods and exits. A few moments later, the kitchen door can be heard to close.* MAX *pulls out his cell phone and dials a number.*)

MAX *(into phone)* Hello? Kawamura-san? Max Yarrow here. I just wanted to confirm our meeting. Is eight o'clock convenient? Fine. You should be prepared, Mr. Kawamura. The price has gone up.... *(pause)* Yes. We have some documentation. As I told you, we've established a provenance. It's more definite than I'd suspected. Whatever you pay for this canvas today, I predict it will be worth twice that amount in a year. *(pause)* As always, sir, I'll let you decide the appropriate amount after you've given the matter further study. Yes. I look forward to it. Half-an-hour, then. *Domo-domo* to you, too.

(MAX *hangs up the phone.*)

MAX *(to himself)* Now, where is that envelope?

(MAX *walks over to the coffee table. He picks up the envelope, and looks at a number written on it.*)

MAX *(into phone)* Room 927, please. Hello, Miss Carson. My name is Max Yarrow. I represent the Hennesy family in connection with *Le Matin au Pont de Rialto*. Or, if you prefer, *On a Certain Morning*. *(pause)* That's right; I heard about your claims, and I would like to discuss the painting with you. Perhaps we can come to an understanding. One that is...morally repugnant, but momentarily beneficial? *(pause)* Yes, yes. I'm glad to hear we speak the same language. I'm a bit tied up at the moment; an unrelated matter involving insurance agents and customs regulations. Can I call you later this evening? Say, ten o'clock? *(pause)* Very good. I look forward to it. Right. Good-bye.

FADE

Act II—Scene II

The lights go up on the living room a short while later. The room is unchanged, except that the painting and easel are gone, and in front of the sofa is an old pine chest about three feet wide and two feet deep. JACK *is standing over the box phonograph; he has just put a record on.*

JACK *steps back just as the first scratches of the record are heard. We hear the same Claire Waldoff record* ELLEN *played earlier. The sounds of the record bring* MAX *into the room.*

MAX What's that?

JACK Don't know. One of the old German records Ellen found. Claire Waldoff. Ever heard of her?

MAX Not that I recall. Did you find anything while you were rummaging in the storage locker?

JACK Yes, as a matter of fact, I found this.

(JACK *walks over to the old pine chest.*)

JACK This was Granma's. She used to keep her photo album in it. It's locked, but I'm sure Ellen knows where the key is. She's the official curator of the family treasures, such as they are.

MAX There don't seem to be many mementos of your father around. You must have been quite young when he died?

JACK Our father, Robert Henry Hennesy, was a lawyer, and a professional contrarian. When we were kids, he left the firm in Chicago that he'd founded to open a small practice in Arlington Heights where we lived. He became sort of the local free law clinic. He never made any money, but he was the self-proclaimed thorn in the side of the local establishment. He was also a drunk, which we didn't know when we were kids—at least I didn't know. It was kind of like the old joke: I didn't know my father drank until one night he came home sober. For us, that discovery came on an October morning when he collapsed in court. He was immediately diagnosed as having liver disease. They found the cancer a week later. Dad spent the next six months in and out of the hospital. There was really nothing they could do, and he didn't have any interest in what they suggested. He just gathered up the courage he needed to accept death.

MAX I take it, K.J. and your father had a rocky relationship?

JACK It was more complicated than that. Everything with K.J. is. You have to understand, K.J. was born looking to improve her station in life. It's fascinating, really, her skill and determination in that way. Since we were kids, K.J. was always in the right social group; hell, she could perceive social distinctions where none existed. I could never understand the "why" of it. Even the nerdy, brain groups like the chess club and the chemistry club were beyond my social grasp. I just hung out at my dad's office, reading my books, watching him study and write. You know, I don't dislike K.J., not really. I just don't understand her philosophy. All that work; toward what? Trying to impress people who are only impressed by people who have even more money than they have.

MAX Social climbing has its place in civilization, Jack. It's an outlet for ambition. A necessary evil; like corporate game playing, or even academic politics; if nothing else, social climbing fuels the arts. New money often goes to develop new artists. The Medicis and the Napoleons have been replaced by the stock brokers and the CEOs and the plastic surgeons. Many important artists have been discovered by the *nouveau riche*, and more importantly, saved from starvation by an investor who doesn't know Winslow Homer from Homer Simpson. I learned a long time ago not to judge my customers too harshly.

JACK And who exactly are your customers, Max? Did I understand you to say you specialize in brokering looted art?

(MAX *smiles.*)

MAX Looted art is an ugly phrase.

JACK But accurate.

MAX Not in all cases. Not even in most. The history of art is, as I said, chiefly commercial. And political. The spoils of war have always included art. The British Museum has the Parthenon tablets; the Louvre has the *Mona Lisa*; even the Metropolitan has its share of back-door pieces. I'm not an opportunist, if that's what you're getting at. But I do understand that the world we live in is messy. We can either retreat from its dilemmas, or do our best.

JACK Does doing your best mean ignoring the truth or just maneuvering around it?

MAX *(chuckling)* Now don't judge me too harshly, Jack. My efforts have been directed at helping your family appreciate the options available with respect to an artistic treasure. I've expressed no opinion as to what I think should be done with the painting.

(K.J. *enters from the kitchen.*)

K.J. I think the old man is here! We saw a car turning onto the block as we were parking.

(K.J. *removes her sweater, which she drops on the sofa. She checks her appearance in the mirror.*)

K.J. Where's the painting?

MAX I moved it into the bedroom. I thought we should hear what Mr. Golian has to say before we show him the canvas.

K.J. I hope we don't regret bringing the old man here.

JACK The man has a name; it's Golian. Karl Golian.

(ELLEN *enters the room.*)

ELLEN Did K.J. tell you? Is he on his way up?

JACK Do you know where the key to Granma's chest is?

ELLEN It's taped to the bottom. But I told you, there's nothing in there but a quilt and some old sheets.

(JACK *reaches under the chest, pulls off a key taped onto the underside of the chest.*)

JACK Did you know there's a false bottom? Granma showed me when we were little.

(JACK *opens the chest. He removes an old blanket, and then a quilt, and few nicely folded linens.*)

JACK Here we go.

(JACK *again reaches into the chest. He removes a piece of wood roughly the size of the chest.*)

JACK And here we are!

(JACK *pulls out the photo album.*)

Guten Abend, Großmutter Feld!

(JACK *sits back on the sofa and begins to study each page of the album carefully.* ELLEN *and* K.J. *approach from either side.*)

ELLEN I've never seen this before.

K.J. Grandmother Feld used to show it to us all the time. Remember, Jack? These must be Granma Feld's parents. I've forgotten their name.

JACK Wolf, I think. Unfortunately, nothing is labeled. All these faces and no names.

K.J. Well, that must be Granma; when she was in her thirties. She looks a lot like Ellen.

ELLEN More like you, K.J.

JACK Here's the picture I remember. The one with the Nazis on the steps.

ELLEN Who's that next to Granpa Feld?

K.J. His father, I think, but…

(The front buzzer sounds.)

ELLEN That must be Mr. Golian. I'll let him up.

(JACK *closes the album, which he places on the coffee table.*)

K.J. Use the intercom. Just to be sure.

(ELLEN *presses the intercom.*)

ELLEN Hello?

(GOLIAN's *voice is heard through intercom offstage.*)

GOLIAN Yes, this is Karl Golian. At your invitation.

ELLEN C'mon up. I'll meet you at the elevator.

(ELLEN *buzzes the door. A moment later—* KARL GOLIAN, *a man in his late seventies, with wild, longish white hair enters. He wears a flannel shirt tucked into brown polyester pants and a slightly different colored brown suit coat.*)

ELLEN Jack, K.J., this is Mr. Golian.

JACK Mr. Golian, how do you do? I'm Jack Hennesy.

(JACK *offers his hand to* GOLIAN. GOLIAN *looks at JACK cautiously. Slowly he takes his hand.*)

GOLIAN Yes, yes. You have your grandfather's face. Your grandmother's nose, though. The Wolfs. That would be your grandmother's family.

JACK We were just talking about them.

ELLEN And this is my sister, K.J.

(K.J. *nods her head in a cold manner.*)

K.J. How nice to meet you.

GOLIAN What is your name again, my dear?

K.J. It's K.J.

GOLIAN No—the letters, I heard. What is your *name?*

JACK Her name's Katrina.

GOLIAN Ah, Katrina. Like your grandmother. You look so much like her.

ELLEN Here, have a seat, Mr. Golian.

(MAX *approaches as the old man sits in the easy chair.*)

MAX How do you do? I'm Max Yarrow. I'm working with the family on some business matters.

GOLIAN Yarrow? What sort of name is that?

MAX Russian, I believe.

GOLIAN Russian Jew, you mean.

MAX Well, yes.

GOLIAN What did it used to be? Yaroslavsky?

MAX *(graciously)* Something like that. It was changed many generations back.

GOLIAN Don't be embarrassed, Mr. Yaroslavsky. There's nothing unusual about changing a name. People have been changing their names for three thousand years. They want respectability. More than a heritage, I guess.

(MAX *is speechless.*)

K.J. Not to interrupt, Mr. Golian, but we were wondering what can you tell us about our mother's...our grandmother's painting? The one you mentioned to Ellen at the funeral. When you spoke to Jack on the phone, you said it was valuable.

GOLIAN First, may I have a glass of water? I'm at the age where all the moisture in my body settles in my feet. My throat is dry as a bone. My feet are like water balloons.

ELLEN I'll get you a glass. Or if you'd like, some wine? Or crackers?

GOLIAN No wine. A cracker is okay.

(ELLEN *runs into the kitchen.*)

GOLIAN I see you've moved the painting.

(JACK *and* MAX *look quizzically at* GOLIAN.)

GOLIAN It's no longer over the mantel.

JACK *(slowly)* Yes. Yes, we took it down.... To have it cleaned. How did you know where...?

GOLIAN Oh, I've been to your mother's apartment before—one time. About seven or eight years ago. Your mother had not been here very long then. We'd met quite by accident at the shopping center a few weeks earlier. We hadn't seen each other for many years. You know, your mother was not so comfortable seeing someone from the old country. *(slight pause)*

Maybe it is more correct to say she was not so comfortable seeing me. When I first arrived here in 1949, she was very kind, but not so warm. Austrians can be like that, so it was not so unusual. Her mother—your grandmother—sent me some little packages of food. They inquired as to whether I needed money or a job. I think your mother gave me an old dining room table and some chairs. Don't misunderstand what I'm saying. Your mother was a kind woman. And concerned. But not so inviting, I guess. When I arrived in the United States, your mother and her parents had already been here for two or three years. They came just before the war ended, I think. Your mother was still living with your grandparents. She was only twenty or so; what a beautiful girl—she was always beautiful. Even when we were children in school together, she had perfect features. I can see that all three of you got your mother's face.

JACK Thanks, I guess.

(ELLEN *returns with a glass of water and a plate of crackers. She hands the water to* GOLIAN, *and puts the plate on the coffee table.*)

GOLIAN I figured out pretty quickly that even though we'd been quite close in Austria, your mother did not really want me to be a part of her life here in America. I think her parents thought this was a little strange, but I understood. Anyway, I seldom saw your family…only a few times, but I did get an invitation to your mother's wedding. It was in 1951, I think. Your mother was working at the Stevens on State Street. Your father was the ideal American. Tall, black hair. Strong face and shoulders. He had delicate hands, though. I'll never forget the wedding. It was at a country club. There was an orchestra, and flowers. They served roast beef, double baked potatoes. I knew then why your mother was no longer interested in the old country. She was in a new world—a much better world. A perfect world, from what I could see. To tell you the truth, I was very hurt and upset to see her get married. Of course, I had a crush on her. I always had, but it was more than that. To know she was leaving our old world forever... Well, it was to be expected.

JACK What do you mean?

GOLIAN In a way, it has to do with the painting. What exactly does it have to do with it...well, that's for you to decide.

K.J. *(impatiently)* Please, tell us about the painting. *(smiling)* I mean, I'm sure you're tired—We don't want to keep you from anything.

GOLIAN Oh, you're not keeping me from anything. My daughter dropped me off—on her way to the Dominick's. She'll pick me up on her way back. Anyway, I like to tell this story. Especially to young people; they think I'm explaining about something that happened on Mars a million years ago. But it was only sixty or so years ago, and there are still a lot of people around who saw it happen.

The Germans took over Austria in 1938. I was sixteen at the time, driving a delivery truck for a small bakery in downtown Kitzbükel. I had attended the same school as your mother. Of course, she was two years younger than me. I didn't know your grandparents then. But after the Nazis took over, they closed down the bakery where I worked. Maybe it was more complicated than that—It was, I recall, a case of their wanting the building for something else—what, I don't know. The Nazis didn't waste a lot of time explaining things. Anyway, I was out of a job, and it looked like I would be conscripted into the Austrian army. But your mother met me in the street one day, and when I told her that I was afraid I would be made a soldier for Hitler, she told your grandmother, and your grandmother arranged for me to go to work at your grandfather's plant.

JACK Plant? What kind of plant? We thought our grandfather was a baker.

GOLIAN Well, yes. He owned a bakery—one of the largest outside of Vienna. He had thirty or so employees. In a big, modern plant, two stories, four delivery trucks. Everything was clean and efficient. And so I was very grateful when your grandmother fixed it for me to avoid the army.

JACK How did she do that?

GOLIAN Well, your grandmother was a very clever woman. She was, in effect, the manager of your grandfather's business. Not that he wasn't a competent man. On the contrary, he was a very smart person, but strictly in business terms. He understood things like gross revenues and fixed costs. Your grandmother, on the other hand, understood the Nazis. She immediately knew that after the *Anschluss,* things would be different in the worst way imaginable. So, rather than fight them, she worked with them.

(ELLEN *gasps slightly.*)

GOLIAN Oh, I don't mean she was one of them. I mean, she knew how to manipulate them. In public, she would stand up to them on little things—administrative requirements, work papers, licenses, that sort of business. The Nazis were very big on paperwork, and record keeping. They were the first tyrants to use paper as a weapon. Anyway, in public your grandmother always challenged the inspectors and other agents who came to the plant. But in private, in private she would give them little…gifts: bread, special cakes, bottles of schnapps and brandy. Make a show of deferring to them. And then, unpredictably, she would be rude to them. Kitzbükel is, or was sixty years ago, a small city, far from Vienna, and far from all of the political activity going on in the country. Before the war, the city lived indirectly on tourism—your grandfather's bread was sold all over Austria, but mostly in Linz and Vienna. For a little while after the Nazis took over, things stayed the same; although business started to drop off; as you can imagine, tourism was a quick casualty of the Nazi take over of Europe. By summer of 1938 most of the bread made by your grandfather's factory was being bought by the government. I had been working for your grandmother in the office for several months, by then. It was difficult to find office people. Almost all of the Jews had left Austria. Or else, they were hiding out—keeping a low profile, if you'll pardon the expression.

JACK What about the Blooms?

(GOLIAN *looks at* JACK *confused.*)

MAX He means the Bloomsteins. Specifically, Joseph Bloomstein.

GOLIAN Oh, yes. Oh, yes. Herr Bloomstein. Well, Bloomstein was one of the Jews who waited too long. He owned a small clothing factory and store. Before the Nazis came, he made dresses, trousers, suits. That's all, I think. Almost immediately, the Nazis gave him orders to make uniforms. Austrian military uniforms. Mr. Bloomstein did what he was asked to do. They didn't take his business away from him—not right away. But, as the weeks passed, more and more restrictions were placed on Jews. First there were curfews, then Jews were prohibited from attending schools, and then they were forbidden from owning property. Many were put in jail or forced to clean soldiers' barracks. *(pause)* Most of these regulations took a while to reach Kitzbükel. But as the pressures on Jews increased, more of them fled, if they could. There was an Office of Jewish Emigration, and in order to leave Austria, you first had to get permission from the Emigration Office—this meant surrendering all of your property; all of your money. It meant leaving parents who were too old to travel; it meant acknowledging that you were not a human being.

JACK Is that what the Bloomsteins did?

GOLIAN I'm coming to that. At some point; it was autumn, I think.

The Nazis finally took over our town. It was then that they closed up the remaining Jewish businesses. How they did it was, they came in on trucks—a whole company of soldiers, all with rifles. They rushed from store to store—they knew which ones were owned or managed by Jews. They went inside and dragged out their Jewish owners by their collars, tossing them onto the street, where they were shouted at. Shouted at by soldiers, and even by old friends and neighbors. *(pause)* One of the first businesses they reached was Herr Bloomstein's. The soldiers knocked Mr. Bloomstein on the head, they punched his wife in the face when she protested; they threw his son and daughter out onto the curb. We didn't understand then that this was a big show—by the SA troops; so strictly speaking, these weren't Germans who did this; they were Austrians trying to impress the Nazis. *(pause)* Anyway, I did not see it all happen, as I was at your grandfather's plant that morning. But a friend of your grandmother's—a Mrs. Hitzmann—she called the plant and told your grandmother what had happened. Mrs. Hitzmann asked your grandmother to go to the police department and help the Bloomsteins. They were all under arrest for having resisted the soldiers, but mostly they were being held because they were Jews and they had not registered with the authorities.

ELLEN Why did Mrs. Hitzmann call our grandmother?

GOLIAN Well, in part because everyone knew your grandfather was an important businessman, and your grandmother had some influence with the local officials. So I drove her into town. That was one of my jobs; to drive your grandmother into town when necessary. But we did not go to the police station. Instead, Mrs. Feld asked me to take her to the offices of Captain… What was his name—Fitzel, I think; Fitzel was our resident Nazi official, he was the Jewish Emigration liaison. He was a dull-looking man. Small, thin, stoop-shouldered, the complete opposite of whatever you think is a frightening looking person. He stayed in his office for the most part. You never saw him on the streets of Kitzbükel. Fitzel was

Austrian, I think, but just barely.

Anyway, I took your grandmother to see Captain Fitzel. She was very angry, but she stayed calm. She told the Captain that it was disruptive to all the businesses in town to use such force against people who had been cooperating with the government. Even if they were Jewish. The Captain just looked at her while she talked. She asked that the Bloomsteins be released on bail—your grandmother herself offered to post the money. The Captain said nothing; after a while, he stopped listening, and began to review some papers on his desk. Finally, your grandmother asked me to leave the room. I did, and she closed the door behind me. What happened next, I can only guess.

I went to wait in the car. About ten minutes later, your grandmother came out. Without a word of explanation, she asked me to drive her to the police station, which I did. It was just two blocks over. She went in, and a minute later—no, less than a minute—she came out; the whole Bloomstein family in tow. Your grandmother asked me to drive them to their home. Nobody spoke. Everyone just looked worried. Except your grandmother. She looked, well, like someone who is in control. Which, frankly speaking, is how she always looked. The next day, the Bloomsteins came to the bakery. Frau Bloomstein and the daughter—who I had known in school—and the much younger brother were leaving the country. They were taking the train to Vienna, and from there—who knows to where? Switzerland, probably. Anyway, your grandmother was quite upset to learn that Mr. Bloomstein himself was not leaving. There were some very worried and strong words said about this. I could not hear everything that was discussed. But certainly your grandmother was upset. I got the impression that she had somehow arranged for the whole Bloomstein family to leave, but that Mr. Bloomstein had decided not to go. He wanted to stay a bit longer. Sell the business and his house. Your grandmother was very much afraid for him. Even though I was still just a teenager—even I could see that Mr. Bloomstein would never be able to sell his store. He was the only one who didn't understand this, or didn't want to understand. Anyhow, Mrs. Feld did not consider it her business to try to talk another person into doing something against their will. So, she merely said goodbye to the Bloomsteins. And that's when they gave her the painting.

K.J. They gave her the painting?

JACK Which painting?

GOLIAN The painting. The painting that used to hang over that mantel. And before that—well, many years before that, it was in your grandmother's apartment. I saw it the one time I visited their apartment after I arrived in Chicago. And before that, the painting was in Kitzbükel.

MAX What did the painting look like? Do you recall?

GOLIAN It looked like fog. Thick fog over a bridge. That's all. That's all I remember.

JACK And you say that Mrs. Bloomstein gave the painting to Granma Feld?

GOLIAN Yes; as they parted. Mrs. Bloomstein handed the painting to your grandmother. It was still in a frame. A very plain frame. Mrs. Bloomstein thanked your grandmother for saving her life and the lives of her children.

MAX So the painting was a gift?

GOLIAN Of course; what else would it be?

JACK Well…it wasn't left with our grandmother for safekeeping or anything?

GOLIAN No. It was a gift. A gift of friendship. Mrs. Bloomstein said the painting had been in the family, and she wanted Mrs. Feld to have it.

K.J. It's ours, then!

GOLIAN Of course, it's yours. It was a gift of friendship. I've often wondered what your grandmother said or did to convince the Nazis to give the Bloomsteins their exit visas, but your grandmother never mentioned the matter again.

JACK No doubt she offered them a bribe.

GOLIAN It's possible. But money was not so valuable at that time. Jewelry; gold currency; small art works—portable wealth that crossed national boundaries undetected were the only valuable items. Perhaps your grandmother offered cooperation of some sort. Who knows? Whatever she did, she did as a daughter of Moses, so anything is possible.

K.J. What do you mean "as a daughter of Moses?" Our grandmother wasn't Jewish.

GOLIAN Your grandmother? Frau Feld? Wasn't Jewish? Of course she was Jewish.

JACK What are you talking about? Our grandmother wasn't Jewish.

GOLIAN She certainly was. Her whole family was Jewish. Everyone knew the Wolfs were Jewish. Your grandmother converted in the mid-'30s sometime—like many Jews did. It was the safe thing to do. Especially if you were married to a non-Jew. Hundreds of Jews in Kitzbükel converted in the mid-'30s; several of my cousins did the same thing; my parents were both dead by the time the Nazis took over, and I didn't know to do it myself. Eventually the Nazis decreed that these converts were still Jews. But a few people slipped between the cracks, and anyway it took a while for the Nazis to track down the converts. That's why it was such a courageous thing your grandmother did. Standing up for the Bloomsteins was very risky. But it was your grandmother's way. And that's why Mrs. Bloomstein gave her the painting. She understood the risk your grandmother had taken.

K.J. But our grandfather wasn't Jewish?

GOLIAN No, as I said, Herbert Feld was a gentile. Presbyterian, as a matter of fact. So your grandfather was not Jewish. But you are.

K.J. What are you talking about? We're not Jewish.

GOLIAN Of course, you are. Your grandmother was Jewish; which means your mother was Jewish. And if your mother was Jewish, then so are you. There's nothing to be ashamed of. (slight pause) You're Jewish; is that so bad? It means you have a special reason to be proud of the painting. It connects you with your heritage; connects you with your people. That's why the painting's so valuable. That's why I mentioned it to Ellen at the wake—I was afraid if you didn't know its history, you might give it away, or leave it locked up in an attic somewhere.

JACK So when you told us you thought the painting was valuable, you meant historically valuable...personally valuable. You weren't referring to its monetary value?

GOLIAN No—I have no idea what it's worth—in dollars. Probably a lot. I mean, I assumed it was expensive when I first saw it. Even in a simple wood frame, I could see it was something important. Your grandmother certainly knew it, too. She tried to persuade Frau Bloomstein to take the painting with her; to use it for expenses. Mrs. Bloomstein could not be dissuaded from giving it to your grandmother. And that is why its value in dollars is nothing compared to what it's worth to your family. To know it represents the lives of an entire family. Mrs. Bloomstein left Austria with her two children. Mr. Bloomstein was put in a work camp; I can't say what happened to him after that; he almost certainly was killed. If not for your grandmother, they all would have been dead. She was a brave woman to offer them help.

ELLEN And what did she do, Mr. Golian? To convince the Nazi captain to let the Bloomsteins go?

GOLIAN Like I said, she never told me. And I never asked. It doesn't matter, does it? Whatever Mrs. Feld said or did to accomplish the Bloomsteins' safety, she did to save the lives of others. And that makes anything possible. Anything she did was a *mitzvah*—that's Jewish for "a good deed."

(MAX *exits the stage for the bedroom.*)

JACK *(matter-of-factly)* So, we're Jewish. *(pause)* Well, K.J. what do you think you're membership committee will think of that?

K.J. Probably the same thing as your tenure committee.

(MAX *returns carrying the easel and the painting.*)

MAX Is this the painting, Mr. Golian? The painting that Mrs. Bloomstein gave to Mrs. Feld?

(GOLIAN *studies the painting for a moment.*)

GOLIAN Yes; that's the painting. I'll never forget it. I'm delighted to see it again—like an old friend. You know, I hung that painting for Mrs. Feld in her office at the plant. At first it troubled her to look at it, but slowly she came to love it. She used to call it…

K.J. *(quietly)*…Her "morning" painting.

GOLIAN Yes, her "morning" painting. *Auf eines bestimmtes Morgan; On a Certain Morning.* So you do know something about the painting.

JACK Just what we remember as kids.

GOLIAN Well, now you know why the painting is so valuable—and so you can tell the story to your children.

MAX There's someone else who'd like to hear the story—the granddaughter of Mr. and Mrs. Bloomstein—her name is MaryAnn Carson.

GOLIAN The Bloomsteins' granddaughter? She lives here in Chicago?
MAX No; California. She's come for the painting; she's making a claim for it.

GOLIAN A claim? A legal claim?

MAX Yes; the young woman believes the painting was stolen from her grandparents by the Nazis, and then given to the Felds by the Austrian government.

GOLIAN Of course, just the opposite is true. Frau Bloomstein was determined not to let that happen. The painting was the only thing not stolen from the Bloomsteins by the Nazis. So the granddaughter doesn't know the story of what happened?

JACK No; we didn't know the story ourselves until you told us.

GOLIAN If she doesn't know the story, then how does she know about the painting?

JACK Well, believe it or not, this painting is by Claude Monet—it's worth several million dollars. Ms. Carson knows it was once owned by her grandfather, and she's been trying to locate it for many years.

K.J. That's why we asked to see you—we wanted you to identify the painting for us, and confirm that it's real; that it really is by Claude Monet.

(GOLIAN *nods his head thoughtfully.*)

GOLIAN Under the circumstances, I wish I could tell you that this painting is a fake; that it is not by Claude Monet—then you would understand its true value; its value in terms of human life—that's the only value which matters. But I can't tell you that; I suspect that this painting is what you say it is, a genuine masterpiece, worth…what did you say? Millions of dollars? Well, that is the curse of young people living in this country today. Money appears valuable while life seems cheap. Well, I guess I have told you what you wanted to hear—a story that confirms your good fortune.

JACK It's not like that, Mr. Golian. We wanted to know who the rightful owner of the painting was, so that we could do the right thing by Ms. Carson.

GOLIAN And now that you know the history of the painting, what do you intend to do?

MAX They intend to sell it, of course. There doesn't seem to be any legal or moral bar to its sale. I suspect Miss Carson will still sue the family once she learns about the sale, but based upon your statement, sir, it's clear who has legal title to the painting. No doubt there will still be some unexpected publicity, once a suit is filed. But that's all.

ELLEN What do you mean by unexpected publicity?

MAX Oh, nothing as onerous as I described earlier. After all, since you're Jewish, no one will attack you for being anti-Semitic.

K.J. Would you please stop saying we're Jewish; we're not; I'm not.

MAX But don't you understand? Your being Jewish is what gives you undisputed title to the painting. It's the reason your grandmother was given the canvas in the first place. It's the reason she risked her own life to help the Bloomsteins. The story of how your grandmother acquired the canvas removes all doubt as to its ownership; it was a gift from one Jew to another. If you're ashamed somehow…

K.J. *(angrily)* I'm not ashamed; it's just that I won't have people saying I'm something I'm not. I…I don't want to hear anymore about…Nazis or history; or paintings, or anything. And I certainly have no intention of telling the world that we're Jews, or that we're anything. None of this is anyone's business but our own. If selling the painting means announcing to the world that we're Jewish, then forget it.

JACK You can't be serious.

K.J. Don't tell me what I can or can't be.

MAX Then what do I tell Mr. Kawamura? Is the painting for sale? Or not?

ELLEN We haven't decided yet; we were going to vote. What do you say, Jack?

JACK Well, I vote—I vote—I guess I vote, yes. It's ours; based on everything I've heard...and seen. I suppose it's ours to sell. We certainly can't afford to keep it. Or give it away, for that matter.

ELLEN K.J.—what do you think?

K.J. *(quietly; almost distractedly)* I vote...no. The painting's not for sale. It's the one thing not for sale in this family. Not tonight. Not ever.

JACK You can't be serious. What about the financial trouble—the legal trouble—you're in?

K.J. My reasons are my own.

MAX Think it over carefully, K.J. Your decision may be irretractable.

K.J. I've made my decision; the painting's not for sale.

JACK It's up to you, then, Ellen? How do you vote?

ELLEN Well... I don't see how we can *sell* the painting. I mean, even if it belongs to us legally, it doesn't belong just to us. It belongs to Granma Feld and to Mr. Bloomstein and to...people who might understand it better than we do. Anyway, I'm not sure we have the right to send a painting like this to someone's house in Japan somewhere. It seems like we should sell it to a museum, or something. Maybe we should talk it over with Ms. Carson. At least see what she has to say.

MAX Then, the question is settled—the painting will not be sold—at least not tonight; and not to Mr. Kawamura.

JACK K.J., you must be out of your mind... You know, for some reason, I don't think that your decision has anything to do with what people might think—there's something else—something you just thought of...or remembered.

ELLEN Be quiet, Jack! Leave K.J. alone. Whatever her reasons, they're as good as any. Not everybody can live up to your ideals, you know. Some of us have families to protect.

(JACK *looks shocked;* K.J. *offers a bemused smile.*)

K.J. You don't have to defend me, Ellen. My motives aren't selfish. Not in the way you might think. It's just that all of this talk has reminded me of Granma Feld, and how we all treated her—how I treated her. I was never...nice to her. I never talked to her. Never let her get close to me.

JACK *(sympathetically)* Well, she was a fairly...intimidating person for a child to get near.

K.J. Not in the beginning. She tried to get close to me; when we were very young, maybe too young for you to remember. She used to smile then; smile whenever she saw us. And she tried so hard to be our friend. But she was just so foreign—I was always scared of her and the more she would try to befriend us the more we would resist. *(pause)*...I remember once when I was in fifth grade—I had stayed after school to be in this recital. Dad was in the hospital at the time, so Mom was supposed to pick me up after the program was over. But something happened to Dad, and she couldn't come. So Granma Feld came to pick me up. Only Granma couldn't drive, so she came to school in a taxi. Everyone could see the cab arrive—it seemed like such a strange thing. I mean, I'm not sure why everyone thought it was so odd, but all the kids were pointing at it, and when Granma got out, and started walking into the building, all the kids started asking, "Who's the gypsy woman?" It was just the way she was dressed, in this thick black dress, and with a shawl. I was just so embarrassed to see her—I didn't want anyone to see me with her. I ran out of the auditorium, and hid in my home room. Granma came into the building and started looking for me. Of course, she couldn't say much in English, except my name. Mrs. Prendergast, the music teacher, tried to help her. But suddenly I could not be found, and now everybody was panicky, wondering where I'd gone to. Somehow, Granma found me in my home room. I was sitting at my desk, crying. She tried to calm me down, find out why I was so upset. I told her to please go; to leave me alone. She realized then what the problem was; that she was my problem. She said something to me in German; I don't know what, and then she left. Mrs. Prendergast came in a few moments later, and said that she would take me home. I guess Granma had explained to her something of what had happened. That was the most horrible thing I ever did to anybody. I never even tried to apologize to Granma, either. She never told Mom about it, at least not what happened exactly. Mom just heard that I had been hysterical, and that there was confusion as to who would take me home. Anyway, after that, Granma never again tried to get close—to any of us. She sort of kept her distance. I was very grateful for that, and still embarrassed.

JACK You were just a kid, K.J. You're not responsible for what Granma was, or became.

K.J. What I really don't need right now, Jack, is patronizing bullshit from you. I know what I did, and how it hurt Granma.

JACK Alright, fine. You hurt Granma's feelings. But unless I missed something along the way, your husband is in the kind of trouble they measure by years. Selling the painting can't hurt Granma now. From the story Mr. Golian just told us, I suspect she'd understand why we have to sell it. Besides, as Max said, we can't just keep it, or give it away.

MAX I never said you couldn't give it away. I just said it would not be nearly as...profitable. You could, should you so desire, sell the painting to a museum for roughly the amount of the estate tax and other costs the sale would generate. It's complicated, and requires the services of pasty accountants and dandruffy tax lawyers. But it can be done, and is done all the time. Perhaps the painting can be donated in such a way as to acknowledge the sacrifices of the Bloomstein family. I'm sure that once Miss Carson knows the whole story, she'd find such an acknowledgment a kindly gesture. Of course, it's up to the family; I'm only here to advise. I might recommend, however, that this would be a good time for us all to lay our cards on the table.

(JACK *looks at* MAX *for a moment, then starts to laugh; a pleasant, "this is all too hard to believe" laugh.*)

JACK Max, do all your assignments become so deeply involved in self-discovery and recrimination?

MAX Not all; but many. As I said before, art is a matter of faith. Perhaps in this instance even more than you suspected at first. But now...

(MAX's *cell phone rings. He takes it out of his coat pocket.*)

MAX Hello? *(pause)* Oh, Mr. Kawamura; where are... *(pause)* Yes, you're all but here. It's the tall red building. Yes, that's right. We'll see you momentarily, then.

(MAX *hangs up the phone.*)

MAX Mr. Kawamura has arrived. There's no point having him up if the painting's not for sale. Do I have your final decision then?

(MAX *looks at the three siblings.*)

MAX K.J.?

K.J. *(distantly)* Call Ms. Carson tomorrow morning. No, tonight—tell her the story; tell her that we'll do nothing with the painting until she's convinced. Then, make whatever arrangements you think best as to how and where the painting is to be donated. Jack and Ellen can decide; whatever they want to do is acceptable to me.

(The door buzzer sounds.)

MAX That must be Mr. Kawamura. I'll go down and give him the bad news—*On a Certain Morning* is not for sale! Congratulations to you all on reaching the right decision. Fortunately for me, my clients are not always so right. Ellen, I'll call you in the morning. Keep your grandmother's painting safe until then. Now, if you'll excuse me.

(MAX *walks toward the door.*)

JACK One more thing, Max—I have to ask. Did you know all of this from the start? That our grandmother was Jewish? That she had been given the painting by the Bloomsteins?

MAX I suspected some; deduced the rest.

JACK Then why didn't you tell us?

MAX How can you tell a person something they already know? Besides, I'm here only to advise and to follow the instructions of my client.

(MAX *walks to the door and exits.*)

K.J. What a miserable night this has turned out to be.

JACK Ellen, you knew Grandmother Feld was Jewish, didn't you?

ELLEN *(slowly)* Mom sort of told me years ago. After Dad died. All those years, she'd never said anything to him about it. I think she was sorry she hadn't. I don't think it would have made a difference to him—I don't know. I think she was embarrassed she'd kept it a secret, and yet I don't think she was really comfortable with the idea that we were at least partly Jewish.

K.J. Why didn't you ever tell us?

ELLEN I guess I thought I was protecting us.

JACK From what?

ELLEN From something that didn't fit into our lives. I always wanted us to be a normal suburban family, and being Jewish—even a little bit Jewish didn't fit.

JACK What makes you think we were normal?

GOLIAN What makes you think being Jewish would make you not normal?

ELLEN I don't know. Being Jewish just seems so foreign; so different from what we were, what we are.

GOLIAN I understand, Ellen. Being Jewish is not so simple a thing, especially for young people. But what choice do you have in the matter? None. Even being a little bit Jewish is enough. Like a drop of blood in a glass of water. Eventually you'll understand it's not just a question of religion. It's cultural; a frame of mind—it's about your place in the world; your place in the universe.

(ELLEN *nods her head.*)

ELLEN It almost sounds like…a good thing.

GOLIAN Some people think so.

JACK (*turning toward* K.J.) What'll you do—I mean, if we don't sell the painting?

K.J. I can't imagine that you care what happens to me.

JACK I do…I mean, goddamn it, K.J., why do we always have to fight about everything? I…I don't want to fight with you. I want to help you. That's the only reason I voted to sell the painting.

K.J. There's nothing you can do to help—nothing any of you can do.

ELLEN That's not true, K.J. Don't just shut us out.

(*The door buzzer sounds twice.*)

GOLIAN That's Margie. She always rings twice. Like the postman. I'll see myself out, if you don't mind. You seem to have a lot to talk about. (*pause*) Before I go, let me say one thing—the three of you are a family; it's something—the *one* thing you have no say in. And in the end, family is all you have, the good ones and the bad ones; they're all you have. Paintings, money, houses, friends, even life itself, it all disappears in a minute. And what you're left with is family. The three of you are too old to pretend it's not true any longer. Now put on a pot of coffee, or better yet open a bottle of Schnapps, that's what your grandmother liked. And talk it out. As my own mother used to say, "Class is how people in a crisis treat each other."

(GOLIAN *gets up; stretches a little; heads toward the door.*)

JACK Would it be all right, Mr. Golian, if I called you tomorrow; I'd like you to look at my grandmother's old photo album? Maybe you can help me identify some of the people in the pictures.

GOLIAN Certainly. But I thought you were returning to Iowa tomorrow morning.

JACK I've decided to stay...at least a few days.

GOLIAN *(nodding)* Call me tomorrow. After eleven; I have water aerobics till then.

(GOLIAN *exits. The three siblings are quiet for a moment.* JACK *walks over to the painting.*)

JACK *(to the canvas)* How do you like that? The painting's real; and we're the frauds. But you're ours; whoever "we" are. Well, maybe something good can be done with Granma's legacy.... (*turns toward* K.J.) What do you say, Ellen, K.J.; should we open the wine you bought? Try to talk things out?

ELLEN We aren't really Jewish, are we, Jack? I'm afraid we're too dysfunctional to be Jewish.

JACK I guess even Jews are dysfunctional, Ellen.

(K.J. *puts on her sweater, grabs her purse.*)

JACK What do you say, K.J.? Will you stick around awhile, talk things over with Ellen and me?

K.J. I...I can't. I have things...I'll call you, Ellen. Later in the week.

ELLEN Listen to me, K.J. You're not walking out of here. You're going to stay and figure this thing out with Jack and me. You can yell, get angry; do whatever you want. But you're not leaving.

(K.J. *starts for the door, stops, looks down little by little.* ELLEN *runs to her, wraps her arms around her, and brings her back to the center of the room.* JACK *walks slowly over to them, puts his hand gently on* K.J.'s *arm.*)

K.J. I hate this family.

ELLEN You mean you hate our family.

K.J. Yes, I hate our family.

JACK If it's any consolation; I think we all do.

(JACK *starts to open the wine.*)

CURTAIN

FELIX CULPA

——Scott Grunow

A fallen angel food cake
upside down on a green bottle:
now she must take

the memory of bright wings
on cards glued with glitter
into the depth of casual things

make the shapes a word
on purple paper
a sign, not a sword:

one sign deep as drains
full and sweet
after the last muddy rains

THE FIRST SUPPER

——Scott Mintzer

The Scheer family was in the middle of the second Seder when the meal was interrupted by the ringing of the doorbell. The patriarch, Emanuel Scheer, got up to answer. He ran a bagel bakery in the checkered section of Brooklyn where they lived, but had closed the bakery for Passover, helping his wife prepare the festival meal instead. Now he was tired, and felt annoyed that they could not even enjoy the fruits of their preparation in peace. As he opened the door he readied a mild but firm rejection to any sales pitch or request for charity. The man at the door was Jesus Christ.

"Good *yom tov*," he said. "May I come in?"

Manny stared at him: he wore a long robe and sandals, sported a mustache and full beard, and dark hair that came down in waves to his shoulders and shined like a shampoo commercial. It took Manny a moment to recognize him. There were certain things about him that looked so human; the hands were calloused, and a few small tufts of soft hair peeked out from his nostrils. But no, it was definitely him. By the time he realized this he found that the abruptness of the appearance and the Jewish greeting had taken him off guard. He opened the screen door and stood aside.

Jesus entered the living room. He was a tall man, and his arms and legs were thin. He appeared in great need of a good meal. He removed his shoes and approached the table, bowing to Manny's wife, Sheila, and their two teenage children. "I was looking for a place to spend the Pesach," he said. "I would be greatly honored if that place could be in your home."

Sheila swallowed and smoothed her skirt. "Well, yes," she said, "I suppose that would be all right, but I would have made more food had I known…"

"I understand," Jesus said. From beneath his robe he produced a half-full box of matzo with seven pieces in it and a jar of gefilte fish and laid them on the table. It was now impossible to turn him away, so Manny brought a chair from the kitchen. He hoped the Finkels next door had not seen their guest enter. They sat down to eat; there was plenty of food, and no one was left hungry. Jesus ate heartily and praised Sheila for her cooking. They talked easily and politely as the evening wore on, and by the time they had finished the macaroons and fresh fruit a luminous moon had risen into the dusky sky. Then they completed the service; Jesus prayed along with them, eating of the *afikomen*, beseeching Elijah to drink his cup of wine. At the end they sang songs, *Adeer Hu* and *Echad Mi Odeya* and *Chad Gadya*. Jesus sang with great feeling, and during the last verse of *Chad Gadya*, when God kills the slaughterer, he seemed deeply moved.

Comfort settled over the table. They spoke to Jesus as one speaks to one's family. "What are you doing here?" Manny said.

"I thought it was time to come back," Jesus said.

"What for?"

"To further what I started."

"Well it seems to be doing just fine on its own," Sheila said. "It's very popular."

Jesus shook his head. "It is not what I envisioned."

"How so?"

He sighed. "I did not hope to see my people split into factions, fighting with each other. I did not hope to see my people perverting their faith into gross intolerance, or using it as an excuse for punishment or prejudice or…"

He choked, and a tear rolled down his cheek. "This is not what I taught to my people. Not this at all." And then, nearly under his breath:

"I only wanted to make my father proud." The rivulet from his cheek descended through his beard, letting a drop fall onto the table, where it mixed with the drippings from the dish of salt water they had earlier passed around. He wiped his face and composed himself. "All I ask is a place to stay for a time, a place to make a new beginning, to consider how I may bring my people together. Your hospitality would honor me."

The family members looked around at each other. "Why this house?" Manny asked. "Why here?"

"I wanted to be with my people," Jesus answered.

They sat in silence. Manny's daughter Marcy held her breath, transfixed. Outside the bushes rustled and the trees swayed in gusts of wind.

"You may stay on our couch tonight," Manny said. "More than this I will not promise." He pushed back his chair and stood, signifying the end of the Seder. Sheila began to clear the dishes. Jesus rose to help her, and Marcy to help them both.

An hour later the elder Scheers lay in bed, the room darkened for sleep.

"Should we let him stay?" Sheila asked her husband.

"I don't know."

"He seems kind."

"He is a complete stranger."

"Some stranger. He's nicer than your whole side of the family."

"But what is he going to be doing while he's here?" Manny asked.

"I don't know exactly. Maybe he can help out with things. He dries dishes very well."

"So he'll be the maid we could never afford."

"Oh, stop it. He's a guest here. But he is very considerate. And Marcy would probably enjoy his company. She's been so restless lately. Anyway, how often do you get to open your home to somebody like this? It's like having a celebrity stay with us. You wouldn't turn out Neil Diamond, would you?"

He sighed. "I suppose not."

"I think it's only right, Manny. After all, he's just a nice Jewish boy."

It was true. He remembered the emotion of Jesus' singing, the fervency of his prayers. There was no slight honor in all of this too; he could have picked any home, but they were chosen. He turned over and drifted off to sleep, dreaming of pigeons on a playground fighting over cookies, those big half-black-and-half-white ones they sold in the Italian bakeries, the crumbs scattered over the pavement, and an old man sitting on a bench in the background watching their struggle and laughing and laughing.

When Manny reopened the bakery a week later Jesus was still sleeping in the living room. He remained ever the polite and considerate guest, always cleaning up after himself, staying out of his hosts' way, folding up the couch every morning and unfolding it himself each evening. He helped out with chores, vacuuming the carpets, watering the plants. He washed his own robe in the washing machine, borrowing a pair of sweat pants and a T-shirt from Jeremy to wear while he waited. Sheila appreciated the help he provided around the house. Too, there had been a rash of burglaries in the neighborhood, and she felt safer at night with a man sleeping so close to the front door. (Who would shoot *him*?) As she had predicted, Marcy also seemed to enjoy his company. She was taking only two spring term courses at the community college, and, not seeing her friends often, appeared to relish having someone to talk to during the day. Her brother, Jeremy, took a more standoffish attitude, avoiding their guest whenever possible. He told his mother that he was sorry they wore the same size in sweat pants.

Early mornings, when the only ones awake were fishermen, paperboys, and bakers, Manny watched over the boiling cauldron of floating doughballs that fed and clothed his family and considered the situation. There was no clear precedent for this. Not to say that there weren't any parallels; he remembered complaining bitterly when Senator Barry Goldwater came to visit his high school, only to have his father tell him, "You don't hafta respect the man, but you hafta respect the office." Really, there could be no doubt that he was doing the proper thing. Did not even the most sanctified Jewish books speak of giving hospitality to those who ask of it respectfully? And certainly this guest was nothing if not respectful. As far as relations went, in fact, the whole family seemed to like him, except for Jeremy, who didn't like anything. Manny admitted that he himself was growing at least a little fond of their new guest, who offered ready compliments to everyone, and even told the odd joke at the dinner table. ("You aren't much like your reputation," Manny had said to him the other day.) Still, he could not deny feeling funny about the whole thing, and when his nosy neighbor, Finkel, president of the local congregation, had asked him, "Who is that guy staying in your house?" Manny had answered, "He's...a cousin. A distant cousin."

"He looks familiar," Finkel had said. "Has he been on television?"

Manny fished the bagels out of the water, laid them neatly on the rectangular metal trays and slid them into shelves in the oven while he pondered. There was a time when he might have relished thinking about all these things, when he had staked out positions and argued them vehemently. But that was before he had had to help his father run the bakery. Now all he knew was these bagels, not that there was any shame in this, but there were *schmendricks* he knew from the neighborhood who went to college and now lived with their svelte wives in condos on Prospect Park. That was why he was so firm about his children's education, though he had to confess that Marcy seemed a bit lost in it at times, and Jeremy, bright as he was, seemed only to get more miserable the more he learned. He would go to college, certainly, and probably an expensive one, if one of these new bagel chains didn't open up here and drive Manny out of business—no, that could not happen. And it was not just the bagels themselves, but the man behind them; his customers knew this. So he boiled, and baked, and in between added the sesame seeds or the chopped onion or the crystals of salt. He thought about adding chocolate chips to one batch, like the new chains did, but decided against it. It would be like putting mayonnaise on a pastrami sandwich.

It was about a week later when Mrs. Cooper came into the store. She was a rotund, elderly black woman who wore a plastic raincoat and a kerchief pulled tight across her hair.

"Good morning, Sadie. The usual half dozen today?"

"Well, now, le's make it a dozen today, but leave out them salt ones, on accoun'a mah high blood pressure been actin' up. An' a tub a'that scallion cream cheese."

He reached into his bins. "Big order today. You making a party?"

"Naw, but ah feels like celebratin'. Ah jest now did have me a revelation right outside mah door. A revelation of the lawd Jesus Christ hisself!"

"Is that right?"

"Yes, ah sure did, an' in the mos' peculiar way. Y'know Tuesday mah li'l dog Rufus got hisself lost an' didn't come home aft'ah let him outside, an' ah got so tur'ble sad thinkin' mebbe he gone f'good. Well, today somebody come t'mah door, ah fig'd it was somebody sellin' somethin', but when ah op' the door what do y'know but they's a man holdin' mah li'l Rufus in his arms like a precious chil', an' he say to me, 'the los' sheep is return to the flock,' an' that man was the lawd Jesus Christ hisself! May ah pass on this very day if ah'm lyin'!"

Manny felt a tingling in his scalp. "Did he have long dark hair and a beard?"

"Yes he did, an' he was dressed all in white too! It was him awright, th'lawd Jesus, he blessed me this day an' bring me back mah Rufus!" She paid for the bagels while she talked. "Now ah know you of th' Jewish persuasion, Mist' Scheer, but tha's awright, 'cause you a good man, an' you always been a good man, so th'lawd Jesus he gon' shine his light on you too, ah know he will! You take care now!"

At home Jesus folded the sheets, watered the lawn. Manny looked hard at him but saw nothing unusual, nothing to betray what he might be capable of, save a serenity that certainly seemed preternatural at times. But it was hard to know really; there was nobody watching him all day.

The following morning the shop door opened to Mark Kapstein, who had grown up down the block from Manny but was now a wealthy accountant preparing tax returns downtown. He wore an Italian suit and had a cleft chin like a gentile. He pretended to patronize Manny's establishment solely out of kindness to an old acquaintance. "Give me a couple dozen, Manny, different kinds. I'm treating the office."

Manny snapped open a large paper bag and began filling it. "So what got into your wallet today?"

"Nothing, thank God. That's why I thought I'd share my good fortune. If it weren't for some stranger's act of kindness I would have been ruined."

"Well thank heaven for small favors."

"Small favors! I almost *killed* a small favor today, a little seven-year-old one belonging to my neighbor, the genius doctor. Who lets a kid that age play outside without supervision? Anyway, he was riding around in a little scooter while I was backing out of the driveway. I have to admit I was maybe a little distracted, thinking about all the late returns to do, and I would have run over that little favor for sure except that I looked in my rearview mirror and some guy in a white robe is holding his hand up like a traffic cop and yelling, 'Stop!' And then I saw the kid come wheeling out from behind me. Oh, can you imagine how awful! And the little tyke's uncle is a lawyer, they would have sued me for everything! But here I am, alive and solvent, thanks to whoever that was, some vagrant walking around in a robe and sandals. He looked like an extra from *The Ten Commandments*. You've seen it, right?"

"Not recently."

"Well, you should. It's a good film. Charlton Heston. Highly recommend it." He gave Manny a twenty and told him to keep the change. "Best regards to the wife and kids."

At home that night, he told Sheila what had happened.

"I've been hearing similar stories. What is he doing?"

"Saving the world one deed at a time. Who knows?"

Manny could no longer restrain his curiosity, and that evening spoke to Jesus as he finished a meditation on the couch. The light was dim, but Manny could see that he had begun to put on a little weight from Sheila's cooking.

"You've been busy around the neighborhood, I hear."

Jesus smiled, his eyes still closed.

"Is there more than one of you?"

"No. Just me."

"Why are you doing this?"

"To bring all of my people together."

"Why not just perform some great miracle?"

"Big things grab people's eyes," Jesus said, "but the little things grab their souls." He laid a hand on Manny's arm; Manny saw the creases of the knuckles, the pale blue veins splitting off from larger ones like underground tributaries. The tendons of the fingers were tense with revelation, the wrist bent with humility. Manny sat there for some time, while a tingling went through his arm, into his body, and slowly subsided. Then he went up to bed, putting his hand on his wife's arm as he had not done in some time.

The days grew longer, and light began to seep into Manny's short drive to the bakery every morning. He could see now that something was happening in the neighborhood. Amid the graffiti on the wall of the junior high school courtyard (it had gotten worse even in the three years since Jeremy had been there), painted over the gang tags, pornographic caricatures and inscrutable symbols was the phrase "He's back!" drawn in a stylized manner, the 'H' broadened and slanted at the top left, the exclamation point transformed into a cross. It was erased the following day but reappeared two days later, this time even larger. He saw it too on a subway trellis as he drove beneath it, and in the corner of a billboard advertising cigarettes. Then the same legend began appearing on stickers that were plastered on streetlights and storefronts, including four on the window of his own bakery. He tried to scrape them off with a razor blade, but they were tenacious, and left a gluey white residue that was even worse than the stickers themselves.

He asked his wife, "Have you seen…these…?"

"All over. They stuck one on my car this morning. I think they know."

Strangers began to stare at him and whisper when he walked down the street. He saw them surreptitiously pointing, heard conversations drop in volume as he passed. People looked in through his store window without coming in. Mrs. Cooper came in one afternoon and fixed him with a serious look, her shoulders squared. "Is it true what they been sayin'?"

"What are they saying?"

"They been sayin' 'at the Lawd Jesus Christ hisself is come back to th' worl', an' that he be livin' in yo' house."

He steeled himself for whatever might happen next. "He is staying with us."

Mrs. Cooper's shoulders dropped, and her jaw sagged with relief. "Well, I shoulda known," she said. "When I heard it I nearly fell out, I said, 'But he such a quiet man, work hard all day an'jus' go home t'his family, an'a Jewish man besides.' But you know the Lawd Jesus said hisself that the meek will inherit the earth, so here it is come t'pass! An' I shoulda nev' thought any different, 'cause even though you a Jewish man, you showin' a real Christian spirit, hostin' th' Lawd's only son an' bringin' his light to th' whole worl'. An' y'know th' Lawd gon' bless you f'that yes he will, an' you will reap yo' reward in th' kingdom of heaven! Now gimme six a' them onion ones, an' yo' blessing in th' bag with 'em!"

Manny stood for a moment, stunned. Then he gave her the six bagels and took the money from her hand, not even counting it. "Praise be t' Jesus!" she said as she left.

The moment lingered with him, bounced around in his head like echoes in an empty room. He was blessed? But he had not received any blessing that he was aware of, nor had he asked for any. And to think that he was capable of *bestowing* blessings was more ludicrous still. If it pleased God that he was a good Jew, gave help and shelter to someone in need, then so be it. But he was not asking for any reward, nor did he think that succoring somebody else's savior was the way to get it. He found himself getting angry at Mrs. Cooper despite himself. Did he have any intention to inherit the earth? And how was he showing a "Christian spirit?" Did the Christians think they had a monopoly on generosity? When our sages had expounded on the virtues of *mitzvoth*, daily good deeds, hundreds of years before the Romans ever built their first cross?

He watched Jesus at home warily. What did he know about him, really? That he had come emaciated, and now was living well; that he had made himself at home in this family; that by day he did small good deeds. To bring his people together, he said. But to what end? Who were his people, and how did he mean to do this? In his nightmares there was mass hypnotism, religious terrorism, his home the next Jonestown or Waco. But in life he saw his guest in the evening, setting the table, cutting vegetables for the chicken soup (pausing every so often to sneak a guilty piece of carrot) and he would chide himself for his suspiciousness. Manny even saw him cut himself once, though he didn't bleed. He was a klutz, no doubt about it. If he terrorized anything, it would be by accident.

In the morning Manny opened the door to leave for work (later than usual—his assistant was doing the morning baking) and found a group of young people seated in a circle on the front stoop.

"What are you doing here?"

"Waiting to see him."

"Who?"

"Christ, our Lord. We heard he was here." The one who spoke was a young blonde with earnest eyes and large, straight white teeth. The rest were also in their twenties, of varying sizes and shades. One of them wore a "He's back!" T-shirt, with the characteristic cross for exclamation.

"I don't know where he is," Manny said, too surprised to think. "Can I take a message?"

"We'll wait," their spokeswoman said. Manny was about to ask them how long they had been there when his neighbor, Finkel, came over.

"I couldn't help but notice all the hubbub," he said, glaring at the squatters. "Are these kids bothering you?"

"I don't know yet," Manny said. He couldn't decide whether to chase them away or invite them in for coffee to diffuse the commotion. Then Jesus appeared beside him in the doorway. The young people stared in shock. "It's true," one gasped. Jesus stepped out into their midst. They leapt to their feet, began crossing themselves, reciting prayers. One bent down to kiss the hem of his robe. Jesus held up a placating hand. "Come," he said, "let's leave our host in peace." They followed him down the block and across the street, in the direction of the neighborhood park. Manny and Finkel stared after them until they disappeared. "What kind of a house are you running?" Finkel asked. Manny went inside and shut the door.

The weather was warming, and people were out in the streets. Mixed in with the children playing hopscotch and the carts selling ice flavored from rows of colored bottles were people handing out missionary flyers and sporting "He's back!" buttons on their collars. Young boys who used to hustle at busy intersections washing windows without permission and then demanding tips were instead selling "He's back!" bumper stickers. The neighborhood weekly paper reported fewer crimes than usual. And was it Manny's imagination, or were they ringing Sunday morning church bells longer and louder now? They seemed to bother him more, in any case, interrupting his morning coffee and newspaper, but to whom to complain? Perhaps to his new guest, though of late he had taken to spending most of every day out of the house, his exploits flagged by further scattered tales of sundry good deeds, maybe apocryphal, but who could tell? One woman was presented with a wedding ring long since thought lost. Another had a pair of torn panty hose miraculously repaired before a dinner party. At home he continued to find time to vacuum and take out the garbage between all his good works. He was present without fail every Friday evening, singing the blessings while Sheila and Marcy lit the Sabbath candles. He had even begun helping Marcy with a paper for her religion class. "You have such good children," he told Manny once. "They must bring you such *nachas*." That the children (plural) brought him joy seemed a strange thing to comment upon, since Jeremy's antipathy toward their new guest was becoming more palpable with each passing day. He would not remain in the same room except at dinner, where he sat sullenly silent unless spoken to, and then quickly excused himself at meal's end. Manny and Sheila were concerned, and it even crossed Manny's mind to ask their visitor to take his leave. "So we should encourage Jeremy to be rude for no good reason?" Sheila said. She had a point; anyway it was hard to justify.

Manny's notoriety continued to mount. More people than ever stared at him on the street. A group of young girls yelled, "He's back!" and waved, disappointed when he did not reply in kind. Others stared in through the bakery window, but never bought anything nor came inside. He began to dread going to work each day. All this time he had fretted about the big bagel chains, not realizing that the worst thing for his business would be to have a messiah living in his house. He decided that he would go to services to lift his spirits.

Sheila said she had a backache, so he went alone. The evening was slightly cool, as though spring were ambivalent about itself. He got to the synagogue twenty minutes before the service was to start, put a *kipa* on his head and milled about in the lobby, where others were arriving and talking. He smiled, wished others a good Shabbat, but no one smiled back at him. They looked down at their feet, avoiding eye contact, and showed their backs to him in circles of conversation. He felt dismayed, then confused; perhaps he was imagining the unwelcome reception? He searched in some urgency for someone to talk to when he came upon his neighbor, Finkel, who as president of the congregation attended services every week. "*Shabbat shalom*," he said to Finkel, offering a handshake. But Finkel would not take his hand. "I'm surprised you would come," he said. He removed a pack of cigarettes from his pocket and walked out the front door.

Manny stood shocked for a moment, then looked around to see whether anyone else had been witness to his embarrassment; no one seemed to be paying him the slightest attention. He walked outside and found Finkel smoking under the pale moon. Neon lights from the deli across the street threw red streaks into the creases of his face. "What did you mean by that?" Manny asked.

Finkel took a deep drag and looked down. "I found out about your friend," he said. "We are very disappointed."

"Disappointed about what?"

"That a man like you would help an opponent of the Jewish people."

"Opponent? Sander, he's a Jew."

"That makes no difference. He has caused us irreparable harm, and you give him the opportunity to do even more. You become his accomplice."

"For giving a little food and a couch to a man who comes to me in need? Should I have slammed the door in his face instead? He even helps with the chores in return! He helps my daughter with her courses. He is kinder to me than you have ever been."

"See what that sort of kindness gets you," Finkel said. He crushed out his cigarette and went inside.

Manny stood again in disbelief. He went back into the temple and saw that services would be starting shortly. But he could not bring himself to go into the sanctuary, nor could he stay in the lobby with the few remaining congregants. He also could not go back outside, so he exercised the only remaining option by going to the men's room. He found Mark Kapstein at the urinal beside him. "Well, well, look who's here," he said. Manny smiled briefly, trying not to look at him. He heard the sink run and then stop. "So what's your angle on this?" Kapstein asked.

"I beg your pardon?"

"This boarder of yours. Is he paying you a bundle? Or did he offer you a free round-trip ticket to Saint Christopher?" He tore off some paper towels and rubbed his hands. "I mean, I'm sure you must be getting something out of this. How'd you get such a golden opportunity anyway? The book rights alone will be worth a fortune. Maybe you can even charge for admission once the word gets out."

"I don't believe I'm hearing this."

"Oh no no, don't get me wrong. I think it's a great investment, really. Almost wish I had a piece of it myself. Even in the non-financial sense, I think it's a great hedge, you know, with the Man Upstairs, just in case it turns out that this guy really is…well, you know what I mean."

Manny came within half an inch of urinating on his own shoes.

"Of course it could backfire, depending on what everyone else thinks of it, but probably it's worth the risk." He turned to leave. "And besides, if ever you forget who you are, all you have to do is look down."

Manny glanced at his own circumcised penis while the door to the room creaked open and then closed. Then he zippered up in a rush of anger and left the synagogue as quickly as he could. The night was warm and tranquil, with no more disquiet than the quick ripple of cars passing, but his mind tumbled madly as a gum wrapper in a high wind. These people were his, he was theirs, had always been. They were his family, but not only them: any Jew who comes to your door in need, that is your family. Yet now, he was their traitor; or their mercenary; it was hard to say which was worse. Enough years we spent wandering in the desert, and running from Inquisitors and Cossacks and Nazis, that they should know the meaning of a little hospitality! No doubt they would be more hospitable had this happened to be one of the Kapsteins of the world, a rich accountant, but no such kindness for the one who feeds them. Let them go without bread for good, an eternal Passover, and maybe they would play a different tune.

On his way home he passed by the park and saw a crowd gathered beneath a tree, lit by a nearby lamppost; he walked toward them, maybe fifty or so, quiet as corpses, their attention gathered on something in the center. They looked behind and parted for him soundlessly, and in the center he saw a smaller group of twelve or so people sitting in a circle on the grass. Directly beneath the tree was Jesus, legs crossed, mouth moving in prayer. Around him Manny recognized several of the young people who had been sitting on his porch in wait. At Jesus' left hand was the young blond woman who had been their spokesperson that morning. At his right hand was Manny's daughter. Her eyes were closed as she listened to him praying. Manny saw her eyes open for a moment, make contact with his. The look on her face was one of deep contentment. Manny felt the tingling, moving upward into his chest. Then she closed her eyes without a word. With a sudden feeling of revulsion, he turned and walked away.

He heard nothing but the sound of his own footsteps. When he got home he turned on the lamp and sat in the living room chair for a long time, without a thought in his mind, and with no more company than the ticking of the grandfather clock. He did not know exactly how many hours had passed until he heard the front door open and close. Marcy entered the living room.

"Where is he?" Manny asked.

"Still praying," she said.

"Why were you with him?"

"Because I wanted to be."

The clock ticked a dozen times.

"Maybe you have forgotten who you are."

"I haven't forgotten. I'm learning it still."

"I do not think he will teach you to be a good Jew."

"Daddy, this is not about Christian or Jew. It's about something bigger. Have you heard what he says?"

"It's not what he says that disturbs me. It's what he stands for."

"He loves us. He loves our people, and he loves our family. I can't see what's wrong with standing for that." She turned and went upstairs.

Manny sat for some time longer, and then went up to bed himself. He lay in bed awake for a while, thinking of all the things he wanted to ask his visitor, then about asking him just one question, the big question, the only one that mattered, maybe tomorrow morning, maybe this very night when he arrived at the door. But he decided that he would not; he did not want to know the answer, and would not have believed it in any case.

He was awakened late Saturday morning by the doorbell, feeling stiff and tired, as though he had coiled himself into a spring and remained tightly wound. At the door was a clean-shaven young man with a small notebook. "Mr. Emanuel Scheer?"

"Yes."

"Is it true that Jesus Christ has returned to Earth and is currently residing here in your home?"

"Who are you?"

"I'm from the *Wall Street Journal*. We're interested to know why he picked your home in this neighborhood to make his return. Any thoughts?"

"Why are you asking me this? And why the *Wall Street Journal*?"

"Mr. Scheer, the *Journal* has always had a great commitment to reporting important news of all kinds. But frankly, my editors feel that any kind of positive news might boost investor confidence and help stabilize the markets." A couple of car doors slammed. Two more people with pens and pads had emerged from parked cars and were coming toward the house. With them was a third person holding a camera. The reporter turned back to Manny with fresh urgency. "Any comments?"

"I'm not going to say anything," Manny said. He closed and locked the door. When he turned around he found that Jesus had been standing not far behind him. "*Gonifs*," Jesus said in Yiddish. "Thieves of other people's lives. They're like a generation of fleas preying on vipers."

"They are here because of you," Manny told him. "Would *you* like to speak to them?"

Jesus bowed his head for a moment in silence. Manny could feel the beating of his own pulse, and then the tingling again, in his chest. "For my children," Jesus said softly, lifting his head. He opened the front door and walked out.

They came then in bunches and droves. They perched on the porch, staked out his car, planted themselves in front of his shop like weeds, returning rapidly and in force whenever the police cleared them. There were cameras, microphones, zealots and gapers in a moving, buzzing swarm. Always there were questions. He kept walking, tried not to answer them. Sometimes he could not help himself. What is a man to do?

"Mr. Scheer, what made you take Jesus Christ into your home?"

"He asked."

"What do you hope to gain by this?"

"Nothing more than was ever gained from kindness."

"Mr. Scheer, are you a saint?"

"We don't have those. Please leave me alone."

"That man be blessed!" He could hear Mrs. Cooper yelling over the crowd. "He be the mos' blessed of the blessed!"

"Mr. Scheer, do you have any financial stake in the 'He's back!' line of products?"

"Mr. Scheer, what did you think of the recent documentary about the Spanish Inquisition?"

"Mr. Scheer, are you a member of Jews For Jesus?"

"For God's sake, no!"

"But don't you believe that the man staying in your home is the son of God?"

"*No, I don't.*"

"But why not?"

"*Because I'm a Jew!*"

He tried to keep working, maintain a semblance of his normal life, but it was not possible. Every day outside the shop people came on pilgrimages, others came to protest, some handed out flyers, some craned their necks and yelled at him and each other. Amid the tumult nobody bought any bagels except Mrs. Cooper, and he was obliged to close. He spent days sitting at home, wondering whether he would ever be able to feed his family again.

He watched television. Every newscast had a feature about the return of Christ; Manny saw his own house on camera while he sat inside it with the blinds drawn, or his own closed shop as the backdrop for revivals, vigils, sermons and celebrations, vendors hawking burgers and bumper stickers and inspirational pamphlets. When he tired of it, he changed the channel, but everywhere it was the same. On HBN (the He's Back Network) they were selling anything imaginable, from Bibles with exclamation cross bookmarks to rosaries to "He's Back!" Wafers 'N' Wine. A brand of inflatable sneakers with little wings on each side called the Air Apparent was on special: a free set of genuflection pads with every pair. When they weren't selling, there were clips of Jesus making speeches, leading marches, holding conferences for the press. There were crowds with him always, chanting, singing. Sometimes they prayed. Sometimes they fainted. Sometimes, depending on the angle of the camera, you could catch a glimpse of the closest circle of disciples, and in some of these shots, Manny saw his daughter.

"It's just a phase," Sheila said.

He remained indoors for so many days that his skin took on a sallow cast from lack of sunlight. Marcy would be gone all day for days at a time, and then she would be at home for days, helping her mother with the cleaning, buying flowers for the table. Every so often he caught her looking at him with the same look he had seen in the park that night: longing, desperate and content, the kind of look one never expects from one's daughter. He would have to avert his eyes. It was like staring into the sun.

Jesus seldom showed up for dinner, and when he did the table was ruled by silence.

"Why are you doing this to me?" Manny finally asked.

"So that the house of Emanuel might live forever."

The house had come to seem like a prison now. The venetian blinds were cell bars, and the guards outside held weapons more dangerous than guns. They would kill each other for a chance to talk to him; meanwhile, his own son would not grant him a word. Manny approached him while he sat in the kitchen eating a sandwich, reading the *New York Times*. On the front page, beside the report of a Jerusalem terrorist bombing was a story about Jesus leading a march into Bedford-Stuyvesant, the poorest neighborhood in Brooklyn.

"This must be hard for you."

He flipped a page but did not answer.

"Do you miss your sister?"

"I doubt she misses me," he said.

"Your mother thinks it's just a phase."

"You have no one but yourself to blame if it isn't."

"What does that mean? Don't tell me you're on their side too."

"For us there's only one side. You just can't see it. Maybe all those years working with dough have made you soft in the head."

"That dough puts food in your belly and books on your shelf!" Manny shouted. "And how dare you speak that way to your father!"

"My father is destroying the Jewish people!" He snapped a hand angrily at the paper. "You see this? Another terrorist attack in Jerusalem? That's nothing compared to this!"

"How can you compare our house to somebody's explosives?"

Jeremy flipped the paper shut in exasperation. The angry arrogance of the gesture threw Manny back with a shock to when he was his son's age, his tongue sharp in debate too, before it was dulled by decades of hard work, the wife, the children. For years he had done nothing more aggressive than try to keep body and soul together. He was not prepared for this. "What's the biggest difference between Judaism and Christianity?" his son shot back at him.

"They believe that Jesus Christ is the son of God."

"To hell with that! I've figured out the real difference now. The real difference is that Christianity is a missionary religion."

"Who has been teaching you this?"

"Nobody taught me this! I can think for myself, and it's as clear as day, if you just open your eyes! Christians run around trying to convert everyone, saving lost souls. It's hard to become a Jew even if you want to! The Rabbi will try to talk you out of it."

"That's because we are chosen. We do not choose."

"But can't you see? That's why we're so outnumbered! It's like the natural selection of religions, and we're losing badly! Soon enough, we'll be reduced to the fringes, and then we'll disappear altogether. And you're helping it along!"

"I have been a good man all my life!" Manny cried. "And I will not turn away a good man for his beliefs!"

"His beliefs! He believes in 'uniting all people,' isn't that what he says? He's going to dilute us, or convert us, and wipe us out! That's how he'll bring us all together!"

"He has been nothing but kind to us ever since we took him in. He cooks, he cleans, he helps out your mother when she's too busy working at the bank so we can send *you* to college! While you, on the other hand, reduce us all to the level of animals, clawing at each other!"

Jeremy shook his head and walked away. "I can't watch you do this any more," he said.

Then he was gone, vanished. Sheila did a careful count, found missing three pairs of underwear, five socks, one pair of jeans and three shirts. No more than a week's worth at the outside, assuming he didn't do his own wash, which he had never done before. They figured he was at some friend's house, cooling off, but after a couple days they called around, and nobody had seen him or would admit to it. He was fine, he had to be; he was too bright a kid to do anything really stupid. But after four days Sheila couldn't sleep. She started crying. "Why did you have to fight with him?" she said.

"He fought with me," Manny said. But what difference did it make? He couldn't sleep either, thinking of Jeremy slumped in some alleyway like a vagrant, or worse yet, in a hospital. At night, lying awake in bed, Sheila tossing fitfully beside him, he stared up at the ceiling and felt it coming down on his head. It seemed to be his fate. But why? he beseeched God. What had he done to make it so? For an answer, his eyes were clouded with tears.

When he could no longer stand it, one Friday night (it was hard to tell the difference between days, now that he had stopped working), he decided to go to the synagogue and seek guidance. He opened the door and found no one. Apparently, he had waited out the media, defeated them by sheer boredom.

Still, he could not help glancing around him constantly as he walked, fearing that every car door slam was a reporter or a protester. His heart felt like lead by the time he opened the synagogue's great front doors twenty minutes before the service. Inside the lobby he got the same chilly reception from the milling congregants that he had gotten the last time. He found an unoccupied corner and stood, watching. Most of the people he recognized; they had bought his bagels, lived on his block. He had fed their children, given them change for the bus. He had prayed with these people, celebrated and fasted with them. To be among them now, and so estranged from them, was almost too much to bear. He turned his face to the floor, and struggled hard to keep from weeping.

A few minutes later, Sander Finkel came in. He saw Manny almost immediately, and Manny could see him take a deep breath and tighten his mouth as he walked directly up to him. "We need to talk," Finkel said. He gestured for Manny to follow.

He led Manny down a hallway to a room used by the officers of the congregation. He motioned Manny into a chair, then sat himself with his hands folded atop the large desk. Manny thought that perhaps his overwhelming sorrow had evoked some pity in Finkel's heart. "Listen, Manny," he said. Then he stopped, pursed his lips and stared at his hands, unable to continue. Manny wondered: was he working up to an apology? Finkel took a breath and looked up at Manny resolutely. "It would be best if you did not come here to worship right now."

Manny fell as silent as if he had been executed. The words that finally came up from his throat must have risen by some natural force, like soda bubbles, since he lacked the will to produce them. "Who says this?"

"Not just me. Many of us. As long as he is living under your roof, at least. I don't think you understand what you are doing to your own people. None of us approves of what you're doing. Some even say that you will finish what Hitler started. I don't say these things myself, Manny, because I try to remember..."

Manny got up and left the synagogue. He walked home with an anger so powerful it made it hard to recognize himself. How dare they! You would think that, if nobody else, a bunch of Jews would have some sympathy for a man who was suffering! But what kind of Jews were these? Petty, ungenerous ones, with short memories, that was clear enough. He would worship at home, then. Or start his own congregation! By the time he got home it was all he could do to restrain himself from launching a rock through the front window of Finkel's house next door.

At home, he found Jesus and Marcy seated on the living room couch, facing each other, holding hands. They looked at each other sheepishly, and then stood to face him. Marcy took a few steps forward. "Daddy, I'm so glad you're home," she said. "I wanted you to be the first to know. We're getting married."

AN EARLY WORK

——M.J. Rychlewski

"Hang that black Irish sonofabitch!"
Hume roars from the Wildcat caboose.
"Can't!" I shout above a clattering herd
of Singer sewing machines gone Zeus.

"They took the gallows out and there's—"
Kant! In the front seat! With my daughter!
His wig is off and they squeal like pre-teens,
arms testifying to the corkscrew air.

"It was rotting!" I screech back at Hume,
still glued to my two loose bolts. "City sold it
to some museum somewhere. Trust me. I tried
to empiricize him once too." "*Ne parle pas* shit!"

It's Jean-Paul Sartre! Why is he sitting next
to me!? "YOU are responsible." He's right.
Hume is squinting into the twisting future
where my kid and Kant whip out of sight

as we shudder through a death rattle
of ball joints, chains, and creaking wood,

AN EARLY WORK

then black down into a worm tunnel
like crop dusters soused on rye. I should

really get off. I mean, I started this poem
years ago—it was an early work, a gesture
from my youth when some punk Irish killer
who escaped the hangman's noose was a sure

sign poetry was an up and budding business
in my mind and not just another excuse for
demolition. Who's that up there puking
over the side? Plato! Bugger! Old whore!

Rubbing against my shadow in the basement
when I was nine. "Oh, you're a dangerous
little tease who likes to rouse my feelings
and cloud my brain. Unbutton my blouse

and strew garlands at my feet or I'll kick
your sweet little boy ass right up the stairs."
"Claire! Claire! Are you safe with Kant?!
Manny! Cover her eyes on the drop!" Where

the hell is René!? He promised he would ride
with me. If my thoughts are good as any man's
how come I got a million of 'em and not one
worth a slug nickel? We whip turn and I jam

against JP, who stinks of stale Gitanes
and can hardly see. "Oh dark, dark, dark,
amid the blaze of noon."
"What the hell?! You're not Sartre!"
Where are my landmarks!?

And why this sick green icky spin of choices
every time we Mickey Finn up a snapdragon
turn? Sunlight glints off a shock of blonde
hair. There! Second car from top! "You son

of a bitch! TOMMY!" O'Connor haunches
deeper into his overcoat. "It's me, you Mick
bastard!" Hume scuttles over the cars, one
claw leaning out, poised for that last quick

inside curl that will give him a clear
shot at my anti-hero's artichoked ear.
"No! No!" I reach. "You could shoot Claire!"
Jesus Christ! Are they all oblivious here!?

"David! Leave it! It was thirty years ago!"
He jerks away. "Fuck you!" His eyes
seethe. "Custom is the only guide in
human life. Custom says someone dies."

FUN HOUSE

─Sari Wilson

Jo worked as a bar girl at Bluebells, a nightclub on a popular Greek island. She was paid to mingle with the customers, encourage them to drink, *allow* them to buy her a drink, speak her few words of Italian or French and smile at their drunken gaffes. She liked the older men best— they were never too aggressive, usually weren't interested in dancing and didn't care much about a girl's looks. Then, as night edged on to morning, she began to look for her secret departing signs: one of the sunburned tourist women arched backwards over the bar, mouth agape, backside spread across the shiny black surface; Gregor the bartender standing over her with his thumbs cradling the opening of a bottle; people rushing around, clapping, laughing, shouting as if in victory. Then Jo knew she could slip out through the kitchen doors unnoticed into the cool night silence, thinking: *fucking lushes, at least I'm not one of those fucking lushes.*

Although she'd been there for almost two months, Jo had never really adapted to the island culture with its mix of excited tourists, paunchy Greek businessmen, early morning market women, and, of course, foreign bar girls. The tourists came and went with the tide: Irish secretaries, American med. students, the occasional international modeling crew. Jo made cracks about each group in turn, at first to the other bar girls and then once she'd all but stopped speaking to them, just to her boss Dino, or occasionally a customer. "Oh God," she'd moan, rolling her eyes. "Look at that! Heinous! Crime! Tube socks to the knee!" She could dismiss an entire country along with an unfortunate fashion choice. "Finland, God. Never, never!" she'd snort, holding her nose and nudging her chin toward a bunch of light-haired people in fluorescent jogging suits. Dino loved her acerbic humor. "You should have known me in top form," she'd tell him, slapping her sturdy chest just above her breasts, a mock display of former jungle triumphs.

Dino was her one approximation of a friend. Dino, with his tacky silk shirts, pleated pants and tapered alligator skin shoes. Dino, who called Jo "little big girl." Dino, who took his time laying the *drachma* in her hand when he paid her, winking at her with his sparkling eyes. Jo knew he was just having fun with her, so she'd squish her face into a pucker and say, "Oh yeah, right. Suck face with you—are you crazy?" Dino would hold his hands to his mouth and gasp to show how scandalized he was and then push at her playfully. Sometimes Dino would smile at her, looking beleaguered, and tell her how brave he thought she was to be in Greece all alone. He envied her that one. "And I'm going all the way to India, too," Jo would remind him, her voice too loud even to her own ears. In truth, Jo liked Dino more than she could admit; she thought everything about him looked so magnificently shiny and well tended. In America, only really rich people looked that way.

Jo's hair, a wiry dark brown marking the territory around her head, forearms and legs (when she didn't shave, which was often), made her distinct among the bar girls who were mostly blonde and from Scandinavia or Australia. That and her bulky form. Box-like, Jo herself thought. Like an empty box, or rather a box containing nothing really useful. Just discarded odds and ends: brittle toenails, a fearful sweat, too-soft skin covered with freckles, the remnant muscular bulk of a mediocre high school field hockey career. Jo told herself that she was glad to be separate from the rest of them, unique and identifiable. But really, she just felt invisible. Even her reproachful comments about the tourists no longer made her feel any more real. Sometimes, in the midst of all the clamor and drunkenness, she felt as if she could drift out of her body unnoticed. Then she imagined herself clearly, stripped of her bad-girl leather and combat boots: an overweight girl with frizzy hair, curiously silent and sad. Her desire to make others laugh was dropping away like an old skin and it often left her scared and speechless.

Behind the stretching of her lips into what she supposed was a smile, Jo was waiting. It was not an active kind of waiting, it was simply the uncomplicated act of living without purpose.

And then one night, Paulette appeared. It was just past ten and Jo was dragging herself down the white-washed steps into the club, the annoying words of an overplayed Madonna ballad an endless loop in her head. The many bars and clubs on the island each boasted "original music," by which they meant a continuously played tape of variously arranged American pop songs sold from behind the bars under the names "Songs of Greece in Summer" or "Songs of Summer" or "Songs of Greek Paradise" or simply "Special Songs." Remembering that she would have to go back someday, to the States, to college, Jo began to frantically catalogue bits of information like this—things that would be just bizarre and stupid enough to amuse her friends back home.

As Jo crossed the dance floor and headed toward the bar on this particular July night, she caught sight of Gregor laughing with a girl she'd never seen before. Girls didn't usually come to Bluebells alone, unless it was near closing time. The back of this girl's big body shook and Gregor's bony nose was screwed up in something like a smile. Her blondish-brown hair fell like a waterfall down her back, thick and heavy, leaving visible only the rump of her Indian-print skirt and her ample cheeks hanging over the stool. A black leotard encased her torso, riding over the various protrusions of flesh. "Big all over, bigger than me," Jo said under her breath.

Jo pulled herself up onto a black vinyl bar stool several seats down from the girl and glanced around the room. It was too early to start working: the Australian girls hadn't arrived yet, and there were only a few jock types at the bar. Jo turned back to the new girl and took in her profile with several quick glances: lumpy nose, full lips, outlandish earrings, a deep tan. *Was she a new one?* Actually, she looked older than most bar girls—late twenties, thirty. Ten years older than Jo. *Not a girl even.* Still, there *was* something girlish about her. She had one of those bodies that come in all shapes and sizes but all say the same thing: I know you're watching so I take my time for you. Jo flushed, but she couldn't stop herself. The woman's fleshy body on the tiny bar stool jiggling with a series of chuckles—it was like a blinding sun: the more Jo knew she shouldn't stare, the more desperately she needed to do so. Jo watched as Gregor slapped the bar and dropped his forehead down onto the hand in front of him, shaking his head. As if she'd told him the funniest joke in the world. Then the woman swiveled her body around toward Jo and gave her an eyebrow-raised, "what-can-you-do-with-them?" look. As if they were old friends. Jo smiled tightly and began to turn away when, with a jangle of jewelry, the woman patted the seat next to her and waved her over.

"Hey, little girl, you're looking lonely," called out the woman in English, smiling and showing several chipped teeth. She was American. Jo smiled back awkwardly, noticing the ache of her mouth in the process. She felt like a minion being called by a queen. Without quite knowing what she was doing, Jo got down from her seat and climbed onto the stool next to the woman.

"Jo no like the others. She stay alone," Gregor said to the woman. Jo was surprised that Gregor had even acknowledged her presence—it was the most interest he'd ever shown in her. Of course, it was nothing compared to the admiring words he bestowed nightly on the Australians who gathered in the corner alcove, drinking prodigiously and free of charge. Well, that's how it was: everything on the house, "no problem," as long as you showed "special courtesy to the patrons," a phrase Dino was fond of saying in an overly enunciated way, so that you never knew if he was being facetious or serious.

When Jo, having taken in the large fruity-looking drink in front of the woman, found her voice to ask for a banana daiquiri, Gregor wrinkled his eyebrows together with displeasure. "Eh? You're no drinking girl!" he shouted. In Gregor's unalterable view of things, all girls were one or the other. Jo got paid in *drachma*—1,200 a night—while the other girls drank free but got no money. It would be too complicated to explain to him that she would pay just like a regular customer. Jo refolded the two hundred *drachma* note she held in her sweaty fingers and tucked it back into the waistband of her skirt.

"Wait, honey." The woman addressed Gregor, "Give the girl a drink." She tilted her head and started chuckling again, for no obvious reason.

The creases between his eyebrows smoothed out. "You pay?"

"Sure." The woman flipped a note at Gregor, who made a grab for it, and although he missed it, shouted "Aha!" and held a clenched fist in front of Jo and the woman. The woman snorted and turned to face Jo. "You work here, honey?"

"Yeah." Jo's voice sounded scratchy.

Gregor made the drink and placed it before Jo, then moved without a word to the other end of the bar. "Well," the woman said when he was gone. She fiddled with a plastic fruit hooked over the rim of her drink and began laughing again. It came from very deep in her throat and had a raspy element to it, like sandpaper against a hard wood. She pulled the fruit from the glass and held it up for Jo to admire, and then inserted it into her mane of hair. A bright red strawberry sat on top of her head. The woman held herself very erect and laughed, face reddening, as if she were engaged in a secret competition with herself.

Jo began to laugh too. What else could she do? It felt so strange to open her mouth this way, letting all the air in. The strawberry rolled off the woman's head onto the floor but sounds kept coming out of her mouth as if she hadn't noticed. Then, as the jiggling of her body subsided and her face returned to its dry brown color, she bent between her legs to locate the strawberry. It lay on the floor underneath her stool. "Oh well," she said, giving up and pulling herself back up, an arm on the bar for leverage. "Got a smoke?"

Jo took a cigarette from the pack in the hand-held purse she'd got in Athens, lit it and passed it to the woman. She saw that the woman's fingers, encased in rings, were callused and the nails were surrounded by a hazy border of dirt. The woman smoked as if it were as necessary as eating.

"Thanks."

"Sure." The smoke from the woman's cigarette, combined with the thick, musty air of the club, caught in Jo's lungs. Then she felt it move down and spread out into her body—just as Damien had told her happened to him in India. She understood what he'd meant now. Only it wasn't love that was filling up her insides; it was this woman's deep, unapologetic laugh.

Damien was the drummer in her roommate's hard-core band. He was an acquaintance who had disappeared over the summer and hadn't returned to school for sophomore year; he had reappeared just as Jo's need to leave was ripening. She'd caught sight of him on the main street of town. He sat in the driver's seat of a '75 Chevy Nova under the grey New York State sky, one hand on the vinyl steering wheel, the other holding a Dairy Queen shake, his head swathed in a white turban.

"So you found enlightenment at Dairy Queen?" she shouted to him from across the street. "Which one?" He gave her a childish smile and she saw that his face looked shiny like a new coin. "Love, man, love. That's what gives you form…substance," he announced as he stepped out of the car into the peaked light of the afternoon and casually kissed her on both cheeks.

They'd gone to a diner just outside town and gotten cheese fries and sandwiches. When Damien got up to go to the bathroom, he took his turban off and placed it gingerly on the table. It came off just like a hat, which surprised Jo, who had imagined it would be an ordeal to put on or take off. Jo saw that Damien's hairline had receded quite a bit and this struck her as perfect: It reflected all those unseen things that must have happened to him—how he'd lived and been changed. While he was still in the bathroom, Jo scooped his turban off the table, closed her eyes and buried her nose in it; a guilty shiver ran down her spine. Jo could smell the world in the fabric. It smelled sharp and sour—like something pickled. It smelled wonderful. When she opened her eyes again, the diner looked tiny and poorly lit—the smallest, most inconsequential section of the universe. "Fucking hell!" she exclaimed.

Damien had told her he'd just returned from India and Pakistan and was drifting through town on his way from New York to San Francisco. He had stopped by to check on his old friends. It'd taken him a year to get his nerve up to go to India, but finally he had done it. He was proud of himself. Jo said she'd remembered hearing that he'd taken off while the band was on tour and they'd had to find a temporary drummer in New York; he nodded gravely in confirmation.

Then he leaned over the table toward her, his eyes gleaming. "Man," he said, "I dress myself in love every morning. I untuck it from my pillow, let it loose from my hair"—here, Jo smothered a giggle—"and I rub it all over my body! Feels so sweet, like little hairy insect paws roaming all over you."

Jo found it hard not to laugh. "What kind of love is this?" she said chuckling. "Like, the cheap nickel-bag stuff or the hard-core expensive shit?" Damien seemed not to hear.

"Brown dusty earth, a pink sari, ochre sky. From a bus window I saw these things…and…my body was filled with an endless love. There on the other side of the world, I found it: a glue, a glue to life!" His voice rose with great emotion and, just as she would with Paulette, Jo felt temporarily speechless. As a tear trickled down his cheek, he added, "So to speak."

Then he looked at Jo as if seeing her for the first time. He said, "Gained a little weight, huh?"

Jo felt her faculties return and quickly retorted, "In your shriveled-up state, everything must look bigger. Don't worry I won't hurt you, won't step on you with my BIG INSECT PAWS." She lingered on the last words. Just because he'd been to India didn't give him the right…. Love, OK, she could accept that, but she was sensitive about her weight. But Damien just started laughing—giggling really—and Jo, mostly out of confusion, found herself joining in.

"I can't believe you just took off," she screamed as they were saying good-bye. "And here you go again!" He grinned and got into the car. "Take me to the world," she said flinging her arms open and embracing the side window of the car. "I'm joking," she added but he was already laughing. He leaned back in the seat and kissed her chastely on both cheeks and drove off. It was as if he had stepped onto another plane—and her body was too heavy and distinct to follow. Despite Damien's foolishness, which, anyway, seemed sort of charming to Jo, he was the first person she'd met who was moving, going somewhere—anywhere. She cried after he left. She gained more weight She tried to throw herself back into college life. She bought a new leather skirt, a brighter lipstick and she stamped more fiercely in the middle of the dance floor.

The dance floor. Well, really just the concave wooden floor of a clapboard house. All the floors of the off-campus houses fell inward at their center. Perhaps it was the weather, or the state of disrepair or just the age of the houses (some of which were a hundred years old) that caused this condition. The students would gather inside the dilapidated houses, in bare living rooms with yellowing and cracked walls and throw their bodies into the sunken centers of the rooms. They moved to the thumping rhythm from the speakers or the crack and whine from the makeshift stage. Jo would fall amongst them, reveling in the closeness, the sweat, the smoky energy. Each submission into this turning pool of bodies caused the concrete-block high school and New Haven suburbs of her childhood to melt further into memory, clearing the way for who she was now, who she could become.

After Damien left, Jo tried to lose herself on those dance floors, in the undulations of the others. It was a last resort. A space not her own—neither distinct nor indistinct. But soon even this sort of immersion became impossible, and the dance floor began to mock her. It became a sunken pit. And as it sank dangerously, she began to retreat to the walls and window sills, her body acquiescing to its own weight; suddenly each limb felt painfully separate.

After Jo secured her leave of absence, she hitchhiked back to New Haven. She worked in a gourmet bakery and an Amtrak depot office and lived at home, saving her money. India, of course, was her destination: that place where she'd seen you could go to be filled up with a most unlikely kind of love. Perhaps there were other unlikely things besides love, things that grew like weeds, untended and magnificent, in corners of the world she'd never heard of.

An agent at High Time Travel, a downtown agency near where her parents worked, tried to convince her that Greece—with a pre-season round-trip special to Athens of only $300—was the place she was looking for. "Not too far from India," the agent said, laughing and showing pointy teeth, "and certainly more of a paradise for a young woman like you." Jo left with some brochures from casinos on Rhodes and for Minoan tours on Crete, tossed them into the garbage at home and opened an Atlas. She traced an invisible line from Greece into Turkey, turning the page to find Iraq and Iran, then Afghanistan and Pakistan, finally reaching a sliver of dark yellow India in the lower right corner. She imagined walking from one country to the next, at each border being greeted by cheering men in turbans. Jo looked around guiltily, as if someone might have caught a glimpse of this embarrassing vision. There was no one else home.

After her visit to the travel agent, Jo was surprised by how quickly her India fantasy became one of Greece. After all, it was also an ancient, dusty country—not as big, but just as unknown to her. During the day at work she'd look up and feel the heat and the weight of this new possibility heading toward her at a mesmerizing speed and she knew she would have to try to grab hold of it, or step out of its way.

It was a late April morning when Jo woke at 3:25 a.m. and in the cool dark boarded a bus to JFK. As the plane for Athens left the ground, Jo felt like she was falling through a hole in the floor, rather than rising. "Fucking hell," she mumbled, gripping the arm rests. To steady herself she counted the rows of hideous not-quite-suburban houses streaming out from under the airplane until they were lost in the clouds.

"Paulette." The woman gripped the cigarette between her lips, squinted an eye against the unfurling smoke, and extended a hand to Jo. Jo shook it, cringing a little at the strength of her grip.

"I'm Jo. Jo Almund."

"Like the nut?"

"Yeah, like the fucking nut. Spelled different but sounds the same. But I'm no nut, let me tell you," Jo said in her super-deep, radio-announcer voice. Paulette fanned the smoke from her eyes and stared at Jo, obviously amused.

"What're you then, a cookie? You look like a tough little round cookie."

Surprisingly, Jo felt no sting in the reference to her body. How could she? Here was a woman bigger than her—and beautiful! Not beautiful like the blonde girls with the icy eyes who she heard on the beach debating which number of sun lotion was better for which body part. ("Twenty for the face, thirty for the nose and tummy, and sixteen for...") She looked at Paulette, her brown skin dusted with a layer of tiny wrinkles. *She* wouldn't use sun block. Just unmediated skin and sunshine, with all the danger and joy of that. Joy! Yes, there was a geyser-like mirth bubbling out of this woman. Jo wanted to dip into it, drink it, scoop it out of the black insides of her mouth and shake it out of her hair, carry it back to her pension.

"A cookie? Umm...yes, that's right." Jo raised a pretend mic just below her chin and resumed her radio voice. "I'm a cookie, you're a cookie, wouldn't you like to be a cookie too?" Jo heard herself. Ridiculous. She was being stupid; she just couldn't help it.

Paulette let out a few non-committal snorts then turned and yelled down the bar, "Hey, more Rosy Cheeks down here!" In a minute Gregor placed two more drinks before them.

"You're American, right?" Jo asked, finding her normal voice.

"Sure am, honey. But haven't been there in years. From upstate New York originally—"

"That's where I go to college!" Jo exclaimed. "I mean, used to."

But Paulette hadn't heard. She was saying: "Greenest county in the country, as far as I can remember. Also poorest. Don't know if it's still so green, but you can bet it's just as poor." Paulette paused, raised her hands to her face and sniffed. "Mm, love that smell of work." She smiled at Jo slowly as if she were remembering something far-off and pleasant.

Jo felt a flush of embarrassment. Paulette had unintentionally reminded her of how quickly she had jumped at Dino's suggestion that she come work at Bluebells. Just a week after she'd met him at her regular dinner haunt. *A little obvious, huh?*

"Yeah, I've got a little jewelry business going," Paulette was saying. "You know, earrings, bracelets, some beads. Mostly earrings. I make them at home back on the peninsula, then I bring them to the islands to sell in the good months. The fruitful months." She said the word "fruitful" in two distinct syllables.

Jo's hands shook as she lit a cigarette. "You live on the Peloponnese Peninsula?"

"Yup. Southern coast. A town a little inland. Best place in the whole world. No one bothers you—even if you want them to." Paulette widened her lips in a smile, the dull pink of her tongue visible through her chipped teeth. There was another odor attached to her, besides sun and dry skin; it was a grassy odor, or maybe one of just plain dirt.

"So, college girl, you here all alone?" Paulette asked.

"Yes. You?"

"Oh well!" Paulette exclaimed, looking pleased with the question. As if *she* had wanted to answer it all along. "That's complicated. All how you look at it. We're all alone really." She leaned toward Jo and ran one heavy arm along the bar in the opposite direction. "I mean, can't hold another one to you for too long, you know? Well, you probably don't know, you're so young." She looked at Jo and began laughing her sandpaper laugh again. As it tapered off, she said, "The short answer? I'm just in for a week or two. I'm staying with him right now." She jerked her head toward the corner of the club where Dino liked to stand, surveying his domain.

"Him?"

"Yeah, Dino. Well, really Demetrius—at least I think that's his real name, but he won't be called that. You know," Paulette said grimacing, "they always want some stupid American sitcom name. Yeah. Dino probably loves *The Flintstones* or something. Ha! At least he's not one of those island-Athenian guys who want to be called Joe or Frank." She sighed and mimicking the sweet overtaxed voice of a sitcom wife, she said, "Whatever you want, honey."

"Whaddya mean, 'staying with him?'"

Paulette raised an eyebrow. She took in Jo's puffy face and frightened eyes. "I'm just staying with him. Just that, no more, honey. Whew!" She did an exaggerated hand-swipe at her forehead, grinned at Jo and lit another of Jo's cigarettes. "He is a pretty one though, no?"

Jo felt her face drawing all the blood in her body. She was suddenly afraid of Paulette's bold, amused stare. No secrets seemed possible with this woman. She wanted to run out of the club into the cool night air. And she might have if Paulette's hand hadn't landed firmly on her back. Paulette leaned close and said resolutely, "Look Jo, Dino's friends with my man."

Jo sighed. She was tired; Paulette's hand was warm on her back. Paulette leant back onto her stool and let her arm drop until her hand rested against the small of Jo's back for a second before she took it away altogether to pick up the ashy cigarette balanced on the edge of the bar. She chuckled to herself softly, then turned to Jo. "Jack, I call him—my man, I mean—though his name is really Jari. He's a sweetie. From Holland. Ever since I was young I've dreamed of a lumberjack man. He'd be chopping trees for me, serving me dinner, running his callused hands over me at night. And Jari's no name for a lumberjack, so I call him Jack. 'Course he doesn't chop trees, but he does do carpentry." Jo smiled tentatively at Paulette, who pulled a stray end of hair out of her mouth.

"Anyway, point is, Jack and Dino are friends from when Jack was running a hostel in Athens where Dino worked. Almost ten years ago. Before I met Jack. Dino was still in school. All the girls liked him then too. But let me tell ya something," Paulette leaned over and with a jangle of bracelets pulled Jo's ear closer to her lips. She whispered, dry and smoky, "He don't go that way, honey. Women, I mean." She leaned back, looking kindly at Jo, who found herself laughing. Jo tried to stop; she was scared the laughter might dislodge the pleasant feeling inside and leave it hollow again. Paulette just sat there by her, silent, smoking. Jo was so grateful to her for existing, for being at Bluebells, for not noticing—or not caring about—the growing group of guys around them, their white sneakers glowing an eerie purple in the club light.

Abruptly, Paulette dropped her cigarette without stubbing it out and, with remarkable ease for such a big-bodied woman, lowered herself to the ground. Jo watched as Paulette adjusted her leotard, pulling and prodding the fabric where it had bunched up around her breasts. Paulette started toward the dance floor. Jo noticed that there were enough men ringing the room that she could start working. *Should* start working. But she found herself unable to conceive of going up to one of them. Instead, she watched as Paulette meandered out onto the dance floor alone and undaunted, arms raised, hips swinging. Jo caught the look on the face of another bar girl across the room as she approached a customer; she saw him smile and lower his beer. She was reminded of the north campus girls back at college who gathered around long-haired guitarist boys in newly starched bandannas, slapping their thighs in tune to their random strumming. She used to make fun of those girls, calling them "Venus flytraps," or screaming across the lawn, "How much are you getting paid to look so STUPID?" Now she realized that her own face probably unconsciously fell into the same tentative suggestion of intimacy as she approached a customer. A tacit requirement of the job.

Jo ducked her head away from Paulette and the other bar girl, and turned to where Dino stood in the half-light of a circulating strobe. She was going to wave out of habit but stopped when she saw he was chatting excitedly with a big Greek lady in a bright green dress. They grinned at each other and hugged. The lady waved as she backed away, shouting something back at him and then blowing kisses until she disappeared into the dark entranceway. Probably some relative, maybe an aunt, or maybe even his mother, Jo guessed, shivering at this thought—Dino's having a mother. The idea of her own family seemed impossibly remote to her.

Paulette had begun slowly swaying in place, eyes closed, to a techno-pop song with a relentless, driving beat. It was as if she had caught a slumbering undercurrent of the song, which she had wrapped around herself like a robe made of soft fabric. Her movements were rounded, circular like her body. The men ringing the dance floor watched Paulette unblinkingly. They didn't laugh like usual when a girl, in rebellion against a group or anger at a boyfriend, started dancing alone.

Oh my God, thought Jo. A fleshy woman dancing by herself at a tourist club on a Greek island. How did Paulette do it? She looked so comfortable, so easy. This image was impossible for Jo to reconcile with the roiling dance floors from college, those disorienting anarchic spaces she thought she had left behind. Instead, she had been shadowed. How else to explain Bluebells' taunting, cavernous floor that stared at her every night? It had been whitewashed so thoroughly, so brutally—as if that could contain what lay beneath.

Jo had managed to almost completely avoid the dancing requirements of her job by clinging to the black Formica strip of the bar and choosing her customers carefully. The bar's polished surface felt safe, wanting nothing more than to reflect back the darkened planes of her face, of all their faces. Nothing given, nothing taken. Occasionally it was unavoidable, though. A customer would become so persistent that she would have to capitulate her fear to his desire. Out on the dance floor, it would start. The strobes would begin cavorting crazily about the room, tricking her eyes and her feet and the vertigo would wash over her. She would find herself grabbing embarrassingly at his elbows for support. The last time Jo had attempted a trip out to the floor with a customer, she was on the arm of a dentist from San Francisco. He'd been nice and gentle. They'd talked for almost two hours—he told her all about his failed marriage—and, against her usual protocol, Jo drank all three drinks he bought for her. She told him of her ridiculous fear of the dance floor, laughing tears in relief to be telling someone. He linked arms with her, flicked open a Swiss Army knife, started singing "lions and tigers and bears, oh my!" in a falsetto and with careful steps ushered her out onto the dance floor. But it was no use. Before they'd reached the center (their drunkenly declared goal), she doubled over, hugging her stomach, and fell at his feet. The shiny tips of his cowboy boots winking at her, mocking her. That asshole!

He'd tricked her! He had reached down, genuinely concerned, to grab her by the waist and pull her up. But she evaded him then, her legs screaming across the floor, up the steps into the cool night air. The stars winked at her benignly and cleared away the authority of all that highly polished boot leather.

But this woman, there is no fear in her movements, thought Jo, as she watched Paulette settle back down onto the bar stool next to her, take several deep breaths and run her ringed fingers through her hair. Her breasts were still bouncing from all the exertion. Gregor caught sight of them and smiled happily. He walked by pointing his index finger at Paulette. "You my favorite girl. When you act like girl."

Paulette smiled at him but it seemed more of a grimace. Jo had left her pack of cigarettes on the bar and now pushed them in front of Paulette without looking at her. She felt strangely shy. Paulette pulled one out of the pack and lit it. She mumbled, "Man, say what you want about me, but I likes my smokes." After a couple of drags, she addressed Jo: "So you're a college girl."

Jo looked up. Paulette was rubbing her tailbone; she looked a little tired. Jo caught sight of Paulette's large earrings—an intricate pattern of beads sliding along interlocking silver hoops. College? Dark rooms with cracking walls, anxious laughter in the nighttime air of the art building parking lot. The necessary assertion: a sociology major. Jo cracked the knuckles on her right hand, then her left. "Yeah. Well. Was. You know. But I'm not fucking going back. No way."

Paulette narrowed her eyes at Jo and for just a moment looked unmistakably serious.

"Come on," Paulette said as she lowered herself from the bar stool. "Let's dance." She put a proprietary hand on Jo's forearm, her silver rings cutting a shiny band across Jo's brown skin. Her touch was promising, a little dangerous. Jo sighed as she began following the thick, jaunty hair moving in front of her. The sounds of laughter swam around her as she ignored the accusatory eyes of all the partner-less men. The air felt as smooth and warm and vein-less as water. When Paulette stopped briefly to wave to Dino—who waved back politely but looked perplexed—Jo realized the ground was still solid beneath her. In a burst of exuberance, she reached out and grabbed Paulette's hand and twirled under her arm in a disco move she remembered seeing girls do in high school when they danced together. Paulette looked back and winked at Jo. Jo was convinced at that moment that Paulette, who was as big and bright as a star, had fallen to earth from the sky for her.

GLACIERS

—Peter Meinke

The wildbearded man
on the corner waves his sign:
*Buy your property now
the glaciers are coming!*
He's taking the short view:
things matter

Some day the world will rattle
like a celestial ice cube but
until then we've got
water in the mountains
porridge in the pot
(if the others guess right
and we scorch to cinders
the point's the same)

I can't blame you but look
some urgency's here:
time is limited Please
come back I'm sorry
It *is* the end of the world
Things matter Hurry *Hurry!*

THE WAY IT REALLY WENT

──Patricia Ann McNair

One thing about cancer—and anyone who knows anyone who's had it knows this, too—it's the name of it that gets you sick. Here's what I mean:

A guy goes through his everyday life, not feeling bad or anything, not feeling anything different at all except one day feeling a little hard bubble of something under his skin. Say he's in the shower, soaping up all the parts he usually does, thinking about how he hates to have to ever get out from under the warm stream of water, hates to have to get a move on and put on his uniform and go sit on the little stool he sits on all day, doing the exact same job he's been doing for fifteen years, selling the same tickets to the same people for the same buses going to the same places—on automatic pilot, more or less, trying not to let it bother him, the monotony, the sameness, but knowing that it does. And then all of a sudden something is different, something has changed. And what it is is this little raising of flesh here under his arm on his side. A pebble, it feels like. Tough under the fingers, but it doesn't hurt. *Huh,* he says to himself and fingers it under the soapy slide of skin before he rinses off and shrugs it off and dries off and goes about his day. Only every once in a while, his fingers find their way back to that spot under his arm, play over the spot, pushing and wondering if the thing's bigger or smaller than the last time he messed with it an hour or so ago. When he gets home he pulls the tails of his shirt out of his pants and steps up close to the full-length mirror on the back of the bedroom door, studies the spot but doesn't see anything, not even the bump of it unless he uses two fingers of one hand on either side of it to stretch the skin back over the area—and then what he sees he can't tell if it's real or imagined it's such a small deviation from the flat, pale plane of his side. *A cyst, maybe,* he thinks, and tries to ignore it, doesn't tell anyone, not even his wife because she'd think he was whining and that makes her mad, and besides it's probably just nothing. And the next day and the next when he takes a shower he presses on it, squeezes it, and gets to doing that so regularly that it becomes part of the routine, as mindless as the act of rinsing the shampoo out of his thick black hair. He still doesn't feel bad, not any more tired or achy than usual, just the pains of getting near forty and not doing enough besides sitting and watching TV and life from his couch at home, his stool at work.

But then one day it hurts. Really hurts. Like a stab of something when he presses on it, a sharpness that radiates up and down from his armpit to the lowest edge of his ribs. He remembers what it was like when he had that Plantars wart once and it got so painful that he could hardly step on the ball of his right foot. And even though it hurts, this thing, maybe a wart, he still doesn't feel too bad, although he has been getting sort of tired lately. But he imagines that's because he doesn't sleep too well anymore. Dreams of dogs biting him and sinking their teeth in under his arm—shining slivers of enamel left in his skin when he finally pulls the beasts away—shake him up enough that he forces himself awake and keeps his eyes wide open and fixed on the ceiling until he's sure he won't fall back in with the dogs again.

So, when it gets to hurting, the man makes an appointment with the doctor. And when the doctor asks, he realizes that he can't remember when he first noticed it, can't remember when it wasn't there, part of him. And after this test and that, the doctor tells him what he already knows, says the word in a stream of other possible words. And the man knows it's this one, recognizes the word that had been in his mind all the while, even though he'd never actually said it, even to himself. And the man's surprised that he isn't surprised by what the doctor tells him. Yet, familiar as the word is when he hears it, it still shakes him up, and he sits for a long while on the cold examining table, left alone in the room to dress. Only he can't move. Not voluntarily. He listens to his mind telling his legs to stand now, his hands to reach for his clothes; he even prods himself *Come on, get going* out loud, but it's like he's stuck there, trapped in the sterile white room by the word, trapped in this body which he thought he knew and trusted. Trapped in the body that had turned on him, and now turned on him again by not standing, not taking him out of there, but instead doing its own thing, shaking uncontrollably from toe to head, shivering and shuddering so hard that the paper of the examining robe rattles in the quiet.

And then, for the first time since he found that little bubble under his skin, for the first time ever, perhaps, he says the word himself. *Cancer*, he says, whispering the name as he shakes in the paper robe in the quiet, white room. And then, when the man names it, that's when he gets sick.

When Jim called before he left work at the station and said we needed to talk, I knew he didn't mean we'd have a real conversation where he says something then I do—but more than likely he wanted me to stay quiet while he talked. I knew something was up, I saw the signs. He'd drift away somewhere while we sat in front of the late news, his fingers strumming his ribs, his eyes blanking out. He wouldn't answer me when I'd say something then, not hearing. Ignoring, maybe. It doesn't matter which. The thing is, we hadn't really talked with one another in months. And now I figured he probably wanted me to sit tight and listen while he said one of those three-word sentences most women live in dread of hearing: *This isn't working* or *I've met someone*. Like I said, there were signs.

The way I imagined it would go:

At Anchors Inn, the only rib joint in town and Jim's favorite restaurant (never mind that I'd given up red meat), he would be on his side of the table looking twitchy, the sweat shining in his thick black curls; I'd be on mine, dressed up for once, figure what the hell, might as well step out of those old jeans and tee shirt I live in mostly and slip into the black mini-skirt pushed to the back of the closet. Heels, too. Figure if it's going to be him leaving me, he better damn sure know what he's leaving behind.

I'd sit on my red vinyl bench across the red plaid tablecloth from my ten-year husband and listen to him hemming and hawing around those words—*This, er, I've, uh....* I imagined when he finally did say it—his brown eyes focused on a spot somewhere off to the side of my head, his Adam's apple bobbing—I'd just smile big and nod nicely, and stand up and lean over to kiss the top of his head. Good luck, I'd say, and leave him there, walk away and leave him getting an eyeful of my good side.

The way it really went:

I sat in the flickering light of the fake lanterns tacked up on the rough-paneled walls and watched Jim squirm. He looked small in his white shirt and black tie, his bus ticket seller's uniform, and damn if it didn't look like he might cry. He kept blinking and clearing his throat, and I waited for him to say something, like it seemed I was always waiting for him. I used to finish his sentences for him; it was as if he just didn't have enough words in him to make it through a whole conversation sometimes. But I got tired of that, like I got tired of the other things: the way he pretended not to stare at every other woman in the neighborhood—from the high school girls working at the Stop'n'Shop with their tight bodies and too-tight jeans, to the new moms pushing their buggies'-full, their ripe boobs bouncing; the nights I went to bed hours ahead of him so he could watch the round-up shows after the games, and then the highlights on the late news, and then whatever sports they'd be playing in some other part of the world in the middle of the night that he could get on that damned cable; the pools of water on the bathroom floor that I'd slip in every morning when I went in after him to pick up his towels, put the seat down, wipe the toothpaste splatters off the mirror. Like a goddamn cliché our life was, and I couldn't even remember anymore when things weren't exactly the same.

But that night at the Inn, things seemed different somehow. And as I sat there waiting for Jim to talk, my heart pounded in me. A good pound.

A life's-about-to-change-get-ready-it's-your-turn kind of pound. It nearly made me giddy. And, God help me, I felt like laughing. But of course I didn't.

"I...," Jim started finally, after our busboy came by to fill our water glasses and put our place settings down.

"-'m leaving," I finished the sentence in my head for him. But I kept my lips pressed tight together. And Jim, after that first false start, closed his own mouth and pushed back into his seat, then opened his mouth long enough to gulp down some water, then closed it again, his eyes skittering around, touching everything but mine.

Maybe I should have left him. Not like the thought hadn't crossed my mind a million times over the last, oh, not ten years (because the first two were actually pretty good I think, I don't remember how or why, only I have this feeling that there was something more than just pleasant about them), but in the last eight years I'd often considered going. Still, there's a certain comfort in what's familiar, and Jim was definitely familiar. We'd known each other since the sixth grade. He was the first boy I let slide his hand into my shirt, under the bra, back in freshman year behind the rear door of the field house. I looked across the table at Jim's hands. At the low silver half-moons under his nails, the ones that meant money or luck, I'd heard somewhere. At the long, sleek white digits fidgeting with the spoon, the knife. His hands were what made me fall for him for real in the first place. Even before that day when he slipped one inside the cool cotton of my bra and it felt so wonderfully warm and smooth, a press of palm so real and alive, like nothing I'd ever felt before. When he slid that palm over my nipple we both took in air at precisely the same moment, a gasp so quick and deep that he just about snatched his hand back, and would have if I hadn't hugged it to me, pushed my whole self up against it and him, wanting the feeling of his electric warmth to take me over entirely until we had to pull apart and run around to the front entrance and get to homeroom before the second bell rang.

His hands were clean, always, the fingers long and solid. They looked good holding things. In seventh grade he came over to our house with a big brown casserole of beans and ham from his mom, an offering of sympathy the morning after my dad died, and when I went to the door and found him there, shifting from foot to foot, his nose red and runny, maybe from the cold October mistiness, I couldn't look in his eyes when he said he was sorry, *You know, about your dad and all, I mean,* so instead I focused in on his hands, white and strong around the heavy brown dish; and they looked so perfect, the nailbeds pink and long and healthy, my heart broke and filled in the same instant, and I couldn't help but crumple and sob, and he dropped that big old casserole, beans and slimy ham all over our front stoop, and he put his hands on me, on my back, in my hair, on my face, and how could I help but love him then?

But all that was years before. Years before we went together, broke up, got back together, had a child, lost a child, and so on. It all somehow seemed like an inalterable progression. After Jim and I were married, we seemed to just keep going on with our lives, nothing changing, unless you count that day of the accident and how after that we clung to each other at first, tried to start over, to have another baby with not a bit of luck, then stopped talking, nearly, and stopped sleeping together entirely, sharing a bed, but not bodies, and how I started stepping out, finding someone or other to hold me, someone or other to want me. So even though I didn't ever go anywhere, I guess I had been doing my own leaving for a while, and now I figured Jim could leave me and we could get on with things.

I watched our waitress at the next table pull a long pepper mill out of her red apron pocket in an elegant arc, and twist the big thing over the plate of a woman with hair so black it was blue. The woman lifted her hand in a small wave. "When," she said.

Jim picked up his menu, put the plastic wall of it up between us. "What're you gonna have?" he said. The first full sentence since we'd been there.

"I'm not too hungry," I said, not even bothering to open my menu. "I'll just go for the salad bar."

"Yeah," Jim said and put the menu down again. His lips pulled down at the corners and a line creased deeply across his forehead. "Maybe I will, too. Red meat's not too good for you."

Now here was something different. Jim was the kind of man who joked about not getting enough fat, not having a high enough cholesterol level. "More salt," he'd say at the movies when he ordered popcorn, "keep pouring, keep pouring! I can still see some yellow from the butter."

And it was at this moment that I got scared.

"Jim—?"

"I went to the doctor today," he said and turned his head toward the bar, away from me. He began to roll up his sleeve. There was a purple patch of skin spreading out from under a Band-Aid in the crook of his elbow. The back of my neck got cold.

And then he said it. Three words, the number I knew there would be. But not the right three words.

"They found something."

An odd sensation seeped through me. I don't know what you'd call it, but I know I'd felt it twice before. That time when my mom came home and told me what happened on the afternoon my dad died on the job, a heart attack that took him down to the cement floor of the bays of the trucking company right before lunch time, made him dead before the first of the guys on his way back from the cafeteria found him down there, cold and totally empty of breath. That time, and the day of our daughter's accident.

My eyes burned, and I swallowed and swallowed, trying to get that thing out of my throat so that I could talk.

"It's just a lump," Jim said finally, reaching one of those perfect hands across the table to me. His fingertips touched the white knuckles of my own hand gripping the edge of the table. His voice was soft now. It sounded young and concerned. Scared, maybe.

"What the hell does that mean, Jim?" And here's the thing; I heard my own voice get too loud, raggedy with edginess. And the feeling that covered me a minute before was burning off into anger. Even I knew this wasn't right, this wasn't what Jim needed from me right then, to be pissed off at him. Pissed off again, for chrissakes. But I was. And maybe I was at least a little mad at myself then for not seeing this coming, for imagining something else, protecting myself from the wrong thing by imagining something entirely impossible, Jim having an affair—boring, settled Jim, as loyal and unambitious as a fat old house dog. Mostly, though, I was mad at him. "What's 'it's just a lump' supposed to fucking mean?"

Our waitress—Emily, her brass name pin said—was at our tableside then, her hand on her pepper mill, just doing her job but caught in our little moment and frozen there, it looked like. It was all I could do not to reach over and snatch the damn wooden pepper club from her and swing it around in an elegant arc over Jim's head. I'll give him a lump.

"Uh, I guess you need more time," Emily said when I turned my face to her. The fire I felt in my forehead must have shone in my eyes. She patted the table twice and smiled her good waitress smile and backed away.

I looked back at Jim, at his skinny neck in the wide starched white collar. His fingers had slipped from my knuckles but his hand stayed stretched across the wide table, the pink pillows of his palm up. He blinked and blinked, his deep brown eyes fogging and clearing; his lips worked like he was trying to say something but couldn't. The spot under the Band-Aid on his outstretched arm looked colored on, a fake bruise. But I knew that this was as real as it gets.

"Ah, shit," I said, when the strangle hold of it all finally let go of my throat. I took his hand in my own, startled by how strange and how familiar the skin-to-skin warmth and smoothness of it felt. Jim tilted his head up and watched me stand. He looked so damn small there surrounded by red vinyl, a boy at the end of the marred arm. "Come on," I said and jiggled our hands held together like a double-sized fist, "let's go home."

Back at the house, we let go of one another's hands just long enough to undress and we got into bed—Jim in his tee shirt and boxers, me in my panties. We got into bed on our backs and on our own sides. Our hands found their way to one another across the span of cold sheet. Jim fell fast and hard into sleep. I lay still and silent, stared at the black flatness of the ceiling and wondered if something as routine as sleep would ever come to me again. And when it did I didn't notice until I was pulled out of it, away from dreams with no movement, still pictures of people and objects vaguely familiar yet unrecognizable. Jim's crying woke me but not him. He whimpered and shuddered, but didn't come to, so I slid over the mattress and into him, pressed myself against the back I'd gotten used to having turned to me at night. Each sob shook me, and I held on, clucked in a way that came natural to me, even though our bodies, pressed together, felt changed. My own softer and fleshier than whenever the last time we touched like this was, his thinner and somehow brittle. His shirt was soaked through so I pulled it up his back and over his head, and in his sleep he let me. The slick skin of him was hot and cold at the same time, but I stayed close until he felt just-right warm against me. The crying stopped and gave way to even breathing, heavy and thick with sleep, and when he's five minutes' calm, I run my hand up his side, smoothing the skin until I feel it. And it's true, there's not much there, a couple of stitches over a pea of sickness, and I wish that I could bite it, take it between my teeth and pull back quick and hard until it's out of him and in my mouth and then I could spit it out. Into the toilet, I think, and I'd flush it away and when Jim woke up it would be gone, and he'd be old Jim again, same old same old, and I'd be Annie, just like before—whatever, whoever, that was.

The surgery came four days later. In the recovery room everyone was smiling, Jim even, ready to believe that was that. "Optimistic" was the word the doctors used then. I wanted to believe, too, but the tightness I'd felt at the Inn had turned into a knot, a hard blister of dread. And then the day after the surgery when they read his tests, the blood work and lymph nodes, they found more.

They say what doesn't kill you will only make you stronger, but I'm not sure that goes for chemotherapy. Jim couldn't eat from queasiness, and after his daily shots he'd vomit up all that nothing. From my cold plastic chair outside the examining room, it was like I could hear his bones rattle with the dry heaves. When he'd come back through the doorway, grey and wobbly, I'd go to him and curl under his arm, make myself a crutch for the slow move down the long bright hallway to the exit. It was like we used to walk, back in high school, wrapped into one another so tightly that if one tipped, both would.

At home one day I heard the shower running, but it sounded like it was falling straight down, like no one was moving under it. I put my ear against the door and listened hard. "Jim?" I whispered against the wood. And then I heard that sound of his crying, a soft whimpering, and the quiet distress of it ran through me like ice water. "Jim?" I said again, a little louder this time, and rattled the doorknob. He sniffed. "Yes," he said. I heard the shoring up under the word, the effort it took to keep it steady. I stepped inside the bathroom, waved my hand in front of my face to clear a path in the steam. "Honey?" I pulled back the shower curtain and found him sitting there on the floor of the tub, knees pulled up to his chest, arms wrapped tightly around them.

"Go away," he said into the space between his knees, and from where I was I could see the white of his scalp through his hair, something I'd never seen before. I stood there, my hand still holding back the curtain, not sure what to do next.

"I said go away." He didn't raise his voice, there was no edge in it, he said it like a plain and simple fact. But I couldn't go.

"Jim," I said again, almost a whisper, running out of words myself this time, and put a hand on the back of his neck. He tilted his face up to me. His eyes were rimmed and red, his cheeks slick with steam and tears and snot.

"I can't even take a fucking shower anymore," he said softly, and his eyes began to fill. "I'm just so damn tired," he put his head back on his knees and his shoulders shook. So I climbed in there with him, right down on the porcelain next to him, jeans, tee shirt, socks and all, pulled him into a circle I made with my legs, into the circle of my arms. We rocked there for a good long while, him crying and me thinking about crying but unable to, I hadn't shed a tear since the news first came. I wasn't trying to be strong or anything—I knew that in some long-guarded, hard-sided spot near the blisterknot inside me I wanted to sob. But I couldn't. And then we lay out long in the tub, felt the water pour down over us, clutched together chest-to-chest, legs tucked up and around one another so we could fit in the small space. When the water ran cold, I reached up and turned it off, but we lay there still, who knows how long; and later, much later, we stood up together and I pulled off my own clothes and turned the water back on and held him with one arm and ran the soap over him with my free hand. Even in its whiteness and stick-thinness, his body felt familiar under my hands, and when I bent to my knees and soaped his balls, his dick, the long, hard muscles of his thighs, I couldn't help but remember the times when we'd done this for fun, lathered each other up and slipped our bodies against one another. And his dick remembered too, because it stiffened some, but not much, and I kissed its little head for old time's sake before I stood up again and hugged Jim to me while I reached around him to scrub his back.

He sagged against me while I washed him, his arms resting over my shoulders and his legs shaking under his weight. But then I felt a gathering of the energy in his body, and he pulled back from me just far enough to look into my face.

"I'm really sorry, Annie," he said, his voice low and thick.

There were a lot of things I'd wanted him to be sorry for over the years. Sorry for not being able to keep a better hold on our daughter. Sorry for giving up on our having another kid without ever talking to me about it. Sorry for my feeling like I had to go out on him, look elsewhere for what I thought he should be giving me. Sorry for standing by while all we had that had been warm and familiar turned to cold, cold routine. Sorry for us. Sorry for me. But this? This was not his fault. There was nothing here for him to be sorry over.

The water poured down on us, cold again, and I moved in for some of Jim's warmth. And when I did, I felt myself slip a bit. Jim lifted a hand to me and I grabbed it, held onto it, and then slid it over my breast. I wished he could push his fingers under my skin and through the bones that cross over my heart and find that knot inside me. I wanted him to rub away its hardness. He cupped his other hand behind my neck, and we pressed together. "I'm sorry," he said again. I wanted to tell him it's okay. *Don't worry, it's okay.* But standing with his hands—those same old perfect hands—on me, holding me, keeping me steady, I couldn't say anything. So I nodded. That's all I was able to do. Just nod. I couldn't do anything more.

SMOOTH SAILING

—Jo-Ann Ledger

"Boat rides! Get yer boat rides!"
Nasal buskers sold
a short tour
of the lakefront:
the boat groaned
against rollicking waters
he and I clung
as summer draped buildings
shivered.

Years later
a night cruise:
polished water
slipped by
clear skies
trailed twinkling fingers
as you and I stood
smiling.

I DIDN'T

──Mary Ruth Clarke

I didn't

hang up said yes I would
would meet you for
coffee I don't drink I didn't

panic, percolated what
you want how to
be what to
offer how to
get out of
what it would
leave me what it
meant didn't

shower, wore the old
bra and dashing chocolate
cape on the train closed my book at

I am trying to heal the fractures
accumulated in a fall from grace

MARY RUTH CLARKE

Lynn says in this New Age the synchronicity of serendipity sprouts
like Starbucks

I didn't
want it but the legs under the
cape walked toward

you I didn't bring an Uzi or pickle
puss didn't

smile when I saw you did

ask what size didn't
say super extra tiny the two
gulp and I'm gone cup I said

Medium

trying to keep my wits
about me didn't look a
way when you

thanked me for coming
apologized for harming
offered reparations

didn't blurt out *like what?* Well.
Yes actually I did but you didn't
know nor did I what you could
do so I said I would keep you

posted also didn't
ask if you were climbing some anonymous

I DIDN'T

twelve steps didn't want to
care I didn't talk too much. Well.
Sure I did but didn't give a
way my power didn't cry nine
years of tears to cry now and didn't

forgive you didn't assume I had to
make an "ass of me and you"
didn't gush

it's all right

you did
harm me
I didn't

list specific offenses you didn't
either we didn't
need to as they squatted on big bright

butts betwixt our
hot brews next to that roaring
glass encased
fire

took
the lid off
tepid is warm
enough didn't
drain it
left the bitter bottom didn't

MARY RUTH CLARKE

embrace you shook
your hand and didn't

run home but wandered retail
therapy bought stuff
let that hot brew run through

BROKEN WING

—David McGrath

"What do you suppose goes on in that house?" asks Harry. "Two women like that, by themselves?"

His wife Mary sits opposite him in the matching beige recliner. She raises her eyes above her Book of the Month Club selection, and she looks at him, he thinks, as an object of study.

"Everything with you is sex, isn't it, Harry?" she says, turning the page. Her book jacket is silver and black, with the author's name, Dean Koontz, in seventy-two point letters, he estimates. Every month it's Grisham or Steele or Quindlen. Thousands of words a day she ingests under that Wal-Mart pole lamp, and he wonders why none of it seems to move her.

"All this time we've lived here, I've never seen a man next door," says Harry. "Those girls are only, what, forty? Maybe not even that."

She remains hidden behind Koontz, but her sigh communicates to him her exasperation, then resignation. "When you help them move the refrigerator today, you can ask what they do. Maybe they'll let you watch."

He imagines their neighbor Clara seated on the sofa, in the early evening, with the curtains closed. She's in a plush terry cloth robe, her long, thin legs crossed, her toenails painted scarlet, the auburn hair unfurled and shining, unhidden by the painter's hat she wears while doing her yard work. Her roommate Helen carries over the bowl of popcorn, watching Clara watch the video of the film *Obsession*, which they rented for tonight. Clara uncrosses her legs as she scoops a handful of popcorn, her robe opening with the movement. Helen smiles, kneeling, moving into the just showered, powdered sweet warmth.

Mary clears her throat as she turns the page.

Harry asks, "When did Clara leave her husband?"

He catches her eyes above the book's spine, but they aim over him, searching the wall above his head for the answer.

"I don't know. A year before she moved in with Helen."

"So that's nearly ten years without a man."

"I've told you, Harry, that women are different."

"Ten years. You think she just, you know, does herself?"

Mary rolls her eyes.

"They have a living arrangement," she says. "Financial, whatever. They're best friends, like you and Ted."

"Ted doesn't have a pussy."

She gets up to leave the room, as he knew she would. Six years ago, it seemed that with their son's death, came the death of something more between them. It was as though the physics involved in the eighteen-year-old's 75mph jet-ski bulleting into the concrete breakwall of the Whiting, Indiana harbor on Lake Michigan, required disintegration of far more than the meager mass of plastic machine and 145 pound boy.

Funny, he understood how part of that mass had to be their love. But as long as they both chose to still live, he thought, consuming food and maintaining a home, and speaking when necessary, and ineluctably breathing, they ought also be fucking, if for no other reason than the brief respite from grief it might give her, in the same way that an orgasm for him during hay fever season in August, would be the only moment of the day when he could freely breathe.

Quite contrary/did Mary this see, he thought. This wife who once upon a time would sleep entangled in his arms and legs, now showed irritation in her eyes and forehead at the mere mention of sex.

Which he does more and more—mentions it. Was he bringing it up on purpose? Maybe it's not a strategy. Maybe he just talks about it because its absence is so big. The way have-not's talk about money. The way a dieter thinks about the box of Fannie May candy in the freezer since Christmas. He likes the candy image. He makes a mental note to remember that metaphor for work. To mention in front of Viveca.

Viveca, who likes to be licked while she's standing up. Who insists on washing her boyfriend's prick in soap and warm water, slow and thorough, before making love. At least, that's what Viveca tells Harry. Well, not just Harry. She informs everyone at the lunch table at Midtown Data Storage—himself and Diana and Rosemary.

Ted, his friend of twenty years who is in insurance, tells Harry these very intimate "news" items from Viveca amount to an invitation, and Harry laughs and tells Ted that he's way off, it's not like that, Viveca is way out of his league, it's just workplace banter, and so on.

Young women speak that way, he would tell Ted. Not like when he and Ted used to take Mary and Jenn to the River View Amusement Park and to the Prudential Building, when they'd have thought the girls sluts if they heard them say fuck, let alone shit; but these girls today, even the college graduates, let the f-word poof out of their pouty mouths—"Fuck that shit!" Viveca says, her front teeth denting her purple painted bottom lip. They talk that way at work, but they really let loose at Alph's, a nearby lounge where they occasionally gather after quitting time, and to which they ask Harry along, mainly, he thinks, because they know he'll gallantly produce his Discover card at the end of their happy hour. So he tells Ted that Viveca and the other girls just think of him like some queer uncle that they talk around, who is good for a laugh and for the tab.

What he tells himself is that Viveca probably makes half this stuff up. Yeah, he thinks she does, but then he sometimes thinks maybe not. Of course, if she were making it up, then Ted may be right after all—that it's a come-on. Ted, who divorced Jenn and knows things since he dates other women, says that since Mary has hung out her "No Fishing" sign, Harry is projecting interest, even if unconsciously; so he receives reciprocal interest.

"Women can smell it," said Ted. "Called phonemes or something."

"Wait a minute. Isn't that a language term?"

"Fuckin' A. The language of love, my friend."

Harry remains skeptical, but bemused. Like the state lottery, or Publishers Clearinghouse: in your heart of hearts, you know it won't ever happen. But at least he gets to hear and see the jackpot each day at work. Viveca's lurid bedroom machinations spoken almost as rebuke through glossy lips constitute Harry's current sex life. Or at least the foreplay, delayed until he gets home, requited in his downstairs workshop. Alone.

It's Saturday morning and already Clara is out in the yard with the hoe she uses to scrape and shovel the dog shit into a plastic bag. She does this first every Saturday, preparation for her other yard work. She wears white shorts, a pink halter, and a white scarf instead of the painter's cap, tying back her reddish hair. Is that because I'm coming over today, he wonders.

She is a tall woman, and Harry uses his hand to shade his eyes and to conceal his appraisal of her breasts, about the size of ricecakes, beneath the pink cummerbund. He likes the way the smooth, tanned skin of her legs disappears into the tennis-white shorts, and how he can see the bottom edge of the bunching of her abdominal muscles above the waist band, the same pale, milk chocolate color.

She is thin-waisted and thin limbed, probably because she's a vegetarian. And one time he had advised her that the Jell-O she was snacking on was made from animal fat. She hadn't known and she thanked him but he regretted causing the elimination of another food from what must already be a very limited and joyless selection.

She has unusually wide hips and a flat behind, like a sewer cover, attributes which he doubts also derive from her diet. Surely, she must get plenty of exercise, running with those two little canine annoyances each evening, and then all the yard work, and the swimming, which is something else she must be doing inside that house, since he saw the truck delivering the swim-in-place pool two years back.

He doesn't feel right exchanging pleasantries while she's harvesting the dog shit, so he waits until she cinches up the bag and places it in the trash can.

"Hi," he says. He's by his own back door and she's in the back of her yard by the trashcans. He likes for them both to have plenty of leeway, then maybe they move closer, depending on her eagerness to talk.

She looks up at him, white plastic frame sunglasses; a style revisited from the 1950s, he thinks, hiding her eyes. She has a sharp pointed chin, an aquiline nose, a cable for a neck. Her giraffe-like proportions and outsized, trapezoidal ass make her, he comes to think of it, like a rather homely, cartoonish figure.

But then she smiles, a slightly shy, mostly lush, ice cream smile, and something from her inside, whatever it is that chooses her clothes and spurs her quick-cat movements, and whatever it is that consumes her consciousness while she brushes her hair to a shimmering softness, and whatever inside her produces the tendency to incline her head slightly down and to the left—something inside that's like a battery emits a fevered purring, secret and physical and warm and dark.

He stands in his tiny square yard on a Saturday morning, his dick as hard as one of the galvanized fence posts that separate them, realizing how sexuality has less to do with the blonde hair and supermodel body of someone like Viveca, than with, perhaps, something hidden and human and vulnerable. Clara reaches overhead to snug her scarf, unintentionally exposing a shadowy patch of underarm stubble.

"Did I see your car towed away on Thursday?" he asks.

She used to stop working to chat with him over the chain link fence. But now she talks while fitting the trash can lid. Possibly she's cool to him since the Jell-O business.

"Uh huh, it wouldn't start," she says. "It cost me an arm and a leg for them to tow it and charge the battery and then call me to pick it up."

Reflexively, he appraises her left leg, the knee slightly bent for leverage in clamping down on the lid. The tendon that runs up the back of her thigh and into the tunnel of her loose shorts, flexes and unflexes. He pauses too long. She is looking back at him.

"Might be a loose wire, some kind of short draining the power," he says.

"They said they couldn't find anything," she complains. With a glint of her smile and a shrug of her bony shoulders, she converts the exasperation with the mechanic to a celebration of human quirks and foibles.

"I suppose I should just be glad it's runnin'," she says.

He thinks that he could be with this woman. Listening to her is like tuning the car radio to light rock—what they call "easy listening"—after escaping the Bach-like dirges through the door behind him. Wonder what happened with the man she was married to, for how long did Mary say, for two months?

"Next time it doesn't start, why don't you call me first," he offers. He can't fix a car if there is really something wrong, but he can look at it. With no man in the house, Clara and Helen are in awe over someone handy like him. Or else maybe they just act that way for Mary's benefit. Acting like she's so fucking lucky, when inside they laugh over their popcorn.

He imagines himself and Clara, in her darkened garage, as he emerges from under the hood in triumph—"Just a disconnected vacuum hose," he might say—and she embraces him gratefully. He can smell the fruity shampoo in her hair. She pulls back to say she already called work to tell them she'd be late, so why don't they go inside, and…

"You have enough of your own to worry about," she startles him back to reality. With a wave of her hand, she heads for the other side of the house, to another chore, and, she is out of sight before he can remind her about the refrigerator. Remind her about the refrigerator? It's a favor he's supposed to do for her. Shouldn't she be reminding him?

A wave of sadness rolls through his chest and head. He sees an overhead image of himself standing in the fenced-in quarter acre lot, a microscopic speck in a checkerboard of a billion squares. Then the wave recedes. Dissolves.

He thinks, Ted has it all wrong. None of these women think about anybody but themselves. Mary, Clara, even Viveca—absorbed in their own one-way lives, their minds closed to the lives of everybody else, by which, he means, mainly, closed to him.

He opens the side door of his own garage and pulls the string of the overhead fluorescent light fixture above the workbench. He should clear the work surface, sort these loose tools and bolts and pieces from his last Saturday project—what was it? But it's a good day for being outside, so maybe, instead, he'll back the car onto the apron and change the oil.

But as he pigeons his head against the driver's window to peer at the odometer, he calculates that he needs to drive another 1,200 miles before the next oil change is due. He repairs to the workbench and picks up an adjustable crescent wrench which he used, now he remembers, to remove the beater bar on Mary's vacuum last week after it became seized with some fibers from a throw rug. The wrench hangs on the second nail above his tool rack, above which hangs his fiberglass fishing rod, suspended horizontally on several nails along its six and a half foot span. That's what he should do, he thinks, drive to the lake and do some shore casting. It's really not too late to leave; he could drive down there, fish a little, stop at that Steak 'n Shake so he wouldn't have to have supper with Mary.

"Like, I know all about those fishing trips," Viveca had said during the office coffee break one morning. It had been a Friday, and Harry had asked the women about their weekend plans: "Sleeping in," Diana had said, and, "No idea," from Rosemary.

Viveca said she planned to go with a new 'friend' to Boogie Nights, one of those cavernous, strobe-lit dance halls modeled after the cinematically immortalized Studio 54 in New York. She'd spend Saturday afternoon getting her hair done.

"Why don't you forget fishing and bring your wife to the 'Nights?'" said Viveca.

"Ehm, very tempting," said Harry. "Let's see: a dark smoke-filled room full of twenty-year-olds, high decibel music, the Pet Boys singing 'Slap Your Bitch Up Side the Head.' You know what, Viveca, I think maybe I'll go fishing instead."

"Eewww, fishing?" said Diana. "You actually kill those things?"

"Not usually. I like searching for them, you know, fooling them. And then there's the surprise when you hook 'em. I don't usually keep them."

"I think he likes the smell," said Viveca, not even looking up. She had been focusing on her nails, spreading the fingers of her left hand, a spiral thread of blue smoke rising from the cigarette held in her right hand. She wore a yellow top, like a man's dress shirt, the top two buttons undone where Harry saw a pale blue vein roll taut and aslant just beneath the skin and down to the first fleshy furrow of cleavage and disappearing beneath the shirt. He raised his eyes and saw her looking right at him.

"My father used to tell my mom he was going 'fishing,' nearly every weekend," she said. Her eyes were slitted, accusing, either of her father or of Harry for being caught staring. "He took his rod, all right, but it never left the car, if you know what I mean."

That explains a lot, thought Harry.

"Sorry to hear that," said Harry.

"Forget about it," she said. "I love my mom, but she's a fucking witch. Impossible to live with."

"I thought you got along with her," said Harry.

She couldn't reply immediately, as she was holding her mouth open, using the flat of her thumb to trim the lip gloss, while she held a cigarette and a compact mirror in her other hand.

"Well, sure," said Diana. "You get along fine with Mother once you move out. Ain't that right, Viveca?"

"Newsflash," said Viveca, snapping the mirror shut with timed emphasis. She used to respond to things she thought obvious with a sarcastic, "Hello?" Then it was "Thank you" for several months, more groaned than spoken. "Newsflash" was her latest.

She picked up her make-up bag, stood up. She looked into Harry's eyes, touched the tip of her pink tongue to her upper lip as she slid her fingertips up and under her black mini-skirt either to smooth or adjust her panty hose, swiveled her hips tauntingly as Diana laughed and Rosemary rolled her eyes.

"Maybe that's what you need to do Harry, baby," she said as she sauntered around the table toward the door. She stopped behind Harry and tugged playfully on his right earlobe. She must have applied a fresh spray of perfume in the washroom, for its warm, lilac heaviness descended and engulfed his head as though he had entered a greenhouse. "Maybe Harry needs to leave 'Mommy,' too."

Diana's laugh convulsed her shoulders, and she stopped short, her quick over-the-shoulder look at Harry telling him all too well the nature of their regard for him. They could have been pubescent eighth graders shining on the school maintenance man.

That scene was from last month, and maybe Viveca was right; maybe he ought to leave Mary. Ted thinks so, too, yet Harry knows that Ted and a number of men and women who made an art out of leaving people, didn't seem much better off for it.

Of course, he had no sense that things could get better at home. She was different—they were different—from the two people who had remained lovers even after their son was born. Even through the crippling mortgage payments and used cars that didn't start in the winter and paycheck battles and grade school teachers that asked galling questions about their home life, through all of that, they still had maintained a romantic sanctuary—an escape, if only to their own bedroom, when she reverted to being the tallish, rangy brunette who would lose herself in his embrace, would abandon motherhood and decorum as she bit through his shoulder flesh in those satisfying moments of self-celebration and absorption and blood. Since the accident, she made even reminiscing about those times feel like some kind of sacrilege.

He may as well go fishing. If there is one thing he has learned, it is… to go fishing when you feel like going fishing. Brilliant, he thinks to himself.

Carrying the rod and tackle box out to the car, he looks at his watch and calculates the time to drive to Lake Michigan, fish a couple of hours, and drive back. He had stopped asking Mary to go after too many refusals, when she'd close her eyes and shake her head, doubtlessly thinking not of a blue lake, but of a sea of darkness and oblivion that had swallowed her child. He, however, felt drawn to it because the city's contagion was halted by its shore, by the sweet water wind that buffeted his face. And maybe because of the same thought which had kept her away, that the last living his boy had done was between the lake's silvery folds.

It had been his son, too, for crissake. But after six years he was tired of all her hurting, of her weakness, while her eyes and her silence accuse him of not caring, of loving less. Why can't she just take the hurt and compress it into a hard black ball of anger deep within, where it's hidden and manageable and, hell, even something strong?

He'd go fishing all right and be back a little after dark, soon enough to watch Mary fall asleep during the news. Or maybe she will have dozed before then, regenerating enough energy to stay up in bed for a change. Maybe if they had a glass of wine.

"Oh no you don't," came the voice from behind him. The warning familiar, the voice familiar; but the two didn't go together. He turned to see Clara with her hands on her hips. Not pulling weeds. Not moving.

"You fixin' to hang up your 'gone fishing' sign, mister, before keeping your promise?" She pronounced "promise" with a breathy first syllable, and ironic fricative—onomatopoetic—the word full of portent.

"You caught me, all right," he said.

"I declare," she said. "When Helen said we ought to hire the he-man next door for the job, who would have thought he'd try to sneak off?"

He-man. What Ted calls a come-on? Or it also could be another eighth grader patronizing the janitor. It's what these women do, tease to please the silly middle aged man, turning on all their charms, mainly because they bet his prostate makes it pretty safe.

He wheels slowly to face her. Hers a wide open smile, big teeth. Brow squinted and glistening in the sun. He remembers now that she was born in Alabama or North Carolina, somewhere down there. Not much trace of accent left, but some of the expressions remained.

"Any other time I'd say git—go fishin', enjoy; but that new fridge is coming, Harry. I can help you some, and I'd bet it would take only a few minutes."

"Famous last words," smiles Harry. Her smile flattens—he can't tell if in confusion or disappointment.

"Let's get her," he says. "I'll just go to my workshop and get the two wheel dolly and be right over."

"I'll be in the kitchen. Just walk in."

Standing in the middle of the workshop, he grasps his shirt at the top button and pulls it away from his collarbone, smells inside. He takes two pieces of Trident gum from the economy twenty pack he has kept on the windowsill, ever since his dentist told him it was a half way substitute for flossing. The red two-wheel cart hangs from a bicycle hook next to the door, but he hesitates before reaching for it. He recalls the advice Ted gave him for dealing with Viveca, to talk to a woman and pretend to listen hard. So he'd ask Clara some telling questions about herself. Not her garden or her new pair of shears, but, let's see, how long do you plan to live here and how many years have you been here, and was it because you suddenly discovered you were a lesbian that you split from your bridegroom after only two months?

On the way to her back door he feels a telltale misstep. Goddamn it, dog shit all right. His fault for interrupting her that she didn't finish the job. He went back and changed into his deck shoes, would probably have to throw the sneakers out—you could never get everything out of those deep treads.

She had told him to walk right in, but he knocks anyway. In all these years, he has never been inside his neighbor's house, nor either of them inside his. Just over-the-fence neighbors. Good fences make good neighbors. The second he violates the fence rule he springs a dog shit booby trap. What else is in store?

"Be there in a second," comes Clara's voice from somewhere else in the house. "Come on in."

The kitchen clean and bright, what you'd expect with two women living together. A thirteen inch television on top of the counter. But he would have expected a different house smell, soapy or flowery, instead of what he scents now. Something oily, perhaps smoked food. Oniony. But from yesterday or the day before. They obviously ate other things besides popcorn.

Clara emerges from the hallway and her scarf is gone. He wonders if she were in the bathroom, smelling under her own shirt. She looks young with her mane of hair stacked and bunched above the ponytail. But out of the sunlight her face is sterner, tired. He'd probably see shadows under her eyes, but her sunglasses remain on. Maybe there's some anxiety at this man filling up her kitchen, the first one in years.

"Had to cage the dogs," says Clara. "They're funny with strangers. I mean, you're not a stranger...."

"It's okay, I know," says Harry. "I'm a dog person. Your place, it's nice."

"Oh, thanks," she says, "but it's such a mess. Changing fridges."

"Yeah. A lot of work."

"Poor Helen. She takes care of most everything inside."

"I didn't see her today," he says, squirming inside at how this sounds. There's an extra second before she replies, and as she does, she looks over at the faded avocado Westinghouse with top and bottom doors open.

"She doesn't normally work Saturdays, but she had a meeting. A half day thing. I expect her soon. You think we need a third person?"

"What? No, I was just...let me slide the dolly over here. You have some tape or something for these doors?"

She brings him a roll of brightly colored red duct tape—what the hell would you use that for?—and they tape shut the doors and he slides the base of the cart beneath the refrigerator. As he reaches over the top to tip it onto the cart, she grasps an opposite corner. She holds her right hand against the olive colored freezer door, and he notices her neatly trimmed nails, unpainted, or else painted clear, and the thin delicate fingers arching in, pressing against the metal, a child's hand, really, in earnest effort. He looks at her face near his own hand on the Westinghouse's top, thought he saw a nervous flicker behind the brown tint of the sunglasses, her lips puckered in and tightly together. He feels something, he doesn't know, like when his kid was small and walked his bike the three miles from school with his pant leg caught in the chain.

"You know, Clara, I'd rather you not be behind the cart."

She nods, keeping her lips pursed, backing up, grateful, it seemed.

"Tell me what's the best way I can help you, Harry?"

Her hands are on her hips again, and he and she are suddenly two stevedores in collaboration and brotherhood—he could joke about anything really.

"You know, you shouldn't be making such an open-ended offer to a man," he says.

Hands still on her hips. She's smiling, but it may only be with her mouth. The sunglasses hide the way she takes this.

"If you can just hold the door open, we'll see if this guy will fit through the jambs," he says.

The refrigerator fits with an inch or two to spare on each side. He bumps it down the stoop without incident, but when he makes the turn to put it out on the street for the garbage men, he senses through his arms and the dolly's handles, the object's momentum and dangerous bulk flirting with a sidelong dive into Clara's Buick Regal. He stops—a hold-your-breath stop, hoping it's not too abrupt, and the Westinghouse leans back straight onto the cart. After he stands it straight by the curb, he slides the cart away and untapes the doors and then uses the red strips to tape them open. Clara is nowhere in sight.

He returns to his workshop and hoists the cart onto its appointed hanger. He can smell the befouled shoe in the workshop and goes back outside. Clara is not at the back door, either. He will go and load the rest of his gear....

"Oh, there you are," she says, holding her back door ajar. "I'd gone around the front and you had already skidoodled. Come up, Harry, and least-wise have a soda or something cool."

"Well, I suppose those fish will still be there," he says to no one as Clara disappears inside.

He targets her door but studies the terrain this time, no booby traps in his path; but he does spot the offending mass off to his right, lines and arrows from his Sears cross-trainer sole stenciled on the flattened brown plateau.

This time she opens the door as he arrives and motions for him to sit.

"Sorry I didn't help you out front, Harry, but this disgusting mess under the fridge couldn't set there another minute," she says.

She tears a paper towel from the under the cabinet dispenser and drops to one knee to swipe hard at yet one more stain where the fridge had rested, a stain Harry can't see. Maybe it's just a smear on the lens of her sunglasses. Or maybe it's a calculated move deriving from Ted's phonemes, as his eyes rest on the bronze arch of her back below the halter, a freckle to the left of her spine just above the waistline. More below? He inventories the colors: pink halter, white shorts, umber hair—Ted will want details.

"What can I get you?" she says. She's breathy after standing up.

"Anything diet," he says. Maybe he shouldn't say that. "You know, just some water is fine, Clara."

She stands on her tiptoes over a red and white cooler on the kitchen counter.

"Got orange juice. And Helen bought some Diet Mountain Dew. It's all ice cold. You sure?"

"Water's fine." She has seemed taller over the fence, he thinks.

She reaches in front with a glass of water and he thinks he smells coconuts. Shampoo? Sunblock?

He waits for her to sit, but she's back at the counter moving things in the cooler.

"That Westinghouse didn't look that old," he says.

"Helen bought it when she moved in. That's ten years."

She closes the cooler lid and leans her back against the counter edge, gripping the rim with her hands. She looks about her own kitchen, a woman who can't stand still. Harry senses that she wishes for the phone or doorbell to ring.

"And you?"

"Me?" She smiles as if awaiting a punchline.

"How long are you here?"

"A year after Helen."

"You moved up from where, Tennessee?"

"Georgia. After my divorce I moved here from Addison. You know where that is?"

"Oh, sure. And Addison. How'd you like it there?"

"What do you mean, Harry?"

"Did you like it? How long were you there?"

She looks at the floor and nods.

"You mean how long was I married, don't you?"

He shrugs his shoulders.

"It's okay; I don't mind. I used to, but it's been a long time."

When she doesn't continue, he takes a drink of water. This isn't going well. He starts to get up.

"I thought you wanted to hear about Stan?" she says.

"No. I'm sorry."

"Sit. I should be grateful that anyone cares to know, really."

Her mouth has shrunk to a pale rose. He can see her neck pulsing.

"I never really dated anybody else," she says. She seems to be forcing herself to look at him now, as though someone had told her, a psychotherapist, perhaps, that forthrightness was the best way to deal with it, even with a neighbor you barely know.

"He was the first man I loved. We were married in August. August 15th. It was September 23rd, a Thursday night, when I listened in on the kitchen phone while he spoke with his ex-girlfriend. It turned out 'ex' was a lie."

She efficiently condenses the facts. More calls, the initial confrontation with Stan, later revelations, dates, the separation, divorce lawyers. It reminds Harry of one of those timelines at the end of a chapter in his high school history book. Just the facts; the blood and gore skipped over, concealed behind her sunglasses.

"It might have been worse," says Harry. "You could have gone months, maybe years without knowing."

Her chin rises. She's thinking about this and he expects her assenting nod.

"No...that's the worst of it," a clutch in her voice.

He should hold her. Or just touch her. It's what people need, as when he and Mary sat in the hospital waiting room. He needed badly to feel her, to hang on. But she shrunk away. She said later it was because she hurt too much.

"I had been so hopeful," she says, "the 'blushing bride.'" Her hands leave the counter edge to clutch her opposite shoulders. She lowers her head and he can see her trembling now, but no tears. He rises from the table, touches her arm. She lets him. He puts his hand on her other arm. She's letting him comfort her. Should her kiss her? Ted says it's all in the timing.

As she looks up at his face, her sunglasses have slid down on her nose so that he can finally see her eyes—pale green. Mossy, but not teared up. Dull. Ten years of betrayal having leeched away the light. And something else in them.

"I didn't even get a chance to have illusions," she says.

When she speaks into his face is when he catches it, a smell of decay like spoiled meat. The mephitic source of what he had smelled when he earlier entered the house.

Then he realizes what the other thing is in her eyes, a pathetic animal kind of thing. Flat. Disconnected. What he has seen in a fish's eyes when it's been foul hooked in the gills instead of in the jaw. Or in a bird's eyes when it can't fly off. He has found them in the yard; a broken wing, a missing foot. You can almost never save them. Any injury fatal.

Viveca is in a bad mood on Monday morning, and Rosemary and Diana talk small and careful. Her legs are crossed as she smokes a cigarette hotly and with no apparent pleasure.

"How about let's get a drink at Alph's after we're outta here?" she says. She flashes one look at the other two women. Harry could be invisible. Diana flips uneasy eyes at Rosemary without moving her head.

"Sure," says Diana. "Sounds good."

Viveca doesn't respond, but she shifts in the folding chair, and now the crossed leg is swinging side to side. A rhythm of thought. Some perceived offense by her boyfriend? Some slight.

"What about you?"

She is not looking at him, but the other girls turn to Harry to wait for an answer.

"You gonna have a drink or are you too pussy-whipped?" Viveca says. She flashes him a glance which he thinks is a challenge, but he can't tell. She is wearing some ensemble of silver and blue eye make-up that is probably the latest rage—Star Trek vogue, or something—but it gives her an odd, hard to read expression. Harry is surprised to see the beginnings of a run in her stocking, a three inch gash rising from the instep of her high heeled shoe.

Were he to join them, he knows what the evening would entail. The secret thrill of wading into the dim scarlet light of Alph's lounge as a companion to three young women. Conversation, liquor, careless words. The illusion of closeness. The reality masked by laughter that comes too quickly. Masked by music. By the astigmatic focus sped by rum and coke. By Alph's smoky haze. And as soon as one looks at her watch, they would all gulp their drinks and scuttle their separate ways, armored anew against tomorrow.

"Not tonight," says Harry. "I'm going home."

Diana exhales smoke in an I-told-you-so hiss. But Viveca looks at him in interested silence, for she must hear it—a note from him that she's not used to, while Harry thinks about the cascade of time that has been wearing away the last chance to fix a broken wing. A slim chance to save her. Save himself.

BREAK

—Tom Montgomery-Fate

Out my window,
after you called, a lone,
wounded house wren,
four ounces of blood and feather,
tried to land on a
quivering black limb
near the top of a maple tree.

He hit the moving target
but couldn't hold; fell
like a startled promise:
two seconds of beating
bits of empty blue
into hopelessness
as the earth soared up to catch
and crush him.

Tiny, lesser-known, essential bones
snap all the time:
while the office coffee machine drips
and honking cars idle on the expressway,
while you rinse crusted diapers or try

to spoon mashed bananas into your daughter's
closed mouth, while you frantically search
for a wad of lost keys, a billfold,
and the delicate, grounding
touch of memory;

and late at night,
while Jay Leno is laughing and you are lying
next to someone you don't know
after twelve years of mending breaks,
reimagining flight,
trying to find a place
to land.

SAWDUST AND CAMELLIAS

—Daisy Lin Shapiro

My mother is tearing our house down with her bare hands. And she's doing a pretty quick job of it, too, for someone who has never lifted a hammer before. Last week she hacked all the furniture in half, and yesterday she dismantled the front door. Neither Dad nor I saw this coming. I mean, it began so innocently.

About three months ago my mom asked for a subscription to *Martha Stewart Living* for her fortieth birthday. This surprised me; it had been a long time since she had shown much interest in sprucing up the house. In fact, she hadn't shown much enthusiasm for anything, it seemed to me, in quite a while. I was excited that she was taking on a new hobby, and I paid for the magazines myself, with money I earned baby-sitting. Little did I know, something had been set in motion that would soon spin way out of control.

I should have seen it right off, in the way she tore into that first issue. Within hours of its arrival on our doorstep, she was on the phone, at the mall, ordering Oaxacan floor tiles, antique doorknobs, and wallpaper of green lamé with red Chinese filigree.

All this was quite a shock. You have to understand, for years our house has looked exactly the same. In the living room a brown velour sofa with white doilies on the armrests sat pinned to one wall, guarded by a dark, beefy coffee table bearing a dried flower arrangement. Leaning against the opposite wall was the mute piano that no one ever played. It was not a big room, and the tan carpet and drapes gave it a dark and sparse feel, like the inside of a hollow tree trunk. In the adjoining dining room, a china cabinet displayed anemic looking cups and saucers, a set that Mom and Dad received as a wedding gift. The dining table was maple.

"Sturdy. Solid," my dad had said with an air of pride. "It has extra leafs to insert, if we have a big party."

I don't remember us having any big parties. Our family portrait hung on the wall above the table. We posed for the shot at a photo studio in town. Mom was sitting down in front, wearing a yellow floral dress, Dad was standing to her left, dressed in a suit, with his hand resting softly on her shoulder like a dead mink, a gesture I've never seen him do in real life. I stood next to Dad and directly above Mom, smiling nervously in the scratchy lace dress Mom picked out for me. Behind us was a neutral grey background, a faux marbled wall panel. That was the way things were, and it seemed as unchangeable as Mom's silence at the dinner table and Dad's corny jokes, but I was wrong.

On the surface, nothing had changed. Dad was working as the sales manager at a plastics company in the city, and Mom worked part-time as a bookkeeper for the Hallmark store at the mini-mall on the main boulevard. She drove me to school every day, cooked dinner, cleaned the house, and never lost her temper—not once have I seen Dad and her fight. Dad says that's because we're a harmonious family unit. Every cog performs its proper function, so even if one cog decides to act up and insist on taking a drum class with its friend Erika, the other cogs just keep humming along cheerfully, forcing the disobedient cog to be quiet and keep up. You can't argue with someone who won't argue back.

As my reward for being agreeable, Mom took me shopping at the mall, and some weekends Dad asked me to go fishing with him. Once, when we were in the middle of the lake, Dad told me that years ago Mom had dropped out of college to come west with some guy, and when he dumped her she got a job at the plastics company and that's where she met Dad. He said he knew right off she would make a good wife. She was a good sport, he said, and she laughed at his jokes. Mom never went fishing with us. She hated the sight of the soft fleshy worms squirming on the hook.

The backyard was where Mom liked to spend her free time, tending to her little patch of green. Nothing serious there, just a few annuals and ferns. The real centerpiece was this camellia bush she planted years ago when I was little. She told me she got the seeds from her mother, who took it from a camellia bush that grew in the back of her house in Louisiana. I met my grandmother once, years ago, and I don't remember much about her except that she had a missing tooth. Just like me, only I lost my front tooth after I fell while roller-skating. She came to visit us but she didn't stay long. Dad called her the dragon lady and said she was a bad cook and always took over the kitchen.

To Dad, a good meal was straightforward; you got your meat, your potatoes, and a side of vegetables maybe.

"I like to taste my food," he said. "But your grandmother, boy, when she came over she started cooking all this fancy dancy stuff... I remember this one dish, a bunch of stuff mixed together—I think it was called "etoofay" or something French sounding like that. But I tell you it tasted like a spicy mud stew. And the fish? As black as charcoal, wouldn't touch it." He chuckled with pride; a man who knows what he likes.

"I like her food," Mom said quietly.

"Well, of course, you liked it, honey. You were raised on that stuff, but just keep it away from me. No, thank you!"

My grandmother never did come back to visit; she passed away shortly after. Mom tended her garden very carefully. She didn't pay much attention to the few droopy plants in the house, but her little patch in the backyard she watered, fertilized, and weeded faithfully. The camellia especially thrived and it grew big and strong and beautiful. Every spring it flowered feverishly, with voluptuous hot pink blossoms weighing down the branches. Mom liked to smell the sweet blooms. One time I saw her alone in her patch and watched from between my curtains as she plucked a brilliant blossom and tucked it behind her ear. She leaned back and swayed dreamily with the breezes, carried away by the scent and color of another time and place. That look on her face. I'd never seen it before. It was not so much a look of happiness or even contentment. I just couldn't pin it down, all I knew was that I had never had a look like that on my face before.

I prayed guiltily that lightning would strike down the camellia bush and that I would grow in its place and be watered by Mom, and bloom exuberantly, unabashedly, and not have her tell me in her cool and patient voice to behave.

One day last winter I came home and found Mom lying face down on the living room floor, tearing violently at the brown shag carpet. "How could you?!" She was fuming at the carpet, tears gushing down her face, her legs kicking. "You killed it. How could you kill it?!" She was flinging pieces of the carpet yarn up into the air. "Stranger! You are a stranger to me!" she said fiercely to the carpet. I felt my blood turn into ice water, and slowly backed out of the living room and walked down the hall into the family room. Dad was sitting on the couch, pretending to read the sports section. The flimsy pages were quivering in his grip like dying moth wings.

"Dad, what's going on with Mom?" I whispered.

"Oh, she's just upset 'cause I cut down her camellia bush."

I drew in a sharp breath. "Why did you do that, Dad?"

"Well, I was building our deck back there and...um...," he stammered, "it was in the way. The wood was all measured out and it was going to take up more room than I expected, and, well, I needed that corner." He shook his head and shrugged.

"I don't know why she's so upset. I mean, it's just a plant, she can always go buy another plant and start her garden on the other side of the deck. Why don't you go talk to her, Katie? Tell her we'll get another plant for her."

I walked back to the living room. Mom was moaning now, her face buried in the carpet.

"Mom," I said. "Please don't cry." My voice was quivering.

"I hate this house," she mumbled under her breath. "It's an ugly place! This is not my house!"

"It is your house, Mom, it is! Please!" I took her hand and held it. She looked up at me, her face swollen and blotched pink with emotion, bits of carpet fiber stuck to her cheeks like huge freckles.

"Look," I said. "If you don't like the house, you can redecorate it. That'll make it all better I bet."

"Yes." She seized upon the thought, wiping her face. "Maybe you're right."

"Just a simple makeover, like in the magazines."

"Yes. A makeover." Mom got up from the floor, straightened the front of her dress, smoothed her hair, wiped her nose, and rearranged her face. Eyes withdrawn, cheeks smoothed out, lips set vaguely horizontal. The face of a cog. "I think it's time for you to do you homework, Katie."

"Um...I have a book report due tomorrow," I offered. "On *Great Expectations*. It's a really long book, but I read the whole thing," I lied.

We walked into the kitchen and Mom started to wash the dishes. I could tell she wasn't really listening to me so I excused myself and went up to my room. I took my favorite dresses and skirts out of the closet and tried them on in front of the mirror. From my window I could see Dad in the backyard, practicing his golf swing.

We never spoke about that incident afterwards and then the Martha Stewart magazines started coming and Mom was suddenly energized. Soon, she began making a few things for the house, like storage boxes that roll underneath the bed. It was pretty impressive. She built a flat wide box with some wood planks and screwed rolling casters in all four corners. She even sewed on a cloth handle that hung over the side so that you could pull the cart out from under the bed more easily. Then she made lampshades out of paper shopping bags and painted fallen maple leaves on them. Green leaves, red leaves, brown leaves. After that, she sewed new drapes for every room in the house. All the sweeping valances and taffeta looked so dramatic it made me feel like I was in a movie where people spoke with European accents.

At first I was relieved that she had something to distract her, but then the pace just kept escalating. Last month, she completely revamped my room in a nautical theme. I don't know where she managed to find a fishnet, maybe she scored it from the fish and chips place down the street, but she hung it over one corner of the room like a huge spider web, then stuck a plastic starfish and lobster up there. She even found one of those wheels that steer boats, with twelve wood spokes coming out all around it, and set it on top of my dresser. My butterfly blanket was stuffed in the closet and replaced with a mermaid bedspread.

"See, honey," she said, mounting a blue marlin above my bed. "This is just like those model homes we saw, each room with a theme." I told her I liked my new room, even though I never much cared for the ocean. It reminded me of the summer I got caught in a riptide and the lifeguard had to come after me with a life preserver.

She decorated the master bedroom á la Louis XVI, with baroque chandeliers, gilded mirrors and pastel wall tapestries showing impossibly quaint scenes of corseted maidens picnicking under the shade of oak trees. Dad, trying to be a sport about it, joked, "That's great honey, but don't you think it's a little much? It's starting to look a lot like a bordello around here!" I laughed obligingly, but Mom did not. She tore out the carpet to reveal wood floors and set to refinishing them. We woke up to the insistent whine of the sander. I opened my bedroom door and clouds of sawdust invaded my lungs and coated me like a powdered donut.

Pretty soon Mom started putting little place cards with our names on the dinner table. She served us multi-course meals on our fine china. Warm spinach salad with goat cheese, candied walnuts, and champagne vinaigrette. Curried scallop canapés. Duck liver paté and aspic. Dad turned to me, a lace napkin tucked into his collar, with a panicked look. He was a man used to his routine. This was not routine.

Then last Friday night we were lounging in the family room, the only room in the house Mom hadn't totally redecorated yet. (Brown leather couch with gold studs in the arms; oak TV console and matching bookshelves, looking dowdy next to new silk wallpaper and rococo drapes.) Suddenly, Mom pointed at the wall, next to the TV. There was a smallish black smudge on the soft green silk. "Where did that come from?" she demanded.

"Oh, um, I think I smacked a fly dead there yesterday," Dad said, barely looking up from his *Fish and Stream*.

"You can't really see it," I said, eyeing Mom apprehensively.

She frowned as she left the room and came back with a damp rag. She started to dab the fly guts gently with the rag. It was a stubborn stain. She rubbed a little harder and when it still wouldn't come out, she got some liquid cleaner and sprayed and wiped the area around it. Only now there was an ugly water stain on the wall. Exasperated, Mom brought down a blow dryer, plugged it into the wall, and started blowing the spot with hot air.

"Hey! I'm trying to watch my show here!" Dad shouted above the din of the dryer.

"You can watch it in the bedroom," Mom said firmly. Dad, sensing her pique, retreated and slumped away.

After a few minutes she turned off the dryer. Not only was the stain still there, but the entire area around it had turned a mottled brown, a sickly ochre color. And the room reeked of burnt paint.

"Shit!" she said. It was strangely thrilling to hear her curse.

She rummaged under the kitchen sink and came back with a flat edged scraper and started grating the wall with it, all the while muttering under her breath, "Smashing flies on Chinese silk! Barbarian!" Then she turned and thrust the scraper at me, "Katie, come help me."

I took the scraper with cold palms and started working on the wall, shredding the wallpaper slowly into lime coconut sprinkles.

Mom shooed me out of the way impatiently after a few minutes and peeled the entire sheet of wallpaper down from the wall, revealing a water stain the size of a basketball. Mom turned pale. She ran to the attic and came back with a chainsaw.

"We'll have to cut it out and replace the drywall. I've seen Martha Stewart do this in the magazines," she said.

She turned on the saw and Vroom! The metal teeth of the saw chomped into the wall. The whole house shook and a torrent of drywall and plaster rained down on my head. Dad ran downstairs, beer bottle in hand, and yelled, "What the hell is going on around here?!"

"I hate this house, I hate this house. It's ugly. Ugly!" Mom shouted and now she was slashing at the wall with the saw.

Dad exploded, "Well, now this has gone too far! You stop this minute, I say. Stop!" He held his hands up to his temples, "I can't stand this anymore!" He stormed out to the RV parked out front and slammed the door shut.

Mom just kept sawing. She sawed across the entire wall, cutting picture frames, paintings, clocks, bookcases and new curtains in half, stripping away the thin white wall to reveal the bare wood supports underneath, the black lining of the outer wall, the snaky wires that crept in between the crevices like blood vessels.

The next day she sawed into the furniture, cutting the couches, chairs, tables, beds into neat pieces as though she were cutting a pie. The rest of the week she concentrated on the doors. She didn't stop with the front door; she took down closet doors, bathroom doors, bedroom doors, screen doors, shower doors.

Now I'm watching her sitting on the left half of the living room couch. Feathers, foam, nails, wires, plaster, wood are everywhere. She is covered in sweat and chunks of the wall are in her hair. She surveys the room with satisfaction. "That's more like it," she says.

I run to my room and unhook the blue marlin above my bed. It has a long thorn growing out of its nose. I hand it over to Mom. She smiles at me and then takes a big hammer and shatters the dead fish into a million shiny brittle pieces. We're stunned into silence by the force of the moment.

Then suddenly she starts to laugh, big guffaws exploding from deep within, and she powers up the chainsaw and cuts into the wall all the way through to the other side of the cheap stucco, in the shape of a circle. I kick at the circle and it falls out like a lid of a manhole. I see the green of the lawn out front. I see cars driving past the house. I see the families in the cars staring at me through the hole in our house. I see the nervousness in their eyes. I crawl out of the hole and wave at them. They keep looking at me and I know that they are confused by the look on my face: the look of release.

THE GIFT
whangai hau: feeding the spirit

──Peter Meinke

The gift grows in the forest
green and gold in the spotted light
of the towering silver cypress
the twisted mangrove

the gift moves toward the empty place:
you moved toward me

When it is full
loved by snake and deer
the hunters come and cup it in their hands:
full they pass it on to the beaded priests

you are a gift of nature:
it is the nature of gifts to move on

In the light
of the one perfect moon
the priests return it to the forest
where it grows again

ANOTHER SON

—Michele Weber Hurwitz

I am pitching to my son on this hot August afternoon. We play on a long stretch of lawn on the side of the house, he and I. It is thick and green and my toes squeeze the grass.

"That was not a good pitch," he tells me madly, with that little boy shake of his head.

"Sam." I look across at him, red-faced and sweaty. I pitch it again. It wasn't a good pitch because he didn't hit it. When he does connect, he somehow manages to hit the balls so that they disappear in bushes, hide in treetops. We find some of them. He hates when he misses, and after he swings the bat at several pitches in a row and the balls fall at his feet and I know his arms are starting to hurt, he tells me he wants to go in for a Kool-Aid.

"I love you a million," he tells me that night from his bed.

"I love you more."

"Will you still love me when you die?"

"I will always love you, Sam."

"Are you in the ground when you die?"

"Some people are," I say.

"Can you move when you die?"

I look at his face. The smooth, still-baby skin, but a face now with edges of something else. "No," I tell him, becoming tired. "You can't move." I pull up his blanket. "Listen, you and I have a lot of years to live and love each other. Let's not worry about dying, okay?"

His brown eyes look up at me earnestly from the bottom bunk. He turns on his side, his face to the wall. "G'night, Mom."

My grandmother lost a son. Not in the way of being dead, in the way of being gone. He left one day, drove from Chicago to Las Vegas, and stopped there, and over the years, had less and less to do with being a son.

Late at night, her phone rings and someone is there. She hears breathing. She swears it is him. Joe, her boy. She says he's checking to see if she's still alive. She must think this so she can believe he still cares, in his own strange way. After all, he's been gone more years than he was with her.

I have a daughter, too, but things are different with her. She is right there, talking, telling, soaking me up all the time. Watching me put on makeup. Asking endless questions from the bathtub.

But, Sam. He is harder to reach, easier to please. He comes with me to the grocery store, patiently walking the aisles with me, standing at the checkout line, so we can stop at the row of prize machines at the exit. He is feverishly collecting miniature baseball hats. I scramble for a quarter, because he needs to get the Cubs.

He is a predictable boy, filled with a sweetness I cannot explain. He eats the same food for lunch every day. He still cries if his sister happens to smack him, and he does not hit her back.

When Joe was young, my grandmother tells me, he used to slip in the narrow spaces between apartment buildings where they lived on the West Side, and hide from her. She would be diligently walking home, from the laundry, or the store—there were always so many chores to do—and here Joe was playing games. She was just becoming angry: "This isn't funny, now, Joe, do you hear me?"—when he would jump out, laughing.

"I was right here," he would say, and throw his arms around her waist. I don't think she laughed.

It was complicated. Joe was told by his aunts on the day of his father's funeral that he was the man of the family now, that he'd have to take care of his mother and sister. He was twelve. So he went outside and got in a fight with some neighborhood kid. They watched from the apartment, all of them sitting Shiva, the aunts, the uncles, my grandmother, my mother.

One of the uncles wanted to intervene. "Don't you go out there, Jack," my grandmother said. Joe's nose was bloody.

"Don't you go out there," she said again. "He's got to fight his own battles." They sat at the front window, the row of faces, and watched until it stopped.

I arrive at Sam's school to pick him up and spy him on the playground. Another boy is bouncing a ball on Sam's head. I sit in my car and grip the steering wheel, fighting every urge to run out there, grab the ball and yell at the kid, and cradle Sam in my arms.

When the fight was over, no one could find Joe. Later in the night, the aunts and the uncles took their overcoats and hats off the bed and left, in two's and three's, and my grandmother found her son in the front closet. He had wrapped himself in his father's heavy brown overcoat and was sitting on the floor. She picked him up, with the coat, and the dried-blood face, and put him to bed that way.

Sam wakes in the morning and comes to sit in my lap. I kiss his nose and hold him as tightly as he lets me until his sister says, "C'mon, Mom, I'm hungry." She is dressed. Sam is in his pajamas, a tuft of hair sticking straight up in the air. These are the times he still looks like my baby.

"Where's Dad?" he asks me.

"He left for work already," I tell him.

"Did the Cubs win?" he wants to know, rubbing his eyes.
"You can call Dad at work and ask him," I say.

There were terrible years after, for the three of them, my grandmother, a widow at thirty-nine, and her two children. My grandmother got a job working as a cashier in her cousin's restaurant. She had finished school only up to eighth grade. My mother, who was older, survived intact somehow. She packed the school lunches, made sure her brother did his homework. She dressed up, lied about her age and got a job after school to help bring some money in.

I want to ask my grandmother when things began to fall apart for Joe. Did she see it happening? Were there any signs? But all I can ask is if she still thinks about Joe.

"Sometimes. Not as much," she says truthfully. "It's a long time."

"But he's your son," I pursue, "your child."

"Just a minute, now," she says, wiping the corners of her mouth with her finger and thumb. "He was the one. He went away, you know. What could I do?"

I look out the window of her apartment, and then look back at her face, heavy with wrinkles from years in the sun with only water and baby oil.

"Gram, I put the milk and the cheese in your fridge, the rest of the groceries are on the counter," I say.

"I went out there to visit him," she reminds me.

"I know."

She gets up to see me to the door. "He was the one," she says again.

My mother writes him letters, once a year, to an address she has in Las Vegas, but he never writes back. She tells him of weddings and births, of divorces and deaths.

I have imagined that I will slip into a cab one day in Las Vegas—

because that's what he does, he drives a cab—and it will be him behind the wheel. I have imagined what I might say, how he might give a second glance in the rearview mirror, thinking I look familiar in some way he can't quite put his finger on.

I have one clear memory of this elusive uncle of mine, who slipped away from the rest who knew him. He was surrounded by too many women, my mother thinks. The aunts. His mother. Even herself. They made him crazy, she thinks. Or he just wasn't strong enough to come out of it.

But what I remember. A tall man, black hair. Playing football in a park with me when I was about eight. New houses. New trees with leaves already lost. A very blue sky. October, maybe. My hair blowing across my face, in my mouth. The hard scrape of the ball against my hand.

There are still more days of summer, and Sam and I are out again, on the lawn. He stands close, right up to me, and measures himself. "I am up to here," he shows me.

I smile and look down at him. "Ready?" I say.

"I'm going to give you another chance, Mom," he says, swinging his bat. "Will you pitch it good today?"

Another chance, yes.

I'll try my best, Sam.

MUSE

—Brooke Bergan

How I hate this silk dress
That conceals a poet
—Yu Hsuan-chi (ca. 843-868 A.D.)

In China the winter plum blossom
whitens toward a pale sky, each chill
petal stung with falling snow, sharp
white against soft white, fades into
translucent flesh, crystal on crystal
snow buds on budding trees in China
when the plum blooms each winter and
everyone is again surprised. Poets

write of this, plum blossoms in snow
their surprise, familiar and strange
"You should not take it for granted,"
wrote Lu You. And Chu Shu-chen, not
expecting their "cold perfume" this
snowy night adorns herself, her love
with white blossoms—and writes.

MY FATHER'S SHOES

a screenplay

──Marco Benassi

Sound of Nailer.

GINO (*voice over*): There's really not much you need to know.

Sound of Nailer.

> TITLE: A Film by Marco Benassi

> > Black

Interior: Shoe Shop (Flashback)

Tight shot of nailer—fades to slow motion.

GINO (*voice over*): This is the nailer. It puts the nails in the shoe.

Gino, eight, watches as Frank, thirty-five, works on a contraption known as the "nailer."

> > Black

Interior: Shoe Shop/Counter Area

Frank, sixty, robust, closes the cash register, puffs wearily on a cigar.

GINO *(voice over):* This is Frank. Frank Fortunato. My Step-pop. When I was a kid...

Dissolve

Flashback: Close on Little Gino's eyes.

GINO *(voice over):* ...it seemed like every guy on the north side of Chicago came to Frank's shop to fix their shoes. These days...

Interior: Shoe Shop/Back Room—Morning

Gino works on the drawing of a unique gym shoe with an oversized heel.

Close up of the drawing.

GINO *(voice over):* ...unless you need a special shoe, hardly anybody fixes their shoes anymore. They just throw 'em away.

Black

Drawing of Gino's Mother.

GINO *(voice over):* This is my Ma. She used to say there's magic in the shoe shop. *(Pause)* She's dead now.

Dissolve

Interior: Shoe Shop/Back Room—Morning

Gino puts down the shoe he's working on and picks up an Italian translation book.

GINO: *Io sono Gino.* (Subtitle: I am Gino)

Title: My Father's Shoes

Interior: Shoe Shop/Counter Area—Later

A boy, seven, sits in the waiting area, a metal crutch next to him. Gino fits a unique gym shoe onto the boy's foot. The boy's mother, thirty, hovers over him. At the front counter, Frank talks on the phone while puffing on a big cigar.

FRANK: Nine-thirty to six. We're always open.

Frank hangs up the phone and begins to spray stretch oil on a black dress shoe.

MOTHER *(to boy):* Sit still now.

She moves to Frank at the counter.

MOTHER: Polish?

FRANK: Stretch oil. It's alcohol. People get older, their feet get puffy. They get sore. They can't walk. So we stretch 'em. We do whatever you want.

GINO *(to boy):* Tight?

The boy shakes his head.

MOTHER: Your Gino's a saint, Mr. Fortunato. I mean that. A real saint.

FRANK: The way business is around here, we need a saint.

Gino walks to the counter and places the boy's old shoes in front of Frank.

GINO *(to Frank):* Pop, are you gonna take me to the airport or do you want, maybe, I should call a cab?

Frank lifts the receiver from the phone and holds it in front of Gino's face.

FRANK: I don't close for nobody.

Gino walks into the back room.

MOTHER *(to Frank):* How much do I owe you?

FRANK: Twenty-five.

He looks at the boy in the chair playing with his crutch.

FRANK: Twenty. Make it twenty.

She reaches into her purse.

Frank hangs up the phone, then lifts the boy's pair of old shoes. He hesitates for a moment, looking at them carefully.

Magical music.

FRANK: Don't worry about him.

MOTHER: I'm sorry. What's that?

FRANK: Your boy, I see good things for him. Real good. You worry, it only makes things worse.

The boy joins his mother at the counter. She smiles, a bit confused.

MOTHER: Thanks.

Frank puts the shoes in a bag and hands it to her. She turns to leave. Frank goes to the cash register, pushes in the drawer and puffs on his cigar.

Black

Interior: Shoe Shop/Back Room—Later

Gino washes his hands with soap at the sink.

FRANK *(off screen):* This broad, she doesn't want to pay 'til Saturday. She always busts my balls. Off the boat, to make it worse. She thinks we're all shoemakers, we're not businessmen.

GINO: I called a cab, Pop, so you don't gotta close the shop.

Frank is at the refrigerator. He closes the door, turns around and notices Gino's suitcase on the table.

FRANK: How can you do this to me? What about bowling?

GINO: Caesar.

Gino removes his worker's smock and hangs it on the shirt rack.

FRANK: Caesar?

GINO: Get Caesar. It's just one week.

FRANK: Caesar? With his hook? Not even for a joke.

GINO: Get Mickey.

FRANK: So, you really think you're gonna find your "real" father? You ain't gonna find *coo cootz*. I think you've been watching too much of that

Jenny Craig.

GINO: Jenny Jones, Pop.

Gino picks up his suitcase and sets it on the table.

FRANK: Yeah, well, whatever. So, you find him, big deal. What are you gonna do? Kill him?

GINO: Look, we talked about this before....

Gino sits and begins to remove his work shoes.

FRANK: I only wanna say one thing: thank God your mother's dead and not here to hear this.

Frank twists a shoetree into a red pump.

GINO: You know, I think, maybe, maybe Ma, she would have understood.

FRANK: So you're gonna meet the great Peppino Sorrentino? You don't like bein' a Fortunato?

Gino puts the suitcase next to his chair and begins to change his shoes.

GINO: Ma said his family, they got money; maybe they own some kind of meat factory or something.

FRANK: Meat? You don't even like meat. I think you're crackin' up. You know, you ain't even been to Wisconsin by yourself. Yer gonna get lost.

GINO: Pop, we need help.

FRANK: We don't need help from nobody!

Frank sits. After a long moment...

FRANK: What you do with shoes, Gino, is an art. You gotta great gift.

GINO: Gift? If fixing shoes is a gift, then I think that maybe I wanna give it back, Pop.

FRANK: What God gives you, you can't give back. You gotta take it and that's it. And shut up! I don't wanna talk about it no more!

Frank turns the shoetree frantically; the strap on the shoe snaps off. He slams it down on the table.

GINO: Pop, I'm thirty-three years old next month. Tell me. Tell me what the fuck great gift God gave me? (*Beat*) God didn't give me this gift, Pop—you did.

Upset, Gino slams one of his shoes on the table.

GINO: I think we should sell the shop!

Frank raises Gino's shoe from the table and stares at it for a long moment.

Magical music.

FRANK: So, maybe, maybe I'll call Caesar.

Interior: Shoe Shop—Flashback

Close on the Cutter.

Little Gino watches Frank trim a sole on the machine.

GINO *(voice over):* This is the cutter. It trims the sole or the heel of the shoes.

Dissolve

Interior: An Italian Bus—Day

Gino rides alone on the bus.

GINO *(voice over):* If you would have asked me right then, I would have told you I fixed my last shoe. *(Beat)* I loved Frank and I knew he missed Ma, too. But Frank was never big on ever tryin' anything different.

Exterior: A City Street, Guarcino, Italy—Same

From the bus, Gino encounters the ancient, Medieval village of Guarcino, carved into a mountainside.

GINO *(voice over):* Truth is, I'm not sure what I was looking to find in Guarcino.

Close up of Gino.

Exterior: Switchback on the Edge of Town—Same

Gino exits the bus.

GINO *(voice over):* Maybe I thought he owed me. Maybe I just wanted to see the life he lived. The shoes he wore. Maybe I just wanted to see what he looked like.

Gino crosses a piazza featuring a busy vegetable stand, then stares at the piece of paper in his hand.

Exterior: Town Street—Same

Gino looks up at an old woman in a window.

The woman meets his gaze then pulls shut the window.

Exterior: Street in the Old Sector—Same

Gino appears in a maze of walkways. A group of children run past him. He begins in one direction, stops, then returns in the same direction from which he came.

Exterior: A House—Day

Finally, he knocks on a door....

A large man, sixty, grey hair, opens the door.

MAN: *Cosa c'é?*

GINO: *Io sono Gino.*

MAN: *Chi Gino?*

GINO: Peppino Sorrentino?

Gino looks carefully at the man, his eyes beginning to water.

MY FATHER'S SHOES

The man holds Gino's face.

Freeze-frame.

GINO *(voice over):* So this was my father.

MAN: No.

The man shuts the door in Gino's face.

Exterior: Frank's Shoe Shop—Later

Mr. Mills, fifty, enters the shop. He's a hurried man, dressed in a dark suit and a fedora. In his hand is a maroon leather briefcase.

Interior: Shoe Shop/Counter—Later

Mr. Mills talks to Frank, who is behind the counter. Frank closes the cash register drawer and lights a cigar.

MR. MILLS: You said it yourself, Frank. The Chinese, they fucked up the shoe business. People don't fix their shoes anymore, they throw 'em away.

A police siren sounds in the street.

MR. MILLS: Boy, this neighborhood has changed. Am I right, Frank?

Mr. Mills takes a mangled black dress shoe from his briefcase and places it on the counter.

FRANK: What's with this?

MR. MILLS: My dog.

FRANK: I know it's a dog job.

MR. MILLS: Every place on this block is a bad check away from goin' under. Frank, look, was there ever a better place to get a hammer than Gus's? Forget about it. Capone used to buy his tools at Gus's. He waited too late, too long to sell, Frank. You know what he got? *Coo cootz.* Nothin'.

Frank picks up the shoe.

MR. MILLS: You know what they opened up there, Frank?

FRANK: What?

Frank focuses more closely on the shoe.

Magical music.

MR. MILLS: A water shop. Have any idea what they sell there?

FRANK: Water.

MR. MILLS: No, Frank, water. You believe it? Water for your heart. Water for your balls. Water for this. Four dollars for a bottle a water. Frank, Frank, listen to me. I got a guy who's looking to buy. So what do you think?

FRANK: I think you got problems with your dog.

MR. MILLS: Frank, there's just no magic left in this place.

FRANK: Your dog don't like you. What do you lock 'im up there? What do you yell at this dog?

MR. MILLS *(loudly):* Forget the damn dog, Frank. I got some papers. I just want you to take a look....

Mr. Mills starts to open his briefcase. Frank stares more closely at the shoe.

FRANK: You got back trouble.

MR. MILLS: What?

FRANK: Back trouble.

MR. MILLS: Yeah, I got a little. Here and there, but...

FRANK: You see the heel on one side? No good.

Exterior: A street in the Old Sector of Guarcino—Same

Gino walks down an ancient staircase. Two men stare at him from doorways.

Gino checks his piece of paper and moves on.

Interior: Shoe Shop/Counter—Same

Frank, holding Mr. Mills's briefcase, is in front of the counter.

FRANK *(demonstrating):* What ya gotta do is this. Change hands every twenty steps. Back and forth. Like a dance. Back and forth....

MR. MILLS: What are you now, my chiropractor?

Frank hands the briefcase back to Mr. Mills and returns behind the counter.

FRANK: Not even for a joke. You can learn a lot from a man's shoes.

Frank lifts Mr. Mills's shoe from the countertop. Puzzled, he examines the stitching around the toe.

MR. MILLS: Frank, maybe you just don't understand the kind of money I'm talkin' about here.

Magical music.

Bingo! Frank, smiling, suddenly understands.

FRANK: You don't wear your seat belt, do you?

MR. MILLS *(still focused on his pitch):* I've got a little flexibility....

FRANK: How many kids you got?

FRANK & MR. MILLS *(simultaneously):* Three.

FRANK: You got three kids. *(Beat)* Wear your seat belt. *(Beat)* I'm serious, here.

Frank rips out the receipt and hands it to Mr. Mills, who is a bit confused. In turn, Mr. Mills takes out a business card and gives it to Frank.

MR. MILLS: So am I, Frank. So am I. Just think about it. It's all I'm asking you to do. Just think about it.

Mr. Mills exits.

Exterior: Shoe Shop—Same

Mr. Mills exits the shop, changing his suitcase from one hand to the other as he walks down the street.

Interior: Shoe Shop—Same

Frank puffs at his cigar, his gaze distant and strange.

Dissolve

Exterior: Peppino's House—Day

Gino stands before the house and knocks on the door.

After a long moment, the door opens. This time, a young woman, Sabrina, twenty-six, answers. Her hair is short and black like her striking eyes. Her pupils carry a mist of emotion as if she's always just finished crying.

SABRINA: *Si?*

GINO: Peppino Sorrentino?

SABRINA: *Americano? (In broken English)* You're American?

GINO: Yes.

SABRINA: Who are you?

GINO: Well, I'm, I'm his son.

SABRINA: Your...your glasses.

Slowly, Gino takes off his glasses.

She looks carefully at his eyes, then smacks him hard across the face and slams shut the door.

After a few moments, the door opens again.

Gino turns his head to see the tattered shoes of Peppino, sixty-five, his "real" father. The shoes freeze.

GINO *(voice over):* So these were my father's shoes. They sure didn't look like the shoes of some rich guy who owned a meat factory.

Dissolve

Interior: Peppino's Kitchen—Day

Gino sits at the kitchen table while Sabrina, smoking and agitated, argues with Peppino. Though attentive, Peppino is focused on Gino, who stands awkwardly, suitcase in one hand, Italian to English book in the other.

PEPPINO *(Italian with subtitles):* My son. Sabrina, he's my family.

Peppino's light, expressive eyes make direct contact with his birth son. Gino moves to the table and sits quietly across from him.

SABRINA *(Italian with subtitles):* Family? We've known him for fifteen minutes and we're family?

PEPPINO *(Italian with subtitles):* Sabrina, it's a sign. It's a sign.

SABRINA *(Italian with subtitles):* A sign. What sign? I think you're cracking up a little. You've been watching too much American television. Tomorrow, I'm leaving for Rome.

Sabrina storms out of the room.

PEPPINO *(Italian with subtitles):* You can't leave now. You can't leave now.

After a long, awkward moment, Gino looks at his translation book, then back at Peppino.

GINO: *Un telephono?*

We hear a phone ringing.

Dissolve

Exterior: Frank's Shoe Shop—Day

Frank answers the phone. He's wearing his bowling shirt, and his bowling bag is on the counter.

GINO *(voice over):* That night, I tried to call Frank. I felt bad missing bowling. I knew Frank couldn't stand Caesar's big hook. I figured he'd never forgive me for missing the big game.

FRANK *(underneath Gino's voice over):* Hello. Hello! *(He hangs up)* Shit.

He grabs his bowling bag and leaves the shop.

Black

Exterior: Sky—Early Morning

The morning sun gradually creeps over the mountain, spilling light onto the quiet streets of Guarcino.

A church bell rings.

Exterior: Street—Same

An old man sweeps the church steps.

An old woman takes in laundry from her window.

Kids run by Peppino's house.

Interior: Peppino's Kitchen—Same

At the table, Peppino flips Italian playing cards over as Gino sips his coffee and bites into a cookie.

GINO *(voice over):* The next morning, it felt strange listening to this guy, my father, who kept talking to me like I could understand a word he was saying.

PEPPINO *(in Italian):* Gino, this is the Ace of Spades, the most powerful card when you're playing….

Sabrina enters with a bag full of clothes and plops it on the counter.

PEPPINO *(Italian with subtitles):* Sabrina, doesn't he look beautiful…like your cousin, Franco?

SABRINA *(Italian with subtitles):* Give me a break! I think he looks gay. Who cares? I'm leaving for Rome.

Sabrina gathers her bag and begins to leave.

PEPPINO: *Basta! (Subtitle)* Stop!

Close up of Gino.

Cut to outside the house. Back inside.

PEPPINO *(Italian with subtitles):* For 150 years, the Sorrentino family has marched together in the procession of Sant'Agnello. You cannot leave. Sunday, we must march in the Sant'Agnello procession, all of us together. Then I will be happy to die.

SABRINA *(Italian with subtitles):* Thank God that Mom is dead.

PEPPINO *(Italian with subtitles):* Your mother would have understood.

Sabrina measures Gino with her gaze.

SABRINA *(to Gino):* Gino, in Chicago, what do you do for a job?

After a long pause, Gino stares at Peppino.

GINO: Well, I'm...I'm a bowler.

Exterior: A Corridor—Day

Sabrina strikes a match off a medieval wall. Gino stands quietly nearby.

GINO *(voice over):* So Sabrina was my sister, half sister, I guess.

They begin to walk.

In the distance, we see a large factory.

GINO *(voice over):* Anyway, she agreed to show me around Guarcino. She thought it would be a good idea to start with the big prosciutto factory.

Interior: The Prosciutto Factory—Day

In a room filled with hundreds of pigs' legs, Sabrina and Gino watch a worker hang a leg on a hook.

GINO *(voice over):* Turns out Peppino didn't own the meat factory. He worked there. Everybody worked there.

The worker tries to give Gino a leg, but Gino shakes his head and retreats backward.

GINO *(voice over):* I guess I would have worked there, too.

Another prosciutto leg slams on a scale.

Another worker, bagging the leg, offers it to Gino, who shakes his head and retreats.

Exterior: The Prosciutto Factory—Same

Sabrina exits the factory. Gino trails behind her, carrying a prosciutto leg wrapped as a gift.

Black

Sound only: SQUEAL!!! CRASH!!!

Interior: Frank's Shoe Shop—Day

Magical music.

Mr. Mills walks to the counter wearing a neck brace. Frank puffs on a cigar.

MR. MILLS: Seriously, Frank. Not even for a joke. How did you know?

FRANK: And the wife?

MR. MILLS: They say she woulda gone through the windshield. You got a gift.

FRANK: It was a bad dog job.

MR. MILLS: What do I owe you?

Frank slides a bag to Mr. Mills.

FRANK: Twenty-five. Just gimme twenty cash.

MR. MILLS: You son-of-a-bitch. You're not gonna believe this....

Mr. Mills begins to recount the accident.

Dissolve

Exterior: Big Fountain—Day

Sabrina, who seems always to be smoking, stands near a stone fountain shaped like a giant pitcher.

Gino, hugging the prosciutto leg, drinks from the fountain.

SABRINA: Not too much. Guarcino water, it's like medicine. The people of Guarcino are so stupid, they no charge money for the water. In Fiuggi, they charge for the water. In Fiuggi, everybody's rich.

Enzo, forty, approaches, holding a bottle of water.

SABRINA *(in Italian):* Hello, Enzo. *(She introduces them)* Enzo, Gino. Gino, Enzo.

ENZO *(in Italian):* Ah, Uncle Peppino's son from Chicago.

SABRINA *(in Italian):* Yes.

ENZO *(to Gino, in his best English):* Ah, Chicago. Bang bang. Al Capone. Michael Jordan. Basket…

SABRINA: Ciao, Enzo! Ciao! Ciao!

She grabs Gino away from Enzo and leads him from the fountain.

GINO: How did he know who I was?

SABRINA: In Guarcino, Gino, everybody knows everything about everybody. *(Then)* Are you tired?

GINO: No.

Sabrina points out a tiny church high in the mountains.

SABRINA: Good. Sant'Agnello.

Extreme long shot of the church.

Dissolve

Exterior: Base of the Mountain—Day

They head up the mountain on a narrow, winding path. Gino, struggling, carries the prosciutto on his shoulder. Sabrina tells him a story.

Exterior: The Mountain—Day

SABRINA *(voice over):* You see how the story goes, Sant'Agnello stayed with all the poor people, the worst. Not even their dogs would stay with them. Sant'Agnello, he stayed. That's why we have the big parade. We walk. That's why my father, he wants me to stay.

Exterior: Sant'Agnello—Day

Sabrina, now carrying the prosciutto leg, effortlessly, makes it to the chapel. Gino trails behind her.

Sabrina leaves the prosciutto on a cement bench. Gino sits next to it, glances at it, then joins Sabrina at the mountain's edge overlooking Guarcino.

GINO: It's beautiful.

Sabrina flicks her cigarette away.

SABRINA: Gino, why did you come to Guarcino?

GINO: I don't know. I guess my mother died and maybe I just, I wanted to see what he looked like.

SABRINA *(slowly):* Gino, Peppino, my father, was promised to my mother when she was just a little girl. And then, he got your mother… *(She gestures as if she's pregnant)*…with the baby. *(Then)* It was the family, Gino. His father and my mother's father, there was the money…. Your mother was poor. They made her leave.

Gino hands Sabrina a picture of his mother as a young woman. She stares at it.

SABRINA: He loved your mother, Gino. *(Beat)* But, he stayed for my mother.

After a long moment, as they look down on Guarcino, opera music begins.

Interior: Frank's Shoe Shop (Flashback)

Little Gino watches Frank hammer the heel of a shoe.

Little Gino hammers a bit himself.

Dissolve

A sequence of quick flashbacks.

Peppino shows Gino how to play cards.

GINO *(voice over):* Not much else happened. I thought of Peppino wanting to walk in that parade.

Picture of Gino's mom.

GINO *(voice over):* I thought of my Ma on some boat with me in her stomach.

Sabrina opening the door to first encounter Gino.

GINO *(voice over):* I thought of Sabrina losin' her mom.

Exterior: Frank's Shoe Shop—Day

Frank and Mr. Mills, both smoking cigars, look up at the sign for the shoe shop. They shake hands.

GINO *(voice over):* And Frank, I started thinkin' about Frank…all alone back in the shop.

Black

Interior: Peppino's Kitchen—Late Night

Gino drops Peppino's weathered shoes down on the table.

He places a bottle of grappa next to the shoes.

Can opener in hand, he begins restoring Peppino's shoes.

GINO *(voice over):* The night before the big parade, I couldn't sleep. Peppino Sorrentino.

Interior: Sabrina's Bedroom—Same

Sabrina drawing on a piece of paper.

Interior: Peppino's Kitchen—Late Night

Gino continues to restore Peppino's shoes.

GINO *(voice over):* He was a nice guy. I figured the least I could do was fix his shoes.

Black

A church bell sounds.

Long shot of Guarcino.

Exterior: Peppino's Steps—Morning

Peppino finishes tying the laces on his beautifully restored shoes. A bunch of kids run by. He looks up at Gino.

PEPPINO *(Italian with subtitles):* Gino, my shoes look beautiful. You're like Michelangelo. Well done.

Sabrina, joining them on the stairs, hands Peppino her drawing of Gino's mother.

PEPPINO: *(Italian with subtitles):* Sabrina. You're an artist. Gino, bring this to your father.

Peppino hands him the drawing.

GINO *(moved):* You're an artist, Sabrina. You've got a great gift.

SABRINA: It's not for you, Gino. It's for your father in America, for doing such a good job.

Dissolve

Opera music continues forcefully.

Exterior: The City Streets—Later

The piazza is filled with people. A little girl drinks from a fountain. The town band rehearses.

Priests hold up the great statue of Sant'Agnello.

Chanting music begins.

Gino, Sabrina and Peppino stand in line for the procession, gazing up at the statue of Sant'Agnello.

Hoards of people march in the parade along with the town's marching band, dozens of priests and the statue of Sant'Agnello, which is hoisted high in the air.

Parade chanting begins.

In slow motion Gino, Peppino and Sabrina walk down the main street with the procession.

Interior: The Shoe Shop (Flashback)

Close up of the stitcher.

GINO *(voice over):* This is the stitcher. To connect the soles with the shoe.

Little Gino watches Frank work with the machine.

Opera music and chanting end.

Dissolve

Exterior: Shoe Shop—Day

Outside the shoe shop, Mr. Mills adjusts a sandwich board sign that says: "Psychic Shoe Readings!" He hands bright red flyers to passersby, which include: a businessman, two young women from a donut shop, and a bicycling ice cream man who pedals by the shop.

Interior: Shoe Shop—Same

Frank, concentrating intensely and puffing a cigar, is holding a young woman's shoe and offering advice to a woman who is being pestered by her young daughter. An older couple wait impatiently in line behind them.

FRANK: Well, I can't say this for absolute sure. But you see this nick here? Right here. On the heel. Your husband, he's a little bit of a pain in the ass sometimes. Am I right?

CUSTOMER: Look at the shoe and tell me if he did it. Because if he did, I'm gonna kill him.

FRANK: Well, let's take a look here....

The shop is filled with people.

WOMAN CUSTOMER *(to husband):* Does it make a difference if it's the right shoe or the left? The right shoe or the left?

Black

Interior: Back Room of the Shoe Shop—Later

Gino hands Frank the drawing of his mom that Sabrina made.

FRANK: She was a beautiful woman, your mother.

GINO: I'm sorry, Pop.

FRANK: For what? Final Game, Caesar bowled 240. Yer off the team.

Frank pinches Gino's cheek, slaps him lightly, then exits with the drawing. Gino smiles and begins to work on a shoe.

Interior: The Shoe Shop (Flashback)

Shots of the nailer, the stitcher and the cutter.

GINO *(voice over):* So there's the nailer…the cutter…the stitcher.

Shot of the finisher.

GINO *(voice over):* This, this is the finisher. The last machine. It's, you know, to shine. To polish. To finish.

MARCO BENASSI

Little Gino and Frank polish a shoe on the finisher.

GINO *(voice over):* There's more. But that's really all you need to know for now.

POETS

─Brooke Bergan

Poets are liars,
Ordinary guys
With extraordinary
Sensibilities talking
To other ordinary guys in
Ordinary language
They can't help
Themselves it just
All pours out
Like a cup
Overflowething
Like an Oprah guest
Like a muzzled woman
Like a windchime in a
Windstorm, poets
Are wise guys
About ordinary things
Where their ideas are
Of order in Key West
For example, they wear
Tight pants so ordinary
Guys will want them gals

BROOKE BERGAN

Too though wishing doesn't
Make it so, deceiving
Either I know one guy
Who lied all the time
Just for the hell of it
I guess because he was
A poet though I don't
Think it made him
A better poet especially
Or worse and another one
Was always getting sick
You couldn't mention
A disease he wouldn't
Get this is called pathetic
Fallacy sometimes when
He was really sick he'd say
It was imaginary this
Is called negative
Capability or a
Sickness of the soul
Which is known as metonymy
Poets have lousy personalities
And want to loaf around
All day talking to
The bottoms of their
Shoes they don't
Make their beds
They don't drink
Water and lots of them
Don't even
Like poems
One poet told me
He only wrote them

POETS

To get rich (ha)
And get laid
Or maybe it was
Famous
He married a poet
So I guess they both
Got laid but she ended
Up more famous because
He died though I don't
Think either of them
Ended up rich since
Only poets who started out
Rich end up rich and not
Even all of them unlike
Painters who can actually
Make money which may
Be why poets like painters
Even sometimes want to be
Painters but not always though
Some are and some think
The two are one
And the same
And sometimes
They are but sister
Arts and sister
Acts are not sometimes
Poets are just plain
Know it alls and
Think poets can do
Anything you can do
Better like play the
Piano when they don't
Know how all it takes

BROOKE BERGAN

Is a little sincere practice
And technique, just
Blunder where angels
Fear to fly right in the
Middle of things
Which is known as *in
Medias res* to mix
Business with
Pleasure is their
Job though it can
Give you a thundering
Headache and
That's the good news.

CONTRIBUTORS

Deborah Adelman teaches writing, literature and film courses at the College of DuPage. Her work includes the books *The Children of Perestroika* and *The Children of Perestroika Come of Age* (M.E. Sharpe), as well as short stories and essays. Her most recent efforts have appeared in *Puerto del Sol, Cream City Review* and *Jewish Currents.*

Marco Benassi earned Masters' degrees in Journalism and Film from Ohio State University and Columbia College. A Professor of Film and Performance Studies at the College of DuPage, he's published more than fifty feature stories in *The Chicago Tribune* and has written and directed three multi-media plays, which were produced in Chicago.

Brooke Bergan is a poet, translator and essayist. The recipient of several literary awards, she has published three books of poetry: *Windowpane, Distant Topologies* and *Storyville: A Hidden Mirror.* Her work has also appeared in such publications as *The Antioch Review, The Chicago Tribune, The Chaucer Review, Religion and Literature, Another Chicago Magazine, Small Press Magazine, Private Arts, Translation Wire, The Yale Lit* and *Poetry East.* Ms. Bergan was the literary editor of *Private Arts* and is currently Director of Publications Operations at the University of Illinois at Chicago, where she also earned her doctorate in English.

Michael Burke's stories, poems and essays have appeared in *TriQuarterly, American Way, Private Arts, Rambunctious Review, Sport Literate, Backspace, Strong Coffee, Bluff City* and *The Prairie Light Review.* His plays—*Wama-Wama Zing Bing* and *Let's Spend Money*—have been produced in Chicago by Strawdog Theatre and OverBored Productions. Mr. Burke is currently completing a collection of short stories.

Cris Burks teaches fiction writing at Columbia College. Her poems have been published in *The Black Maria, Thunder Egg, Ambrosia, Emergence* and *Shooting Star Review*. Her short stories have appeared in *Hair Trigger, Kaleidoscope, Short Fiction by Women, Emergence* and *The Thing About Love Is....* "Song of the Jeweled Bird" is an excerpt from a novel-in-progress.

Mary Ruth Clarke is a screenwriter and playwright who dabbles heavily in writing poetry as a diversion from writing dialogue. Her autobiographical play, *The Backache*, was recently selected as part of Prop Theater's National New Plays Festival. Her film *Meet the Parents*, starring Robert De Niro, will be released this fall.

Robert N. Georgalas is an award-winning author who teaches film, literature and writing courses at the College of DuPage. Among the publications in which his works have appeared are: *Urban Spaghetti, Hair Trigger, Rambunctious Review, Sport Literate, Willow Review, Arizona Literary Magazine, F. O. C. Review, The Prairie Light Review* and *A. U. Review*. His screenplay "No Giants, No Babies, No Killers," is currently under consideration at 20th Century Fox.

Scott Grunow has an M.A. in English literature from Dominican University. His previous studies included a semester at the University of London studying the seventeenth century metaphysical poet Henry Vaughan. Mr. Grunow works in corporate America but is a displaced academic in the most profound sense. He has several obsessions, the most current being Italian dramatic mezzo-sopranos of the 1930s and 40s.

Glenna Holloway, a recent Pushcart Award winner, was founding president of the Illinois Poetry Society in 1991. Her work has appeared in *Western Humanities Review, Georgia Review, The Hollis Critic, Notre Dame Review, McCall's, The Saturday Evening Post, Michigan Quarterly Review* and *Good Housekeeping*. A resident of Naperville, Illinois, she is also a six time winner of the Chicago Poets and Patrons' "Best of the Best." Earlier this year, Ms. Holloway took top honors at the NALPW Biennial 2000 in Washington, D.C.

Michele Weber Hurwitz has been writing since she was ten. She remembers how proud she felt when a story she wrote in fifth grade won a school contest. That feeling still remains in her writing today. A columnist for Pioneer Press newspapers, Ms. Hurwitz has written articles for several national magazines. She has three children and is thrilled that her oldest daughter has inherited her love of writing and reading.

Jo-Ann Ledger was born in England, but now resides in Glendale Heights, Illinois. Editor of *The Prairie Light Review* for three years, Miss Ledger's work has appeared in *Community College Weekly, The Prairie Light Review, The Darien Progress*, and *The Thing About Love Is....*

David McGrath has written stories and essays for *Artful Dodge, Sport Literate, The Thing About Love is...*, and *The Chicago Reader*, among others. His travel essay "The Purest Sport," appeared in the June 2000 issue of Arizona's *Carefree Enterprise*. When he is not teaching literature at College of DuPage, he writes a little and splits wood a lot in his forest cabin near Lake Superior. He has just completed work on a novel entitled *Siege at Ojibwa* and can be contacted at ovid6@juno.com.

Patricia Ann McNair teaches in the Fiction Writing Department of Columbia College, Chicago. Her work has appeared (or is forthcoming) in such publications as *American Fiction, Sport Literate, Other Voices* and *The Fourth Genre*. Ms. McNair's essay "And These are the Good Times" was nominated for a Pushcart Prize in 1998. She is also the recipient of two Illinois Arts Council awards.

Peter Meinke has published numerous books of poetry as well as fiction, criticism and children's verse. His short story collection, *The Piano*

Tuner, won the 1986 Flannery O'Connor Award for Short Fiction. A recipient of two poetry fellowships from the NEA, in addition to many other awards, he directed the writing workshop at Eckerd College for twenty-seven years, retiring in 1993. Since then he has been writer-in-residence at the University of Hawaii, Austin Peary State University in Tennessee, and the University of North Carolina at Greensboro. Mr. Meinke resides in St. Petersburg, Florida with his wife, the artist Jeanne Clark.

Scott Mintzer grew up in Brooklyn, New York and was educated at the University of Michigan and the University of Chicago Pritzker School of Medicine. He currently lives with his wife in Los Angeles, where he is a neurologist specializing in epilepsy at UCLA Medical Center. His first published story, "Insurance," appeared in *The Thing About Love Is....*

Tom Montgomery-Fate, a professor of English at College of DuPage, is the author of *Beyond the White Noise* (1997). Essays from his book are included in *Across Cultures: A Reader for Writers* (Allyn and Bacon), *Manoa* (University of Hawaii Press), and *International English* (NCTE). His work has also been cited in *Best American Essays* (Houghton Mifflin). Recent efforts have appeared in *Manoa, Mothering, The Chicago Tribune, Sojourners* and *The Thing About Love Is....*

George Einar Nelson comes from a missionary family and spent part of his childhood in Brazil working with Kaingaing Indians on a reservation near Argentina. A native of Chicago for most of his adult life, he has been practicing Buddhism in the SGI organization since 1974. Through chanting, he has come to understand that demons are simply gods with an attitude, that the world—the whole universe, bright and dark—is an expression of his own life on the inside. As a writer, he likes stories that reconsider reality and ask questions rather than answer them. His previous work, "Time Pieces," has appeared in *Off the Rocks.*

THE THING ABOUT SECOND CHANCES IS...

Nicolette Roberts is a respected poet. Kissed early in life by wanderlust, she has traveled the world in search of the perfect place in which to write. At present, this former New Yorker resides in a Tuscan hill town. "Words flow easier here," she says. "Then again, maybe it's the wine." Listed among her favorite authors are: Céline, Stendhal, George Eliot, Mark Twain and Lewis Carroll.

M.J. Rychlewski has published fiction and poetry in *American Pen, Conversation, The Yellow Press,* and *Private Arts*. His first book of poetry, *Night Driving,* was published by the Wine Press in 1985. He lives with his wife and daughter in Chicago.

Deborah E. Ryel grew up in upstate New York and now lives in Wheaton, Illinois. She has been writing poetry since grade school and studied briefly under Ralph Mills. Her poems have appeared in *The Prairie Light Review, The Writer, The Spoon River Quarterly, The River Oak Review,* and *The Thing About Love Is....* "The Pilot Study" was inspired by a Doris Lessing essay.

Connie Scanlon is a Chicago-born Irish American, who enjoys writing poetry in Grayslake, Illinois and County Sligo, Ireland. A 1998/99 America's Best and Pirate's Alley Faulkner Society finalist, "Haiku" is her first published poem.

Daisy Lin Shapiro is an award-winning broadcast news producer in Los Angeles, where she lives with her husband Aaron and studies writing under Aimee Bender. She was born in Taipei, Taiwan and immigrated with her family to California when she was nine-years- old. "I remember the first time I encountered a slice of Kraft American cheese; I had never seen anything like it, so I peeled back the plastic and took a bite of the floppy orange square, and that's when it hit me just how far from Taiwan I had gone." "Sawdust and Camellias" is her first published story.

Dorothy Terry is a public relations consultant and writer who operates her own business in Chicago. She has also served as a network television writer for the National Broadcasting Company. Dorothy wrote her first poem at age eight and was a contributor for *Child Life* magazine where several of her early works such as "I Had a Cat Named White Face" and "My Easter Hat is Pink and Rosy" were published. Her poetry has also appeared in the *Journal of the Silverado Roughwriters*, St. Helena, California, and has been read at The Clearing in Door County, Wisconsin. Upon her graduation from Northwestern University, she was awarded the Isabel Lovedale graduate scholarship in Oral Interpretation of Poetry. She lives in Chicago and at her farm in Door County.

E. Donald Two-Rivers is an Ojibwa poet, playwright, storyteller and writer. Raised in Ontario, he currently resides with his wife and children in Chicago. Mr. Two-Rivers has published two books: *A Dozen Cold Ones* (poetry) and *Survivor's Medicine*, a collection of short stories which won the 1999 American Book Award. At present, he is the director of Chicago's Red Path Theater Company, with which he is currently performing his one man show, *Peeking Out of Amerika's Museums*.

Edward Underhill is a Chicago lawyer who holds a keen interest in writing and writers. His short fiction has been published in several law-based periodicals, and he is currently focused on the craft of playwriting. His first one-act play, *Curse the Darkness*, was produced in 1997 by a local theatre group. Another of his scripts, *The Last Word*, saw print in the anthology *The Thing About Love Is....* Underhill can be contacted at eunderhill@masudafunai.com.

Sari Wilson held a Provincetown Fine Arts Work Center Fellowship and the Patricia Rowe Willrich Fellowship in the Stegner Creative Writing Program at Stanford University. She has worked as a magazine researcher and an ESL teacher in Prague. She has also lived on an Israeli kibbutz and has traveled throughout Southeast Asia and the Middle East. Her fiction has appeared in *New York Stories* and *Maxine: A Literate Companion for Churlish Girls and Rakish Women.* In addition, she has collaborated with cartoonist Josh Neufeld on stories for his comic book, *Keyhole.*

Ellen Zalewski was born on the cusp of happiness. She is an avid traveler and finds it difficult not to be continuously planning travel events. Ellen lives on the south side of Chicago in a ranch style home with her dog, Buckaroo.

To order copies of either *The Thing About Second Chances Is...* or *The Thing About Love Is...*, visit your favorite bookstore, Amazon.com, or send $19.95 (Illinois residents add $1.75 sales tax) plus $3 shipping and handling to:

Polyphony Press
PMB 317
207 E. Ohio St.
Chicago, IL 60611